SUNDAY ZEBRAS

by

Art Holst

Art Holst

Forest Publishing
Lake Forest, Illinois

Copyright © 1980 by Art Holst
All Rights Reserved

Printed in the United States of America.

No part of this publication is to be reproduced, stored in a retrieval system or copied in any form without permission of the author.

Published by
Forest Publishing
222 Wisconsin Avenue
Lake Forest, Illinois 60045

Dedicated to my wonderful wife Margie and to our four children Jeff, Julie, Suzanne and Karen. Thank you for allowing me to roam with the Sunday Zebras this past quarter of a century.

Acknowledgements

I would like to acknowledge the following for their contributions to this book:

"Spike" Claassen for his special help in the writing.

Joan King for her talented help in proofreading and correcting the errors that officials never make.

Art McNally, supervisor of officials, the National Football League, for his encouragement and help.

Norm Schachter for his knowledge of professional football and his help to all officials.

And finally, as a group, all of the officials, players and coaches at all levels, who have been a part of a career that I wouldn't trade for any tangible treasure.

TABLE OF CONTENTS

	Page
Preface by Frank Gifford	9
INTRODUCTION	
The Zebra: Animal or Man?	12
CHAPTER ONE	
What A Way To Make A Living	14
CHAPTER TWO	
Everyone's Gotta' Start Somewhere	27
CHAPTER THREE	
Getting In Shape	43
CHAPTER FOUR	
The Early Days	57
CHAPTER FIVE	
It Just Grew And Grew	68
CHAPTER SIX	
My Debut	84
CHAPTER SEVEN	
Football Fields Ain't For Grazing	101
CHAPTER EIGHT	
Murphy's Law Again	121
CHAPTER NINE	
The Game... Brought To You By...	138
CHAPTER TEN	
Trench Warfare	155
CHAPTER ELEVEN	
Camp Charley-Horse	178
CHAPTER TWELVE	
Everyone Talks About the Weather, But	192
CHAPTER THIRTEEN	
It's No Popularity Contest	206
CHAPTER FOURTEEN	
All The King's Men	223
CHAPTER FIFTEEN	
It's A Grand Old Game	244
The NFL Digest of Rules	Appendix

PREFACE

Any NFL fan worth his weight in Dallas Cowboy tee shirts will, in all probability, shudder at the thought that an NFL official could 1) spell enough words to put together a book, 2) find anyone foolish enough to publish it, and 3) even consider that said book might be entertaining, humorous, and thought provoking far beyond the depth of the game itself.

Art Holst, however, has accomplished all of the above and much more in SUNDAY ZEBRAS, and its careful reading by the legions of American football fans could well be the first step in detente between "fandom and officialdom."

I, for one, have never had a problem with the Zebras either as a player for twelve years or as an announcer for another dozen years. On the contrary, as I've come to know many of them personally, my respect and admiration have grown by leaps and bounds. A quick glance at the biographies of the league officials would tell you that the NFL, under head man Art McNally, has collected a unique and talented crew. While they come from all walks of life, the one common denominator seems to be they are proven successes wherever their life's work has taken them.

With this in mind, one has to wonder why in the hell they would ever subject themselves to the waves of abuse that constantly wash over them during the course of a game. Fans, players, coaches — all get into the act; and for three hours each Sunday during the course of the season, of prime concern for each of these groups is the ancestry of the Zebra-shirted few who agitate and infuriate so many.

Art writes about the "whys" . . . and so much more. He recalls hilarious anecdotes dredged from his years of prowling the professional gridirons. He captures the role of the official in those "crisis" seconds where a judgment has to be made which can affect the outcome of not only the game at hand, but a team's entire season.

The "much more" is Art's own philosophical outlook on life which is woven throughout the book. It is in this area where one, regardless of prior prejudices concerning officials, might arrive at the conclusion, "Hey, those Zebras ain't so bad after all." In any event . . . before you burn it, read it and you'll probably love it.

FRANK GIFFORD

ART HOLST and friend, FRANK GIFFORD. Gifford, who wrote the preface to **Sunday Zebras** *is a Hall of Fame man in every way. The former star halfback for the New York Giants is ABC's Monday Night Football correspondent and a true gentleman.*

INTRODUCTION

THE ZEBRA: ANIMAL OR MAN?

On a green veldt in East Africa late on a steamy afternoon, a zebra mare labors to bring her foal into the wild world of the Serengeti plain. Instinct for survival, a knowledge of the terrain and a keen awareness of the predatory animals will allow this tiny creature to reach adulthood. He will be immediately recognized by his black and white stripes, his speed and his ability to function with the herd. This wild, four-legged zebra is a common sight on the beautiful Serengeti plain.

Here in the United States you will find another species of zebra, over ninety in number, and while they do not band together in large herds, you will find them in groups of seven, frolicking on a lush green veldt of their own, crossed by white stripes and having at each end two yellow upright poles with a yellow crossbar between them.

The upper torso of this genus of zebra is also striped black and white, but he has only two legs to get around on. Nevertheless, he has speed, as well as a keen awareness of the larger forms of animal life with whom he shares this veldt. The veldt or field is surrounded by thousands of fans, for it is the arena of professional football. Here the zebra is seldom cheered, often booed, always blamed, but nothing will deter him from frequenting the green of this weekend world.

It is in this world that I have functioned as a National Football League Zebra for the past fifteen years. How is a man "born" into this world? What other fields does he roam before he pirouettes on a field with the biggest and fastest of the armored Homo sapiens? That's part of the story and I'll touch on it as we go along.

This story, however, is not just the story of my life and my experiences in the National Football League. It is also the story of great athletes, whose spirit and will to win is the driving force that places them in the hall of heroes. It is the force that has brought success to men and women in all walks of life. It is the force that enables those fortunate enough to possess it to overcome disaster or adversity in any form, pick up the pieces and return to the game, bloody nose and all. These are the winners. These are the individuals to be emulated, whether they are athletes, industrial leaders or the bull fighter who puts mustard on his sword.

Vince Lombardi demanded "The Second Effort" from his players. He always got it and he got championship football teams, too.

If this book can inspire its readers to apply that second effort to their own lives and their adversities it will have been worth printing. At least I can hope that this book will cause you to think more about a positive attitude. Remember, nothing worthwhile in this world comes easy. God gave us two ends. One to sit with and one to think with. Our fate is determined by the one we use most. Heads we win, tails we lose.

CHAPTER ONE

WHAT A WAY TO MAKE A LIVING

An old mathematical equation says that "the whole is equal to the sum of its parts and is greater than any one of them." This book gives accounts of great performances by great players and great coaches, and their relationship to the seven Zebras trying to maintain the equilibrium of professional football games played across the length and breadth of America each fall and winter. These parts then come together to become the greater whole of the game itself and what it means in terms of our free way of life.

I've often been asked by many people as I fulfilled speaking engagements across the country, "What's it like to be a part of the greatest sporting event in the history of mankind?"

I could talk for hours on the subject, but perhaps it can be summed up by my emotions when I was one of the officials for Super Bowl VI, played at Tulane Stadium in New Orleans. At about five minutes before opening kick-off, we were standing on the fifty-yard line, facing about forty brand new American flags snapping in the breeze. It was a gorgeous day and as the last few bars of the National Anthem were played, a half dozen Air Force jets screamed over the field on a low fly-by, then peeled up and away, skyward.

It was a very emotional moment for me, for I was proud. Proud of my country and proud of the sport I was privileged to represent. Granted, we live in an imperfect nation, run by imperfect people. It has always been thus and always will be. But, in spite of its faults, it still represents the best system for distributing wealth and happiness that man has ever known. My own personal happiness, contentment and self-esteem are provided by my God, my country, my family and my profession, and when football is numbered among those four blessings, it is quite clear how I feel about this great spectacle.

Oh yes, I'm a religious man, a Presbyterian elder and sometime lay minister. In fact, most officials are regular churchgoers. At Super Bowl VI, I worked with three Catholic officials and even though I am a Presbyterian, I went to 5:00 p.m. mass with them on Saturday, and again at 8:00 a.m. Sunday morning. I figured I'd need all the help I could get for that game. You can't get too much religion. Indeed, sometimes I even go to the synagogue. I don't want to be left out of heaven on a technicality!

Needless to say, I love the game of football, and I think one of the big reasons is that football respects the dignity of difference in people. We do not play average teams in the Super Bowl. We play the best, and they are made up of athletes of assorted sizes and colors, denominations and skills. Catholic, Protestant, Jew, black and white, old and young. We have a place in football for a kid who can throw a ball, but can't catch it; another who can catch a ball, but can't throw it. We even have a place in football for a kid born with only half of his right foot, nothing from his instep forward, and only a stub for a right arm. When he told his parents he wanted to go out for high school football, they were all for it.

The years passed. It was 1968 and the Detroit Lions were playing the Saints in New Orleans. The score stood at 16-14 in favor of Detroit, with two seconds left to play. The same kid, now a man, playing pro football, kicked a 63-yard field goal to beat the Lions, 17-16, and with that kick, Tom Dempsey kicked himself right into professional football's Hall of Fame.

And which foot did he kick the ball with? Not the good one. He kicked that football with the bum one. He took his biggest liability in life and turned it into his greatest asset. There's a lesson there. A very uncommon man, with a very uncommon handicap, but also with a very uncommon talent.

Vince Lombardi, the great coach of the World Champion Green Bay Packers, once said, "The disgrace in life is not in falling. The disgrace in life is not rising after you fall." There's a lot of truth in that, for life is like football, a game where you get knocked down and keep getting up again.

Vince Lombardi said, "Winning is not everything. It is the only thing." That certainly is true in football, but another Lombardi-ism applies to life as well as football. "I think a boy with talent has a moral obligation to fulfill that talent . . ." Certainly he has — and even if you can't win you can take comfort in the knowledge that you gave it your all. The disgrace is not in losing — it's in giving up too soon. That's a Holst-ism!

Emlen Tunnell, the great Giants and Packers defensive halfback of the fifties, a terrific punt return man and vicious tackler, once said he wouldn't quit football until he was fifty. "Your body may go," he said, "but the will to win doesn't."

On the other hand, Y.A. Tittle, quarterback for the New York Giants in the sixties, admitted it was time for him to quit when another quarterback, much younger, came to him one day, seeking permission to date his daughter.

There are many outstanding plays that come to mind as I reflect on incidents of success and failure, but one of the plays I shall never forget occurred in St. Louis in 1965. The Pittsburgh Steelers were playing the St. Louis Cardinals. The score was 17-13, Steelers over the Cards, with 37 seconds left to play, no times-out remaining and with the clock stopped. Into the game for St. Louis came number 3, Bill Gambrel, a five-foot-ten-inch flanker back. As the ball went into play, Bill faked the opposing cornerback, got a half step on him, leaped on the eight-yard line, made a one-handed catch of a pass from Charlie Johnson and went into the end zone with the winning touchdown.

Bill had dropped three passes earlier in the game, but that didn't matter. Everyone forgot about those three. The only pass that's in the NFL highlights for 1965 is the one he caught. And that's the only one that should be remembered, for Bill didn't commit the one true failure of not getting up and trying just one more time.

Football? It's beautiful! It's a game of achievement. A game of strategy and tactics! The game plan, the quarterbacks outthinking their opponents, the ball carriers outmanuevering the opposing tacklers, and the men in the line carrying out their bone-jarring assignments with skills sometimes lost to the public eye. They are the true, unsung heroes of the game. From the official's-eye view, the performance of each player, melding as a team, presents an awe-inspiring portrait of a most sophisticated piece of machinery. How can anyone not love football?

But a football team has no room for the mediocre because, as with any group of highly skilled professionals, a team — like a chain — is only as good as its weakest link. This old adage applies whether you're talking about seven football officials, eleven players, a grocery store or a giant corporation.

When I went to college, we had what should have been the greatest football team in our history. We boasted two guards, about six feet three, two tackles who weighed about 260 pounds each, an end who could run like a gazelle and a fullback who was built like a gorilla. We lost ten straight games, because we also had a quarterback who stuttered and a center who was ticklish!

Football is a tough game and it is played by tough men. Yet, despite all their toughness on the field, many are gentle people off the field, and most of the players I know possess a fine sense of humor as well. Paul Hornung and Max McGee during their playing days with the Green Bay Packers are fine examples.

McGee was well known for his sense of humor,

as well as his ability to catch passes, particularly when the going got tough. On Monday morning, as the story goes, Packer Boss Vince Lombardi called the offensive unit of the Packers in for an 8:00 a.m. skull session. The reason was obvious, for they had been guilty of fumbling, missing blocking assignments, and in his opinion had played miserably during a Green Bay loss the day before. Lombardi was a stickler for promptness and was present awaiting his players at 7:45 a.m. His idea of being on time meant you were there fifteen minutes early. Old fashioned? Maybe so, but it produced three straight world championships.

Well, be that as it may, there they all were at 7:45 and Lombardi, who had mellowed some after a good night's sleep, thought he would open the meeting with a bit of humor. Placing a football on the table in front of him, he said, "Gentlemen, I've thought it all over and now feel that your poor performance of yesterday was all my fault. I simply have not taught you well enough, so this morning we will go back to basics!" And with that, he grabbed the football from the table, held it high and declared, "Gentlemen, this is a football!"

There was a moment's silence, then from the back of the room came the voice of Max McGee, "Would you slow down a little, Coach? You're going a little too fast for me!"

That was McGee. Hornung? He, too, could always see the lighter side of anything. I recall a game in Green Bay in 1965. My position was on Green Bay's side of the first half and after the Packers were introduced, they were all shouting or clapping, and some began "popping the pads" of a teammate. You've seen this at a game, before the opening kickoff. Several players will pair off and take turns whacking each other on the shoulder pads to condition each other, mentally, for the violent contact to follow.

On this particular day, I was nervously shifting my weight from one foot to another, while Hornung was "popping pads" with his Packer pals. I turned quickly at the sound of one tremendous pop and watched as Paul got popped again. Hornung glanced my way, grinned and declared, "Ref, that's the hardest I'm gonna' get hit all day!"

To professional football's everlasting credit, it never had a color line that had to be broken. The truth is, the sport thrives on what I have often called the "dignity of difference" among humans. Great teams are welded together by a marriage of many talents. Some players can throw the ball, others are best running with it. Some players catch the ball better than others and some can only kick it. Football has never had a color barrier. In fact, Jim Thorpe, an American Indian and one of the world's greatest athletes, was one of the NFL's founding fathers.

Blacks were a part of it from the beginning. The one-year-old Akron, Ohio, Steels listed Fritz Pollard, great running back from Brown University and Paul Robeson, Rutger's talented end, who later became a world-famous singer, on their 1921 roster.

In 1922, when the struggling American Professional Football Association reorganized and changed its name to the National Football League,

Duke Slater, huge tackle from the University of Iowa, was the bulwark of the Rock Island Independents' line. Jim Thorpe, of course, was there from the very beginning and in 1922 organized the Oorang Indians, a club that was made up almost entirely of redskins.

It was a little different in baseball. Not until 1946 was the color line broken. That was when Branch Rickey, the daring innovator who at that time directed the fortunes of the Brooklyn Dodgers, signed Jackie Robinson to a contract and sent him to Montreal of the International League. The following year, the young, black infielder was playing at first base for the Dodgers. Prior to Robinson's signing, there were reports that some blacks had played in organized baseball as Indians, Cubans, or whatever, but never as negroes.

In football, just as it was among players, so it was with officials. Burl Toler, an outstanding player for the great San Francisco team of the mid-1950's, won promotion to the ranks of NFL Zebras after the 1964 season. He officiated his first game in professional football in August of 1965 and was my roommate for his first two years in the league.

Major league baseball quickly signed Emmett Ashford of the Pacific Coast League late in 1965 and brought him into the American League as an umpire for a few games in September, but he did not actually become a regular arbiter until 1966.

I got to know Toler well during those first two years when we shared hotel rooms. Never, except for those tense moments before his first regularly scheduled game, did I hear him refer to his color, nor have I ever heard any player or fellow official mention it. But just before that first game, as we left the dressing room for the playing field, Toler said to me, "I know when I step into the field, every spectator in the stands, every reporter, every TV announcer and every arm-chair quarterback, watching the game in his living room, will say, 'There he is, the first black official.'"

There may have been some tension earlier that summer, when officials held their annual clinic and rules discussion on just what was in store for him as a Zebra. But he eliminated any such fears by a single comment.

Mark Duncan, then the director of officials, was lecturing to us on field dress and emphasized that from that moment on, there would be no variation from the standard dress. "In the past," he said, "some of you have worn one style of cap that differed from the others. No more of that! You will all wear the same style from here on! In the past," he continued, "some officials have worn black stockings with three white stripes, others solid black, while still others, the regulation black with two stripes. Regulation black with two white stripes is what all of you will wear in the future!"

Toler raised his hand and asked, "Mr. Duncan, could I save the price of stockings by just wearing two strips of white tape around my black legs?"

There was no more tension or apprehension. We all knew that Toler had passed every test on the rules and mechanics of officiating in the college ranks. Now we knew that, no matter what his or our color, he was one of us. Toler's advancement to the NFL was a gratification to all who knew his story.

Burl had been a six-foot-three-inch, one-hundred-ninety-pound center for the San Francisco University team of 1955. He was one of the big draft choices of the Cleveland Browns after that season, but suffered a serious injury of his left knee in the *Chicago Tribune's* All-Star game of 1956. He never played a minute of professional football. After his injury Toler stayed in football as an official among California colleges and high school ranks and ultimately became principal of one of San Francisco's junior high schools. Now Burl has joined the ranks of NFL Zebras, and we're lucky to have him.

Because of his foot speed, Toler has always been a head linesman. Not many fans realize that prior to the 1978 season the head linesman had to be the fastest man on a crew and was responsible for judging all the action on his side of the field from the line of scrimmage to the goal. However, now with a seventh official added, the head linesman is not required to cover the entire sideline.

One of my first assignments as a line judge was at a Green Bay-versus-Vikings game in Minnesota. My position was directly opposite that of Toler who was officiating as head linesman. Minnesota was on the offense and faced a third-down-and-five situation. The Vikings sent their fullback crashing through the line and both Toler and I, simultaneously, but on opposite sides of the field, agreed that Minnesota had failed to make the required yardage by about a foot.

Toler placed the ball on the "forward progress" spot we agreed had been the point of advance, but it did not please one of the biggest and strongest of the Viking linesmen. "We made the first down!" he insisted. "You guys moved the ball back by at least eighteen inches!"

When the player persisted in his shouting, adding a few expletives, Toler silenced him by snapping, "He was stopped here!" as he pointed to the ball, "and we've both got it! We've got it in black and white!"

Incidentally, many people wonder about the placing of the ball. Does it go where the ball carrier's knee hit? Not necessarily. The ball is placed at its most forward point at the time where something, other than the ball carrier's hand or foot, touched the ground.

Toler's quick wit never has left him. At dinner one Saturday night, before a Sunday game, the entire Norman Schachter crew was at the time where line judge Bill Schleibaum was telling a story, complete with gestures. At the end of the tale, Schleibaum threw up his arms, as if signaling a touchdown. In doing so, his right arm struck the tray of a waitress behind him who was busily serving ice cream sundaes. The only two goblets left on the tray went sailing through the air before shattering on the floor. One ball of vanilla ice cream, however, made a high arc over Toler's head and plopped into his hand as he was reaching for a cup of coffee.

Toler looked at the ball of vanilla ice cream in his hand, then looked at the rest of us before turning to the waitress in mock disappointment, saying, "But I ordered chocolate!"

Blacks were not numerous in the NFL until after World War II, but in 1967, when the NFL and the rival American Football League announced their impending merger, 29.8 percent of the players under contract were black. This is according to Buddy Young, formerly a hero at both the University of Illinois and in the pro ranks shortly after the war and now an official of the NFL.

Young, who is himself a negro, estimated that half of the current NFL players are black. The Office of the Commissioner of Baseball states that the percentage of blacks in the 1977 major league season was 18.9.

Talent, the ability to do the job, along with necessary experience, are the fundamental ingredients in putting a team together. This is a basic truth in football and in life.

As there are certain qualities that football players must have to play the game, there are certain terms that readers and spectators need to know in order to appreciate football. In case you run into these terms as you read this book, here are Zebra "daffinitions" to help you:

Kickoff: An event that occurs while you're finding a place to park.

The Long Bomb: A jumbo bratwurst with sauerkraut.

Officials: Myopic fans who can't find seats.

Audibles: Names players call officials.

Tight End: A receiver picked for his ability to look rejected after dropping a forward pass.

Red Dog: What a tight end drinks.

Quarterback Sneak: The other team's quarterback.

Interference: The hat worn by the lady in front of you.

Running Back: The act of returning from the john.

There will be no written test on these; they're just important to know!

CHAPTER TWO

EVERYONE'S GOTTA START SOMEWHERE

The first time I started hollering at everybody was on the night of April 20, 1922, in Galesburg, Illinois. It was then that I was ushered, protestingly, into this world. I bring up the fact that I was born, just like real people, because there are many individuals who will swear that football officials, basketball officials and baseball umpires are not born at all, but are found under rocks, created by the devil to wreak havoc on their favorite teams. Contrary to this belief, I entered this world normally, albeit noisily.

I guess I loved sports from the time I could crawl. Perhaps I inherited this love from my dad who was an enthusiastic Sunday afternoon league ball player. I didn't see him play too often, as his career was cut short during one game by a fast ball to the head. Perhaps I make too much of it. After all, we come of good Swedish stock. In the days of the Viking, Holst head was often used as a battering ram.

I grew up during the depression — the good old days when the most popular kid in the neighborhood was the sole owner of a bat and ball.

As I look back on those happy times, I can't remember ever being without a ball, bat, glove or football, no matter who owned it.

Those hot, lazy Illinois summers were times of real joy. My pals and I played baseball every day, and when autumn rolled around, it was football in the side yard.

School was another matter. I had a world of desire to participate in sports, but I had a physical problem. I just would not grow! I can remember the junior high basketball coach throwing his arm around my shoulder one day and saying, "You're a good little basketball player, Holst, but you're too small. I'm going to have to cut you."

I was crushed! My world had collapsed! But had it really? After all, that was only one man's opinion. If one door is locked, maybe another will open. Even then, I felt that if you want something desperately enough, you will find a way to get it. Somehow I'd find a place for myself in sports.

There's an old saying that goes, "Defeat is only bitter if you swallow it." Now that I reflect, I believe that with that rejection, the seeds were sown that would eventually blossom into a fifteen-year career as a National Football League official.

Adversity can be a negative factor in our lives, but it can also be a highly motivating force. I wanted so desperately to be a good athlete, but by the time I reached my senior year in high school I was a 110-pound failure. However, time has a way of changing things. When I finally graduated from Knox College in 1943, I had grown into a 134-pound failure — but "hope springs eternal."

In high school, the closest I came to starring in

basketball games was playing French horn in the school band. I led the league in sour notes for three years — a record that has never been touched since.

Baseball was not a varsity sport during the depression years. However, I did manage to play on an American Legion team which, at that time, was the closest thing to organized baseball available. The desire to participate in some way in organized athletics never left me, and I've often thought about the rewards of determination. Sometimes we tend to be too careful. We avoid trying to achieve for fear of failure, or we quit trying because of failure.

To me, human personality, or the sub-conscious, is, in fact, success oriented. If we program our goals and adopt the attitude that failure is not failure at all, but a step toward success, we have then progressed over half way to our desired goal.

Once, many years ago, Thomas A. Edison was asked, "How can you keep searching for the solution to the electric light bulb after hundreds of failures?"

He replied, "I have not failed! I have succeeded in finding hundreds of ways that won't work. All of those experiments have put me closer to the one way that will work!"

I am reminded of a story that typifies a dedication to failure. It's about the businessman who couldn't sleep because of a false impression his business would soon fail. He visited his doctor who, after examining him, could find nothing physically wrong. The doctor sent him home with the advice to take a warm bath and count sheep when he retired. The man went home and tried that remedy, but in a week he was back.

"Did you take a warm bath?" the doctor inquired.

"Sure did."

"Did you try counting sheep?"

"I'll say I did," the man replied. "I got up to 50,000, then I sheared them. With all that wool I made 50,000 overcoats — and what kept me from sleeping was, where am I gonna sell 50,000 coats?"

Throughout my pre-college and college years, I maintained my interest in athletics. In the latter I earned my only varsity letter as a member of the Knox College golf team. Knox College is a small liberal arts college in my home town of Galesburg, Illinois. I mention Knox College because of its great curriculum, for it was there that I first learned that the pressure on the cork of a champagne bottle is 57 to 64 pounds per square inch.

Golf was no breeze. I had to wage a tough battle to stay on the team. My handicap was three — my woods, my irons and my putter! In one match I lost two balls on the first hole — and I was putting at the time! Well, perhaps I stretched that story a bit, but truthfully, I did have to work hard on my golf game to keep a place on the team.

Mastering golf was tough enough, but to add to the stress, I endured a French teacher whose name has, thankfully, faded into oblivion. This cretin had the warped impression that all competitive sports were bad. His attitude was trouble enough, but to say I was a student of French would be charitable. I was not interested in any foreign language — including English which was giving me enough headaches. Well, this wretch called me in one day and stunned me with, "If you'll voluntarily drop off the golf team I'll give you a 'D' in the course. If you don't, I'm going to flunk you and you'll be kicked off anyway!"

Beautiful? That's like asking a man if he'd prefer a 100-pound stone wrapped around his neck or his feet encased in a barrel of concrete before being tossed overboard at sea. I didn't have a chance.

I knew nothing about "Possibility Thinking" as a practiced method and I was thirty-five years away from meeting the Reverend Dr. Robert Schuller, who coined the phrase. But I headed straight for Athletic Director Dean Trevor's office and told him of my conversation with the French professor. I was scheduled to be on the golf course at that very moment, for team practice as well as the weekly competitive round that would determine who would play in the next match.

Trev's blood pressure must have jumped forty points when I dropped that little bomb on him. "You go right out to the golf course!" he exploded, "I'll handle the French teacher!"

I'm not proud of the 'D' I received in French, but I'm very proud of Athletic Director Dean Trevor, who must have realized what a crucial point this was in a young man's life and went to bat for me. I'll never forget him and we remained friends until his death a few years ago.

Somehow, in 1943 . . . I graduated from Knox College as an ROTC infantry officer candidate, and Uncle Sam was waiting for me with open arms.

Who can forget those dramatic posters inundating the country in those days, depicting Uncle Sam pointing at you and declaring, "Uncle Sam

Wants You!'"? In my case it was certainly true, for I graduated in June and by July I was an infantry PFC at Camp McCoy, Wisconsin. I was gathered up with many other young men from colleges and universities in the Midwest and we were slated for Officer's Candidate School at Fort Benning, Georgia. Some of us were to be put down eventually in places like Normandy Beach, the Siegfried Line, Hurtgen Forest and Bastogne. Many of these, my good friends, gave up their lives in unknown actions in France, Belgium and Germany to preserve the liberties America stands for.

This is not a book on war, so I'll dismiss my participation in that deadliest game of all by declaring that I worked in the Replacement Training Program at Camp Hood, Texas, before going overseas to the European Theater of Operations in February of 1945. Before I embarked, however, a few other items of some interest occurred. I was commissioned a Second Lieutenant of Infantry and I married my college sweetheart. Margie and I have spent over three happy decades together. She is a lovely lady and the mother of our four fine children. We had thirteen months together before I went to Europe and it was to be seventeen months before I would see her again.

In May, 1945, the war in Europe ended and after a few months of occupation duty near the German-Austrian border, I was transferred to 3rd Army near echelon headquarters in Munich. My timing was great for, coincidentally, the call had gone out for basketball players for our headquarters team. I arrived in Munich a day before the first game, and being in excellent physical condition by this time, I immediately signed up and drew a uniform. The hands that hadn't touched a basketball in three years were soon joyfully passing, dribbling and shooting the ball.

I was pleasantly tired after that first night of practice, but by the following morning, long-forgotten, little-used muscles were sore enough to convince me that perhaps I wasn't in as good physical condition as I had thought.

The next night I was enjoying our first game from a vantage point on the bench. With muscles that were still sore, I was content to sit out the contest to its conclusion. This notion was dispelled at approximately one minute into the second quarter when the coach beckoned to me and suggested I go into the game. I gave a sickly grin, kneaded my charley horses and trotted out on the floor.

The defense must have been lousy, for three of my first four shots plummeted through the hoop. I even added one out of two free throws before my aching muscles began to warn me of an impending strike. I looked to the bench imploringly, but the coach was grinning happily, well-pleased with himself. There would be no succor from that point, and I would just have to forge on.

After nearly five more minutes of play, I staggered to the bench and rasped hoarsely, "Take me out!"

The coach, without changing his happy expression, replied, "Stay in there, Holst! You're doing fine!"

My chest was burning, I could not get enough breath and after one more trip down the floor, I called time out, crossed over to the coach and sobbed, "I think I'm dying!" His grin faded.

Mercifully, he took me out and I wheezed and trembled on the bench for the rest of the game. That "great physical condition" I thought I was in was only a myth. My chest burned and my heart pounded all night and the next morning my cigarettes went into the wastebasket. It took a few days for the ache in my muscles to subside and a week later I was a starter.

Although I was a player, this was really my first exposure to officiating. Looking back, I am sure my conduct was that of an obnoxious jerk at times, as I second-guessed our officials. However, it would be nine years later, when I began an officiating career in basketball and football, that I would realize how stupid I was, as a player, concerning the rules and the art of officiating.

The following spring the 7th Army merged with the 3rd Army and we moved to Heidelberg. One day while playing softball on the post's very large athletic field, I noticed a group of G.I.'s at the far north end, working out on the hard ball diamond. After one game ended, I wandered down there and discovered that it was the 3rd Army Headquarters baseball team practicing. I watched with great interest. As they were about to end their practice, a second lieutenant turned to me and queried, "Ever play baseball, Captain?"

I replied that I had, but not for four years.

He nodded and said, "Grab a glove and take some infield."

I did and it was a great feeling to be going for ground balls again and racing out for short pop-flies.

After awhile he said, "Grab a bat!"

In a few seconds I was at the plate for a few practice swings while the lieutenant assigned one of his pitchers to throw some to me. The first few pitches completely eluded me as I swung at them wildly, but soon I was getting my eye on the ball and hit a few loud foul balls. Finally, I swung at another pitch and heard a beautiful "crack" as the Louisville Slugger met the ball. Joyfully, I watched it clothesline to center field. I didn't hit many more that solidly, but my batting efforts did prompt the lieutenant to ask me to try out for the team.

All candidates who made the team were to be relieved of their present duties, and their new assignment would be playing baseball exclusively for 3rd Army Headquarters Baseball Team in the European Baseball League.

What an incentive! I made the team, and after about ten days of practice, orders came through relieving me of my duties as Highway Transportation Officer of 3rd Army Headquarters. I was simultaneously "attached unassigned to the 755th Field Artillery Battalion, (a mythical unit) for the purpose of playing baseball." The other candidates and I could now exchange our weapons for bats, our shells for balls, and for our defense, a serviceable baseball glove. What a way to end an army career of nearly three years!

The team had its own bus, painted in 3rd Army colors with the circle "A" insignia. My teammates were a great bunch, and I was fortunate enough to room with the great St. Louis Cardinal pitcher "Red" Munger. He would rejoin his major league club in time for the 1946 World Series against the

Boston Red Sox.

Most of the players were college or minor league athletes and completely dedicated to the sport. We practiced every day that we didn't have a game, and I soon ended up as a reserve infielder and first base coach. I would have made the first team if it hadn't been for two problems. I couldn't hit a fast ball and I couldn't hit a curve! But then, I didn't feel too bad. After all, even Mickey Mantle, the great home run hitter, struck out more than 1,500 times in only fifteen seasons!

We played against teams that had players on their roster who were either well known already, or soon would be. Cal McLish was one of them! He was a pitcher who could throw with either his right or left arm. He would pitch part of a game against us left-handed and after we got a few hits ol' Cal would switch to his "Major League" arm and our hits soon became misses.

In July of 1946 my orders came through reassigning me to the States for an honorable discharge from the service. My sudden departure propelled the team into the European Theater Championship. I never could figure out how they managed to do that without me.

Finally, in civilian clothes at last, I would concentrate my attention on what I would do for the rest of my life. I decided to enter graduate school at the University of Illinois until I could make up my mind. My lovely young wife and I moved into a third floor walk-up apartment that was on a par with the fun house at an amusement park. Among its many features was a gas cooking stove with no knobs. However, my wife simply used a pair of pliers to turn it on. I was turned on to school and to the adventures of a part-time salesman. This is where I learned the importance of developing a natural personality, how to plan my work and how to organize my time.

Within ten months, the sales job became more exciting and demanding, so I decided to leave school and enter the competitive world of commission selling, full-time. It was in commission selling that I met Joe Frank, who was an excellent high school basketball and football official on the side.

It's funny how little things can change a person's entire life. One day I was complaining to Joe about how out of shape I was. We talked about it briefly, then Joe suggested I get a license to officiate high school football and basketball. He declared, "That'll put you in shape, and keep you there, if it doesn't kill you first." While I was mulling that one over, the Army was precipitated into another mess, this time in Korea. I was summoned once again to see what I could do to straighten things out. However, the Army doctors checked me over and decided that the hills of Korea were a little too steep for a guy in my physical condition. So, out of the army and to a civilian doctor for some advice.

After the doctor looked me over, he asked, "Holst, are you living a normal life?"

I stiffened. "Certainly," I replied, with some pique. "I sure am!"

"I thought so," he growled. "You'll just have to cut it out for awhile! Lose some weight and get a lot of exercise!"

What did he know, I thought. Hell, I get enough exercise on my job, getting around, meeting people. For a couple of years Joe Frank kept selling me on the benefits of officiating, and only when I began panting while tying my shoe laces did I begin to take him seriously. Finally, when I realized he was not going to give up, I sent my application and five bucks to the Illinois High School Association and back came the rule book, case book and football test.

Knowledge is the first prerequisite for success in anything — be it selling, medicine, law or officiating. I say *pre*-requisite because it is *pre*-supposed that we know our jobs, whatever that job may be.

That first test impressed me with how precious little I really knew about the football rules. It is an open book test, as is our annual NFL test, and like the NFL test, it is a dilly! After hours of sweating over those questions, into the mail went the answers and a week later I had my card as a "registered" football official in Illinois. There are three levels: Registered, Recognized and Certified.

Now, where do you start? In my case, I went to the Champaign Officials Association meeting and, after paying my dues, announced my interest in working. Joe Frank, who accompanied me to the meeting said, "Why don't you come along with Emmerson Dexter (later to become mayor of Champaign) and me to Rantoul on Friday and we'll ask the coaches if you can work as a field judge."

I said, "Fine! When do we leave?"

That Friday was a cold, rainy September day and it got more so by evening. When we got to the dressing room in Rantoul at 6:30 p.m., Joe asked Bill Walsh, who was head football coach at

Rantoul at that time, if I could work, and he replied that it would be okay with him if the Leroy coach agreed. The Leroy coach did and I dressed for my first experience as a Zebra.

The weather was terrible! Rain and more rain! By the time the game ended I was ready to take a fresh look at my new career. This was to be only one of many bouts with the elements, and I was soon to learn that rain, heat, snow and frigid temperatures are all part of a football official's life. Watching an early winter snowfall through the picture window and in the warmth of my living room is wonderful, but that same snowfall while working a football game is miserable!

One thing you learn fast as an official: always expect the unexpected! That means being as well prepared as possible to deal with frustrating problems as they arise. For example, you're undoubtedly familiar with those thin plastic bags for luncheon sandwiches. They also serve as the waterproofing between two pairs of socks when officials are faced with a cold, slushy football field.

What about those plastic dry cleaners bags? We've used them as waterproof jackets by simply slitting openings in them for arms and head. Then slipping them over our shirts and underwear, but under the Zebra shirt, we had added protection from the elements. Now I use a regular plastic rain jacket designed for football officials. We also wear waffle-weave, insulated underwear, which provides light-weight protection from the cold and does not reduce one's mobility much.

Anticipating problems is the mark of a person who has it all together, whether he or she is a good salesperson, businessman, housewife, teacher, football official or clergyman. I add clergyman because I am reminded of the minister who anticipated problems on a certain Sunday when he was going to ask the congregation for a large contribution. Summoning the organist to his study, he said, "On Sunday, when I ask those in the congregation who wish to contribute $25 or more to stand up, be sure you play something appropriate.

"What would you suggest?" asked the organist.

"Something they're familiar with," replied the minister. " 'The Star Spangled Banner' will be fine!"

You have to think ahead! That's why the bag Zebras pack for a game each week has everything in it that might be needed. It must include a long-sleeved shirt, a short-sleeved shirt, long underwear, rain gear and so on. In short, you must prepare, in advance, to meet any conditions which may arise.

During the early pre-season games in 1965, I was assigned to officiate at a night game in Green Bay, Wisconsin, between Vince Lombardi's Packers and the New York Giants. It was a cold day in early September and every official brought his long-sleeved shirt — except the referee, "Red" Pace. He was the supreme optimist and brought only his short sleeves. I told him, "Red, you remind me of the guy who fell out of the 20th floor window and as he passed the 4th floor, grinned and yelled, 'So far, so good!' "

Of course, we all had to dress alike, so we were forced to wear our short sleeves. I damn near froze! However, I did manage to sponge a short-sleeved, waffle-weave underwear top from the Packer trainer and it sure helped. Incidentally, I still have it, and it bears the number 64. In case you've forgotten, that number belonged to that great offensive guard, Jerry Kramer. Trouble was, Jerry was about 255 pounds and I weighed 170, so there was room for me and enough extra space for my wife, had she been along.

That's one experience that sticks with me, and maybe, through the years, I've profited from it. Nevertheless, I still feel that whoever said, "Experience is the best teacher" is off his trolley! It's simply not true! It is the most expensive teacher in the world and can lead to any number of mistaken conclusions. For instance, a cat that jumps on a hot stove lid will never jump on a hot stove lid again — but the same cat won't jump on a *cold* stove lid either!

Officiating mechanics — the art of being in the right place at the right time and seeing the right thing at the right time — is a product of the experiences of countless officials in the NFL over a period of sixty years. So you learn from the knowledge of others, too. Others like "Shorty" Ray, Ron Gibbs, Dan Tehan, Emil Heintz, Norm Schachter, Art McNally and a host of fine officials whose knowledge and experience have helped make the game what it is today.

A businessman, a salesman, a manager, all must be knowledgeable about the past and have learned from it in order to function most efficiently and profitably in the present. The same logic applies in planning for the future. A "game plan" for the future which does not consider the experiences of the past is not a game plan at all — it's a guessing game.

The other extreme, of course, is being lulled to sleep by adopting the philosophy, "If it was a winner last year, then the same things will work this year." Responding to change is a vital part of any business that wants to survive and grow. Television's impact on NFL football is a perfect example. Attendance at games has grown with the growth and sophistication of the television coverage. The "instant replay" started in my first year as an NFL official. The microphone on the referee started in 1974. These ideas and many more were adopted to bring the fan in the stadium and those watching TV better coverage of the game — to make it more interesting and more understandable.

What can you learn from past experiences — and the experiences of others (positive and negative) in your business so that you can serve your market better today?

CHAPTER THREE

GETTING IN SHAPE

Theologian Tyron Edwards once said, "A sound mind in a sound body; if the former be the glory of the latter, the latter is indispensable to the former." And how true that is! A healthy body sharpens the mind! Health through exercise makes the blood sing and sharpens the thinking process.

"I've just got to get back in shape!" That's another quote, but it's said too often and rarely carried out. If I had ten bucks for every time I've heard those words, I could buy a gold bicycle, a platinum fishing rod and retire in luxury! My friend, there is only one way — START TODAY AND WORK AT IT!

In general, the American male is in woefully poor physical condition. He has been sold a life of comfort, convenience and ease until he has reached a point in his mid-forties and early fifties where he is a very enlarged shadow of his former self.

Getting into proper physical condition is an absolute must for a National Football League Official. What each individual does to accomplish this is his own business, but the results are the business of the National Football League and specifically

Supervisor of Officials Art McNally and his two assistants, Jack Reader and Nick Skorich. A full physical is required each June and woe be unto those who carteth too much fat.

In my opinion, physical conditioning — or more specifically, the lack of it — is a major problem in business and industry. I must admit, however, that there is some hope. Many companies are beginning to see the light and have programs of diet and weight control, exercise and recreation. Over four hundred major companies in the United States now have exercise facilities to encourage executive fitness.

Everyone who exercises has his or her own favorite method. Some folks jog; some play tennis; others prefer calisthenics. I'm a bike freak myself. To me the bicycle is an ideal conditioner. I try to ride at least six miles a day. Whenever possible, I up that to twelve or sixteen miles a day. I do it all in one trip, not in several short ones, and I ride at a good pace — a mile in about five and a half to six minutes, or about an hour and twenty minutes total. Of course, it is difficult to maintain this schedule while traveling, and it isn't always possible to do it every day; but if I can ride three to five days a week, I'm more than ready when the pre-season games begin in August.

Whatever your method, be it bicycling, jogging, swimming, or whatever, start slowly and work up. A good physical examination by a competent doctor is the mandatory first step. If you choose the bicycle, start with about two miles. Measure a mile with the family car, or better yet, install an odometer on your bike. Odometers are accurate and they'll tell you how far you've gone. That in itself will be a motivator for your next ride. Spend a couple of days at two miles, then up it to four. A few days at four and you'll be up to six. Six miles in thirty-five minutes is a nice period of exercise.

After a few days at six miles, stop for a drink (water, if you please), then climb back on your bike and do another four miles. A few more days and it will be sixteen miles. You won't believe how much you can eat, how good you will feel and how your body will begin to look a little more like it did when you were nineteen or twenty years old.

In officiating a pro football game, we cover about four to six miles a game, and some of it comes in hard bursts of speed to keep up with a streaking Walter Payton or a fleet flanker like Cliff Branch. If you've neglected your biking or jogging, you've "had it" when you take the field on a 90⁰ August afternoon with the artificial turf surface shimmering at a toasty 140⁰. It's too late then to realize you didn't get the "machine" ready.

Oppressive heat is hard on the officials, but it is even tougher on the players. In the mid sixties I officiated a game in Washington where one player lost over twenty pounds in just three hours. I lost a modest eight pounds that day.

Heat is not all bad, though. It can provide some opportunities for the wry humor that is an integral part of pro football. In 1965, my fellow officials and I worked a game in Baltimore. The field was like a furnace and the humidity was closely akin to a steam bath. A half-hour before game time we gathered for the coin toss. (Now it is done three or four minutes before kickoff). The winner of the toss would have the choice of kicking, receiving or choosing a goal.

Referee Norm Schachter nodded to the visiting captain and said, "Call the toss as the coin is in the air!"

"Heads!" came the cry as the coin spun in the hot, humid air and dropped to the ground.

Schachter looked and declared, "It's tails!" and turning to Baltimore Captain Johnny Unitas, said, "You win the toss, John. What'll you take?"

Without a second's hesitation, Unitas replied, "Norm, we'll take the shade!"

Sometimes I wonder if there would be an improvement in productivity, absenteeism and the sheer joy of working if the men and women of America were motivated to prepare their bodies as if they were to be called to officiate a game of football or actively participate in a sport? I wonder what would happen if our diets were rich in green vegetables, fresh fruits, lean meats, poultry and fish, and much lower in starches, desserts, sweets, alcohol and junk food?

Even if a person weren't called upon to perform with the stamina of an athlete, he would at least add years to his life. Ron Gibbs, one of the best referees ever to work pro football, was an active official even into his early sixties. People ask me, "How did he do it?" The answer was clear, "Because he was ready, physically, to do his job!" Are you? That's a blunt question, but it deserves an honest answer and immediate corrective action if the answer is negative.

Whipping yourself into good physical condition is hard work. Staying in good condition after you get there is relatively easy. The first requirement is a thorough physical examination by a competent doctor. Once that is done and he decides you're not too far gone to start a regimen of exercise, it's simply a matter of getting started. Don't waste another second. Get started now!

I used to jog to get into shape, beginning my routine immediately after my physical each April. I'd take it easy at first, by running fifty steps and walking fifty steps for a mile. When I surprised myself by surviving this, I increased the running to sixty steps and decreased the walking steps to forty. A few days later I'd run seventy steps and walk thirty, then eighty and twenty, ninety and ten. After a few weeks I could jog the entire mile, of which almost half was uphill. The next phase was to increase my speed, so that I would do 1.2 miles in ten minutes and do it five times a week.

One of the obstacles to jogging is making too much of it. Many men and women make it a time-consuming process by hopping into the family car and driving to the nearest school track or gym. I started from my own front door and jogged down the street. An added benefit when taking this route is the enjoyment of birds, trees and neighbors who are on hand as you go flitting by. Even the inevitable dogs. I have always felt that the dogs yapping at my heels helped condition my psyche for the yapping crowds who would disagree vehemently with my decisions once the season started.

Now, before you start dreaming up excuses for not being in shape, believe me when I tell you I've heard them all! "I can't find the time!" "My wife keeps me too busy on those 'honey-do' projects!"

"I'm too old!" "Too fat!" or "Too tired!" The truth is, we are subconsciously using our time to fit our own priorities. Think about it! A ten-minute martini is the one-mile jog! So is the six o'clock news on television. So is that cigarette you shouldn't be smoking anyway.

Think about it! Isn't it more important to increase the ability of your muscles and joints to function effectively for long periods of time? Isn't it more important to improve the efficiency and capacity of the heart, lungs and other vital organs? Of course it is! Go put on your jogging shoes!

Tony Veteri was the head linesman on our Super Bowl XII crew. If you have ever watched Tony work, you have seen him follow a wide receiver down the sideline on a long pass play. He is *always* with the receiver and, bear in mind, Tony is in his mid-fifties, running with a man young enough to be his son. Granted, it is his job to stay with the receiver, but to do that, he pays the price by keeping himself ready at all times.

In the National Football League, it is an individual responsibility to stay in shape. NFL officials are spread across the length and breadth of the continental United States and we have no one to enforce a conditioning program. We must discipline ourselves, not just for our well-being, but because we owe it to our fellow officials, the players, the coaches, and most of all, the fans, who expect us to be in top shape. A professional job of officiating a fast game demands it!

Getting into top physical condition is but one facet of an official's preparation for the season. Putting the grey matter in shape is another.

Knowledge of the rules is mandatory and football is a very complex game that demands constant rules study. Thought officiating was a guessing game, eh? Not so! Each year, around the first of May, we receive a test of about two hundred multiple choice questions. This mental hernia is devised by Norm Schachter, a top expert on football rules. He develops this test each year from cards that have been filed over the past seasons. Actual plays which point up a particular rules interpretation are recorded by Norm.

Sound enticing? Well, for you football fans, I'll pass on ten typical questions. Read them over carefully and circle (a), (b), (c), or (d) — whichever answer seems correct to you. If you decide that none of them is correct, use the space marked (e) to fill in your answer. Good luck! The correct answers are listed on the page following the questions.

1. (2nd-goal on B ½ yard line — 5 minutes left in 4th quarter) QBA1 tries a sneak but the ball leaves his hands just as he is tackled at the scrimmage line. The ball rolls into the end zone when the referee blows his whistle as he saw A1 stopped, but didn't know the ball had dropped out of his hands just as he was touched. B falls on the ball in the end zone. The line judge had raised his hands for a T.D.:
   (a) Touchdown
   (b) Touchback
   (c) A's ball — 3rd-goal on B1
   (d) A's ball — 3rd goal on B½ yard line
   (e) _____

2. (2nd-10 on 50 midway in the 1st quarter) Team

A has eight men on the scrimmage line and flexed End A2, who is the wide man on the right side of the line, starts in motion prior to the snap. A2 takes a forward hand off from QBA1 on the A45 and fumbles the ball which rolls to the A48 where B1 bats the ball to the B45. A2 picks up the ball and runs to the B41:
(a) A's ball — 3rd-1 on B41
(b) A's ball — 2nd-10 on 50
(c) A's ball — 2nd-15 on A45
(d) A's ball — 2nd-15 on A45 (blow whistle as A2 moved)
(e) _____

3. (3rd-6 on B8) QBA1 falls back to pass to the Tight End A2 who is in the end zone. A2 grabs B1 and pushes him out of the way to make a cut toward the corner of the end zone. A1 can't get the pass off and runs for a score.
(a) Touchdown — Kickoff A20
(b) A's ball — 3rd-16 on B18
(c) A's ball — 1st-goal on B15
(d) A's ball — 3rd-13 on B15
(e) _____

4. (4th-10 on A30) B1 gives an invalid fair catch signal on the B35. Just as he is reaching for the ball, A1 tackles him. B1 then catches the ball on the B34 as he is falling to the ground.
(a) A's ball — 4th-10 on A30
(b) B's ball — 1st-10 on B30
(c) B's ball — 1st-10 on B35
(d) B's ball — 1st-10 on B34
(e) _____

5. (3rd-14 on A4 in 1st quarter) QBA1 fakes a

handoff and drops back into his end zone to throw a pass. He is tackled and fumbles in the end zone and the ball rolls toward the side line. The ball is on the one yard line when A2 tries to fall on the ball, but it squirts away and hits the shaft of the goal line marker and B1 falls on the ball in the end zone. A3 had clipped before B1 fell on the ball and before the ball had hit the shaft.
(a) Touchdown — Kickoff 50
(b) Touchdown — Kickoff B35
(c) B's ball — 1st-10 on B35
(d) Safety — Kickoff A20
(e) _____

6. (3rd-5 on B30 in the 3rd quarter) A1 catches a backward pass on the B35 and runs to the B25 where he fumbles the ball. A2 pushes B1 from the rear on the B22 to shove him out of the way so he can recover the ball on the B20. He then runs for a score. The back judge had seen A3 go off the field on the wrong side prior to snap.
(a) Touchdown — Kickoff A30
(b) A's ball — 3rd-10 on B35
(c) A's ball — 3rd-15 on B40
(d) A's ball — 3rd-12 on B37
(e) _____

7. (4th-6 on B24) Tackle A1 (no. 78) enters the game and goes into the huddle without reporting to the referee and then takes a Tight End position. Field goal is blocked and the ball bounces on the B40 where B1 pushes A2 from the rear which shoves him away from the ball. B1 then tries to pick up the ball on the B40 and

bats the ball to the B30 where A2 picks it up and runs to the B15.
(a) A's ball — 4th-5 on B24
(b) A's ball — 1st-10 on B15
(c) A's ball — 4th-21 on B39
(d) B's ball — 1st-10 on B24
(e) _____

8. (4th-1 on B28) Team A shifts and comes to a stop for one second. End A2 then goes out along his line and stops. Halfback A3 then moves backward and the ball is snapped less than one second after A2 stopped. QBA1 sneaks to the B27. Linebacker B1 had jumped into the netural zone but moved back off the neutral zone before the snap.
(a) B's ball — 1st-10 on B27
(b) A's ball — 1st-10 on B27
(c) A's ball — 4th-6 on B33
(d) A's ball — 4th-1 on B28
(e) _____

9. (3rd-5 on 50) On the last play of the game, Team A is behind by a point and neither team has any time-outs left. QBA1 throws a forward pass to Flanker A2 who catches it and runs to the B8. B1 had blocked Wide Receiver A3 who had been split 6 yards from his tackle. He had blocked him below the waist on the scrimmage line.
(a) Game over
(b) A's ball — 1st-10 on B35 (untimed down)
(c) A's ball — 1st goal on B4 (untimed down)
(d) A's ball — 1st-goal on B8 (untimed down)
(e) _____

10. On a kickoff to start the second half, A1 is offsides. B1 tries to pick up the ball in the end zone and accidentally kicks the ball which rolls over the end line. B2 then clips A2 on the B4.
   (a) B's ball — 1st-10 on B2
   (b) B's ball — 1st-10 on B10
   (c) B's ball — 1st-10 on B20
   (d) Safety — Kickoff B10
   (e) _____

1. answer D - A's ball - 3rd goal on B ½ yard line
2. answer C - A's ball - 2nd-15 on A45
3. answer E - A's ball - 3rd-8 on B10
4. answer D - B's ball - 1st-10 on B34
5. answer E - Safety - Kickoff from A's 10 yard line
6. answer B - A's ball - 3rd-10 on B35
7. answer E - A's ball - 4th-11 on B29
8. answer B - A's ball - 1st-10 on B27
9. answer E - A's ball - 1st-10 on B's 45 (untimed down)
10. answer E - Rekick-A-35

Well, fans, how did you do? If you've checked the answers, you can now match your knowledge of the rules with the table below.

0 -1 Wrong: Expert — Get in shape! Football needs you!

2 - 3 Wrong: Very Good — You'll win most of your bets on the rules.

4 - 5 Wrong: Good — You not only enjoy the game, but you speak with some authority.

6 - 7 Wrong: Fair — You enjoy football, but don't expound on the game.

8 - 9 Wrong: Poor — You're in the sportscaster's

range. If your voice is abrasive and you know a lot of long words, apply for the job on Monday night football.

10 Wrong: No rating — watch soccer.

The test which comes down from the league office and Norm Schachter burdens an official with countless hours of hard work. I begin by answering all questions without the rule book. Then I check the doubtful ones against the rule book — usually about twenty questions. Finally, another official and I get together to compare answers and argue out our differences. He is Dick Jorgensen, a referee, but during the business week he functions as a bank president.

Gene Barth, another referee from St. Louis, sometimes comes up to meet with us. He is the president of an independent oil company. Both men are excellent officials, successful businessmen and good citizens. Surprisingly, in spite of the fact that all three of us are veteran officials, we will differ on the answers to three or four questions. Football is a very complex game, ruleswise, and sometimes we argue heatedly over a particular answer. However, honest differences of opinion between co-workers is a strength for any organization and should be encouraged.

A sales force, a company or a crew of football officials comprised of "yes" men is a poor substitute for the strength of a unit whose members know they can speak up without suffering ridicule. I spoke before a company a few years ago and at the conclusion of my talk, a bright young fellow approached me with an idea he had for his company. The more he talked, the more I realized he had thought out everything carefully, and knew what he was talking about.

I said, "Why don't you try it out on your boss?" His boss was the vice president of sales.

The young man smiled patiently and replied, "He'd laugh at me or ridicule me in some other manner. I've never known him to respond enthusiastically to an idea from anyone below his level."

What a pity. Oliver Wendell Holmes summed up this kind of situation very well. "Many ideas," he remarked, "grow better when transplanted into another mind than in the one where they sprung up. That which was a weed in one becomes a flower in the other, and a flower again dwindles down to a mere weed by the same change. Healthy growths may become poisonous by falling upon the wrong mental soil, and what seemed a nightshade in one mind unfolds as a morning glory in the other."

Our crew has a completely open line of communication between all seven of us. There is no question that this relaxed atmosphere which was established by our referee, Bob Frederic, number 71, has helped all of us many times.

I recall a game in Houston in 1971 when one of the crew called a foul for grabbing a face mask. A face mask foul can be a five-yard penalty or a fifteen-yard penalty if the official believes it's flagrant. I was near Bob as he began to walk it off. "Face mask — fifteen yards!" he said.

Very quietly I inquired, "Did you mean five yards, Bob?"

"That's right!" he replied, "Five yards!"

That's all there was to it. No big fuss. Nobody made to look bad — just a crew of Zebras working together to keep it a game and not a riot.

Briefly, that characterizes the NFL official — the ability to think and do. Both mind and body must be fine-tuned to function properly. The rigorous action on the field and the instant decisions that must be made demand it! Good physical condition clears the mind and enhances the powers of concentration. It is as true in the world of business as it is in the world of sports. Preparing yourself physically, as well as mentally, for the demands of your job will sharpen your zest for decision making and reward you with the knowledge that you have performed your work to the best of your mental ability.

So, whether you choose jogging, biking, tennis or swimming to improve your physical condition, don't put it off any longer! Do it now! You'll be proud of the new you!

CHAPTER FOUR

THE EARLY DAYS

Like Caesar's wife, a National Football League official must be above suspicion.

At every NFL game played in recent years, there is a crew of officials on the field in the full gaze of the 50,000 or so spectators, perhaps several million television viewers and one dyspeptic observer with an occasional ulcerous complex. He is there to find out if there is anything wrong. In all probability he is a retired NFL official and had developed under the same espionage system. I am now one of them.

This observer charts and notes the position of the field officials on every play, their response to the snap of the ball, their attention to details, their technique in declaring a rules infraction and their attitudes towards each other and to the players. After the game, he files his report with Art McNally, currently the supervisor of officials at New York City headquarters.

With this report in hand, Art McNally and his assistants, Jack Reader (a retired NFL referee) and Nick Skorich (former head coach of the Philadelphia Eagles and the Cleveland Browns) along with Mike Lisetski (a retired field judge) will view the game film and draw up a conclusion. Then the entire package will be air expressed to the location of the crew's next game, where it will be studied by the crew involved.

I knew when I became a Sunday Zebra in 1964 that the officiating was as perfect as humanly possible, but I never realized to what extent the NFL went to keep it so! An NFL official must be perfect in his debut, yet must improve each week! In fact, if you press me a bit I'll insist that the crews are absolutely perfect! Well, almost! But how did they get that way?

In my own case, a part of my early officiating experience included ten years of high school and college basketball. The "round ball" game has a great leveling effect. You can work the best basketball game possible and half of the crowd will swear on the proverbial "stack of Bibles" that you favored the winners, or that you were a "homer." Moreover, they all know that you are totally blind and should show up with a white cane or a dog — or both.

Even though basketball is a serious game, there is that bit of inside humor at all levels of officiating. I used to work basketball and football games in our own Mid-State Nine Conference out of my present hometown, Peoria, Illinois. There were five high schools in Peoria at the time and the one that served our part of town is Richwoods High. Back in the late fifties Athletic Director Bill Hughes was a good friend of mine and that friendship extends to this day.

Bill always sent a printed reminder card to the officials, noting the date and time of the game. But always — always at the bottom of my reminder post card, he would print, "P.S. Bring seeing-eye dog!"

Unquestionably, all basketball fans *think* they know the rules, while all the coaches and players are positive that they, themselves, do. What is overlooked is that there are intricacies in basketball rules that escape the eyes of coaches, too.

Years ago another official, Bill Hemphill, and I were working a college game in Jacksonville, Illinois between MacMurray College of Jacksonville and Augustana College of Rock Island, Illinois. It was a rough, hard-played game with more than its share of fouls. Late in the second half with a close score, one of us called a "common foul" on a MacMurray player. The "common foul" carried a one-shot penalty with a bonus shot if the first shot is made.

We lined up at the free throw line and I handed the ball to the Augie player for the free throw shot, which he promptly made. Just as the ball slapped through the net, Hemphill, who was under the bucket, blew his whistle and cried, "All right, you two! You're both out of the ball game!"

Surprised, I asked, "What's that all about, Bill?"

He replied, "Those two guys have been elbowing each other all night and I told them five minutes ago that the next time they did, out they'd go! Well, they did it!"

The place went up for grabs. The gym turned into a mad-house and the coaches, Bill Wall of MacMurray and Lenny Kallis of Augustana, were on their feet. I said to Hemphill, "Bill, you play

Andy Frain usher and get them seated, and I'll administer the free throws."

At this point no one knew what was to come except two Zebras. We shot the second free throw of the bonus, which the player also made, and then I called for the Augustana captain. I said, "I want any player in the game for your team to shoot two more!" The expulsions constituted a "flagrant double foul" and when coupled with a "common foul" become what is referred to in the rule book as a "false double foul." In this situation, you shoot all free throws and jump the ball at center.

Now was a good time for an official to be somewhere else. When Augustana went to the line for two more free throws, the hometown faithful went berserk. Some guy yelled, "Light a match, Ref, yer in a tunnel!" There were other admonitions, both clever and unprintable. Nevertheless, we moved the game along. We shot the two at Augie's end which made a total of four. Three of them were made. I then crossed over to the MacMurray captain and said, "I want anyone from your team to shoot two free throws at your basket!"

As we approached the free throw circle, my good friend, Bill Wall, the MacMurray coach, stood with knuckles on hips, coat off and tie undone. Glaring at me, he yelled, "Art, what in the hell are you doing?"

I walked over to him at the sidelines with the ball under my arm and replied, "Bill, we're about to shoot our fifth and sixth free throws during the same dead ball. Now if you don't sit down, we're going to set a new intercollegiate record and shoot seven!"

The capper to this strange but true story occurred later that evening. As we were dressing after our showers, the assistant coach for MacMurray came into the dressing room and said, "Coach Wall sent me. He looked the play up in the Case Book and you guys were right!"

I said, "You go back and tell Coach Wall that's what he's paying us for."

As we left the dressing room to start back to Peoria, Hemphill and I happened to walk out behind the Augustana team. They had lost by a few points and were naturally disappointed. Coach Wall and Coach Kallis of Augustana were walking together and we overheard Wall say, "Lenny, the officials were right on that call."

Without even looking up, Kallis shook his head and murmured, "They couldn't have been!"

It may have happened before or since, but I have yet to find a basketball official who was in a game where six free throws were shot during the same dead ball. Thank God the exact play was in the basketball Case Book.

Wall is now employed by the United States Olympic Committee and I occasionally see him on an airplane as he also travels a lot. Inevitably, the unusual multiple free throw incident comes up and we enjoy a good laugh together.

My high school officiating was all I had hoped for and more. I learned early that you don't perform this kind of job with the expectation of praise.

As I mentioned earlier, officiating is the only career I know of where you are required to be perfect the first time out and then get better as you go along! If you do everything right, you're like Raquel Welch's elbows — everybody knows you're there, but nobody gives a damn! If you do anything wrong — or anything someone thinks is wrong — you are treated like a puppy who has just committed its first social error on the new living room rug. What in heaven's name brings men into this thankless business? I think it is a deep love of the game and the pride in doing something well under great pressure.

I have always felt that I want to please myself, Art Holst, first — to have that self-satisfaction that comes from doing a job right. Number two, I want to please my fellow officials on the crew. The greatest feeling in officiating is to walk off a field after a game and not want to change a thing, knowing that every flag thrown, every signal given, every whistle blown, was right. Realistically, that is not always the case. But the striving for it, the effort, the dedication to be 100% right — that's always the challenge.

Think about it! Isn't that true throughout life? One missed block can screw up an otherwise perfect play. One missed appointment in business can lose a big sale. In flying, one mistake can be fatal. Charlie Jarvis, a speaker friend of mine, who is one of the best, is also a great humorist. One of his many talents is piloting his own plane. On the instrument panel he has a little sign that reads, "One crash can spoil the whole day!" Ain't it the truth?

So the "high grass" leagues (the small towns with poor lights), where the Zebras gather in the fall to officiate the small high school games, are the fields on which the habit of good officiating is developed.

When I began my officiating career, most high school games used three officials — a referee, an umpire and a head linesman. The larger high schools and small colleges added another, thus making it four. He was the field judge. It is at these high school games that officials learn the fundamentals of good football officiating. *The most important game being played anywhere on that weekend is that game!* Whether the game was between Princeville and Chillicothe High School in Central Illinois or the Chicago Bears playing the Green Bay Packers. As far as the teams involved are concerned, their game is *the* most important game on earth and deserves the best possible job from the officials.

We have a saying in football, "We are only as good as our next game!" This is true in any endeavor. As a salesman, personnel manager, secretary, surgeon or business executive, *you* are only as good as your next sales interview — your next management conference — your next letter — your next operation — or your next decision. Make it your best. No matter how impossible the task may seem, give it all you've got! A half-hearted effort is worse than no effort at all.

I am reminded of a classic story where the individual players gave their best. Most players do. They can't help it. It's a matter of pride. There was a football game played in 1916 that was hopelessly one-sided. Little Cumberland College of Lebanon, Tennessee had accepted an invitation to play Georgia Tech. In her salad days Cumberland had a great team, but now she had nothing but her old reputation and sixteen battered players. Nevertheless, Cumberland packed up their gear and limped to Atlanta, where the big game would be played.

In those days, college coaches picked up players wherever possible. The strict rules we are familiar with today never existed then. Just about anyone could play, and sometimes even the coaches played. Cumberland's coach at that time was a native of Dallas named Butch McQueen. The story goes that when a reporter asked him how he managed to pick a winning team year after year, he replied, "What I do is take a tour of the countryside and look over the farm. Whenever I see a farm boy plowing, I ask him the way to the nearest town. Now, if he points with his finger, I leave him. If he points with the plow, I take him." That old story has also been attributed to Bernie Bierman of Minnesota — and many others.

Georgia Tech fielded thirty players and Cumberland was now down to fourteen, having lost a few on the way. The game was a disaster from the beginning. Tech scored 63 points in the last period and another 63 in the second. One hundred-twenty-six points by the half! Nevertheless, the pitiful few of Cumberland fought their hearts out. They were simply outmanned and outplayed. But they never gave up. Despite injuries and humiliation, they kept coming back.

The third period was just as disastrous as the previous two. Georgia Tech scored another 54 points. Still Cumberland didn't know they were beaten. With the score now, Georgia Tech 180, Cumberland 0, the teams lined up for the final quarter. It should never have been played, but the gallant men of Cumberland took on the steam roller once more.

No Hollywood ending here. No rash of scoring of the underdogs. Just a super exhibition of guts and determination. Tech piled up another 42 points and the final gun sounded. The final score: Georgia Tech 222, Cumberland 0. And not one first down was made all day!

All kinds of records were set that historic day, but the one that did not get into the record book was the gallant stand made by that little team from Cumberland. Their performance was a good example of the positive mental attitude which can give your business and personal life a new quality that you never realized existed. What's more, your level of self-respect will rise to the brim.

Confidence and self-respect are born from experience. I was a field judge much of the time in high school football, and although the job lacked the glamor or the referee's position, I was gaining valuable experience in judging those downfield pass interference calls. A young official has to learn to look away from the ball and the ball carrier in order to get an overview of what the other twenty or so players are doing. The awareness of the wild zebra is developed in the repetitive learning process while in the protection of its mother and herd. It's the same in flying. The student does the same thing over and over again under the watchful eye of a competent instructor until he can do it right *all the time*. This type of experience is necessary and vital for a football official.

The rules state that all offensive backfield players (except the quarterback, who is in position to receive a hand-to-hand snap from the center), and the two men on either side of the line are eligible pass receivers for the offensive team. I hasten to add that, naturally, all defensive players are eligible.

Question: Suppose the snapper (usually called the center) snaps the ball from the end of the line? Is he eligible? The answer is "yes!". There is no rule which dictates that the ball must be snapped from the middle of the line.

The Detroit Lions used a play wherein the ball was snapped by the end, during the 1975 season. Although I did not work any Detroit game in which it was used, Detroit Coach Rick Forzano did alert me that the play might be used in the Astrodome when Detroit played Houston in 1975. The point is that you have to know these details about the game — right now, without the rulebook — and be ready to recognize them and make the correct call. It's the old story, "Don't call 'em like you see 'em; call 'em right!"

Learning to "call 'em right" begins at the high school level in officiating. When I talk about high school football officials, please bear in mind these men learned their craft at $12.50 to $20 per game and drove from 50 to 150 miles round trip on Friday and Saturday nights to gain experience — to develop the habit of being right. To paraphrase Charles Kettering, the great inventor at General Motors, "Luck is what happens when opportunity meets the prepared mind." Or to put in Vince Lombardi's words, "Winning isn't a sometime thing, it's an all time thing!"

How true, and I'm deeply grateful to the hundreds of high school coaches and officials who patiently watched my early errors and helped me to grow to full stature as an official — a line judge in the National Football League.

CHAPTER FIVE

IT JUST GREW AND GREW

College football, originally a blend of rugby and soccer, is generally regarded as having been born in 1869 when Rutgers and Princeton tangled following a fall baseball series that failed to determine which team was superior. Others say that Harvard and McGill University in Canada played the first game. Most all historians agree, however, that 1869 was the year.

From the beginning, football was played hard. It was a very emotional game in those days, perhaps even more so than it is today. For example, the Army-Navy game of 1893 stands out as one of the biggest "donnybrooks" in the history of the sport. Both teams were equally powerful, and both determined to win. All of the care and training by their respective academies to mold them into officers and gentlemen went out the window, as they slugged and maimed each other throughout the game. Even the cadets and spectators in the stands were infected by the mayhem and began to misbehave.

Then an astonishing incident occurred. A brigadier general, so incensed with the way things were going, summarily "decked" a too-vociferous admiral. This deed immediately netted him a challenge to a duel. Fortunately for both, they were such lousy shots that only a few twigs on nearby trees were shattered.

Unfortunately, the news of this caper and the misconduct of players and spectators during the game reached the ears of President Grover Cleveland, who issued an order that the annual Army-Navy game never be played again. After a five-year cooling off period, however, a new chief executive, President William McKinley, rescinded the order and allowed the traditional contest to resume.

If 1869 was the year football was born on the college gridiron, it didn't take long thereafter that high schools embraced the sport and soon each village and hamlet had its own team. Here was the ultimate foundation for professional football. Most especially was this true in Pennsylvania, upper New York state and Ohio.

As the sport gained in popularity, it would soon follow, naturally, that play for pay would open up the mad, mad world of professional football. John Brailler, who learned some football at Indiana State of Indiana, Pennsylvania, and later was quarterback at the University of West Virginia, is regarded as the original athlete who played for pay. Brailler, who later became a Latrobe, Pennsylvania, dentist, was guaranteed ten dollars to guide Latrobe in its August 31, 1895 contest with Jeannette, a neighboring village. (Both towns are less than fifty miles from Pittsburgh.) Latrobe in 1896 prided itself on the fact that every member of its town team was accepting pay — football's first all-professional team. (Latrobe has since become reknowned because of a golfer named Arnold Palmer.)

The sport was on its way. It spread throughout the eastern half of the United States with the speed of a measles epidemic, centering primarily in Ohio.

Philadelphia's baseball immortal, Connie Mack, organized the Philadelphia Football Athletics and claimed the 1902 world title at the end of the year. But it was another Philadelphia team, the Nationals, which lost to Syracuse with Glenn (Pop) Warner in the lineup, 6-0, in New York's first Madison Square Garden and pro football's first indoor game. It was a social event with the officials wearing high hats, tails and white gloves — a far cry from the Sunday Zebras of today.

Bidding for the most talented players, Sunday by Sunday, soon threatened the sport. Massillon, Ohio, had 45 players on the bench, but used only 15 in one game, thus ensuring that they would not be available to the opposition. The Columbus Panhandlers, a team of railroad men with seven players named Nesser in the starting lineup, played against Knute Rockne, later to become Notre Dame's great coaching genius. They played on six consecutive Sundays and always in a different uniform.

Things got so bad that finally, on September 17, 1920, the pioneering fathers met in the Hupmobile garage of Ralph Hays in Canton, Ohio, and organized the American Professional Football Association. It is not recorded whether or not they had a chaplain bless the meeting, but they did manage to get underway before twelve noon with a bucket of beer on each fender of the two cars on display. Toward evening, when both the beer and daylight were gone, the Association had been organized with Jim Thorpe, the great Carlisle halfback, as president.

Unfortunately, Thorpe was a better player than executive and at the end of the season the Association was reorganized with Joseph F. Carr elected president. He remained head of the group, which became known as the National Football League in 1922, for nineteen years. He calmed the troubled waters by compelling the clubs to recognize the contracts signed by players of other clubs and to keep hands off players with college eligibility remaining.

The first few years of Carr's reign were rocky ones financially, but pro football struck a gold mine in 1925 when Harold "Red" Grange, a University of Illinois sensation during his entire collegiate career, signed a contract with the Chicago Bears a day after Illini's final game of the season against Ohio State.

The crowds now began clamoring for tickets. In his first game as a pro at Wrigley Field in Chicago, Grange accomplished little, but his share of the gate receipts came to $36,000. The "Galloping Ghost," as sportswriters referred to him, was paid by the game and soon amassed a fortune. He lured 35,000 to a game in Philadelphia and 24 hours later he thrilled a crowd of 70,000 who watched him score against the New York Giants in the Polo Grounds. For carrying the ball in his first pro season, "Red" Grange collected an incredible $300,000, but he had given football its needed shot in the arm.

The game rolled along, gathering momentum, during the ensuing years. Then in the waning weeks of 1932, the division of the NFL into eastern and western divisions was accomplished. This act established a format that continues today. During the 1930's the Bears, Green Bay and the Giants dominated the league.

The next decade opened auspiciously when the Bears, playing what had often been called the "perfect game", crushed the Washington Redskins, 73-0 for the 1940 title. Despite this debacle, Washington was a contender most of the way through the turbulent years of World War II. The NFL's own private war with the All-American Conference ended when it was taken over later in 1950 by the older circuit. Cleveland, best of the teams to move into the NFL from the All-American Conference, had things its own way for the next ten years, but in 1960 another professional league appeared. It called itself the American Football League and immediately began clamoring for recognition.

On the playing fields of the two rival loops, most of the interest was focused on Wisconsin's Green Bay Packers, under the tutelage of the great Vince Lombardi. The Packers lost to the Philadelphia Eagles, 17-13, for the 1960 NFL championship before winning the crown in 1961, 1962, 1965, 1966 and 1967. In addition, they defeated Kansas City of the AFL, 35-10, in the first of the Super Bowl series which began after the 1966 season. The following year they defeated Oakland in Super Bowl II. Shortly after, Lombardi announced his retirement as head coach of the Packers.

Finally, the two leagues announced plans for a formal merger in the mid-summer of 1966, which would be completely effective in 1970 with a realignment of clubs.

The speed with which professional football captured the imagination of the sports-loving population of the United States has often been attributed to television. The Sunday afternoon scheduling of inferior programs has now been replaced with action-filled coverage of NFL games, with the various TV networks paying millions of dollars for the privilege.

And what about television? Has it, with its millions of arm-chair quarterbacks, hurt physical attendance at NFL contests? Not in the least! In 1934, the first year attendance figures were kept, the NFL teams played 61 games with an average paying attendance of 8,770. In contrast, the 1976 figures for the 28 clubs playing 290 games was 15,071,846, an average of 51,972. This includes pre-season, play-off and Super Bowl X games.

Obviously, television has gathered many new fans to football. The excellent direction, camera work and instant replay has taught the viewer what the game is all about. So much so, that his next step is opting for the excitement and color of the game at its source. Even the lady of the house, if not already a fan, becomes one in self-defense. When you can't beat 'em — join 'em!

Women are learning that football can become their arch rival. A bit of fictional fun in this regard involves a group of Sunday fans gathered in their usual box. They never missed a game, sleet, snow, cold, ice, but this Sunday one of the group was missing. "Hey, where's Harry?" inquired one of those present.

Another replied, "Didn't you know? He's getting married today at 2 o'clock."

"Aw, fer cryin' out loud," the first guy complained, "he'll miss the whole first half!"

No one is certain just who officiated the first game played in the newly-organized American Professional Football Association back there in the late summer of 1920. There had been two meetings prior to the inaugural games to devise an agreement on rules, but the names of the men who were to enforce them have been lost as hopelessly as the name of the guy who invented the wheel.

But there were great officials from the start. Perhaps they were not as polished nor as well versed in the code as those of today, but they approached their tasks with a love of the game, and managed to wield a style of authority that created respect.

A case in point: Norman Cahn was either a referee or an umpire as the situation demanded. If he stood on your toes, which he was not loath to do, he might hit 5'1". If he carried a pair of shoulder pads under each arm he might push the needle of the scale to 140. He could easily stand in the shade of most of the men who had to obey his whistle. Cahn's personality was as fiery as his vocabulary. What's more he had a quick mind which permitted him to find a solution to any problem he might encounter. It didn't matter to Cahn, who officiated for twenty-three years in the NFL and its antecedents, that some of his solutions were never included in the rule book. What the hell! Whatever worked!

Back in the early days there was an intense rivalry between the Chicago Bears, owned by George Halas, and the Rock Island Independents. Each club had a great center and the two men were mortal enemies.

Louis Kolls, later to become an umpire in the major leagues, snapped the ball for the Independents. He hailed from little St. Ambrose College of Davenport, Iowa, an institution which has never shaken the football firmament with its prowess. George Trafton, now in the professional Football Hall of Fame had the same job with the Bears. He was a product of the University of Notre Dame, then as now, a member of the gridiron elite.

Cahn refereed one of the games and told his aides, "We'll just let these two kill themselves, if necessary. Otherwise we'll be calling double fouls all afternoon!"

He could be as wise as Solomon, too, when it involved coaches and owners. He was the referee again in a game in which the Bears tangled with the Detroit Lions, guided by the legendary Potsy Clark. Coaching from the bench was not allowed at the time, but Halas and Clark didn't care. They vied with each other, sneaking down their respective sidelines and trying to hide behind the light towers which ringed the field, all the while shouting and inspiring their teams.

Cahn watched the charade for some time, then erupted. He called the two coaches to the center of the field and introduced the two to each other. "Doctor Livingston," he said, turning to Clark, "meet Mr. Stanley. Now the two of you keep the hell off the sidelines and go to your benches! From now on you get 15 yards each time you move!"

They obeyed.

His lack of size was a constant irritant to Cahn. Cal Hubbard, who Cahn once called the smartest player he ever met when it came to the rules of the game, never missed a chance to needle the official with the differences in their sizes. If there was a rules dispute while a game was in progress, Hubbard would pitch into it. All during his long career as a tackle with the New York Giants and the Green Bay Packers, he would listen to the official's interpretations and then usually end the conference with, "The little boy is right! Let's play football!"

Once when the Packers were entertaining the Bears at Green Bay, Cahn took time out to lecture an errant Chicago lineman, who equaled Hubbard's six-foot-five-inch height. Hubbard trotted over to the scene of the debate. Both players towered sixteen inches over Cahn. Hubbard listened briefly, then put his arms under the referee's waist and lifted Cahn at least two feet off the ground before saying, "Now, little boy, tell the guy face to face!"

Cahn's reaction? Years later Cahn told Howard Roberts of the *Chicago Daily News,* "When Hubbard picked me up, it made me feel ridiculous, but when he dropped me on my head, it made me damn mad!"

Today, of course, laying a hand on an official is grounds for a 15-yard penalty and disqualification. An early trip to the showers.

Cahn had absolutely no objection to using profanity to get a point across and only once in his long career did a player get the best of him. Joe

Stydahar, the mountainous tackle from West Virginia University, was just the opposite. He never used profanity and would not permit its use within his hearing.

In an early 1936 game Cahn blew his whistle and dashed up to Stydahar, baying, "What the hell do you think you're doing out here?"

Stydahar blanched, then looking down sternly at the midget-sized referee, he admonished, "Mr. Referee, I don't swear, I don't curse and I refuse to answer questions from anyone who does!"

Cahn quickly deleted the expletive.

But this kind of situation can be turned around. Officials aren't as salty as you might think. Actually, we're a religious lot. Tom Thorpe, not related to the famous Jim Thorpe, was a very religious man and proved it one day when a player stepped out of line. The particular player that Tom confronted was unusually profane and as the action got hotter, so did his language. Thorpe warned him several times, but it did no good. Finally, exasperated, Tom threw him out of the game.

He was immediately swamped by the player's teammates, the man on the bench and the coach. The player wanted to know, "What rule did I violate?"

Tom gave them all a cold stare and snapped, "The Golden Rule! Now get off the field!"

Dan Tehan, later to be elected Sheriff of Hamilton County, Ohio, for twenty-four years, joined the NFL staff in 1930 at the age of twenty-two, and did not retire from active officiating until 1964. During those years Tom Thorpe and Tiny Maxwell dominated in the East. Tehan was a press box observer of officials for the NFL for another fifteen years — a remarkable record.

Jim Durfee was also somewhat of a legend as an NFL official. He was from Chicago and a friend of Joe Carr, then the Commissioner of the National Football League. Durfee worked many of the tough ball games back at the time and had the reputation of being very proud and arrogant. It was also said that his reading of the rule book was confined to infrequent occasions, so he was known to improvise.

Once in a New York — Pittsburgh Steeler game, the Giants broke through just as the Pittsburgh quarterback was getting ready to pass. The quarterback quickly threw the ball to the ground and Durfee called it a simple incomplete pass. The Giants were hollering for an intentional grounding penalty.

"No, No!" said Durfee positively, "I could see the quarterback's eyes and he had no intention of grounding it!" He made it stick but Steve Owen, the head coach of the New York Giants, cast a vociferous dissenting vote.

Actually, there are many things an official sees on the field which lead him to a "common sense" decision, not supported by the view of the coach, the spectator or the television camera. I have seen a defensive man do everything to "bridge" a runner already down to avoid piling on. To the fan, the camera and the coach it looked like unnecessary roughness but the official is in the best position to see the play — so, no foul!!

Durfee once chided a player who insisted that an opponent had been out of bounds during a play but had re-entered the field to recover the fumble.

Durfee would have none of it, saying the play was covered under Rule 5, Section 3, Page 23 of the rule book. That settled the argument. Later, however, the player hunted up a rule book and learned that Rule 5, Section 3, on page 23 explained: "No player shall wear equipment, which in the opinion of the referee endangers other players, and all men must wear on the back and front of their jerseys, identification numbers."

Following World War II, referees Ron Gibbs and Emil Heintz dominated the scene until their retirements. Between 1942 and 1960 Gibbs refereed all but four of the NFL championship games. Five in a row at one time, four straight another time. He was an NFL referee for 25 years — from 1939 — 1963.

Heintz' career paralleled that of Gibbs. He joined the NFL the same year, but retired a year earlier after having worked nine consecutive Pro Bowl games.

Another of that vintage was referee Harry "Bud" Brubaker. I was privileged to have served on his crew in 1969 — his last year as an active official. He admitted to only one bad call in his NFL career. En route home from Baltimore's blanking of the Cleveland Browns game, 34-0, in the 1968 NFL title game, he was asked how the Colts would fare against the New York Jets in their game coming up in two weeks.

"The Jets haven't got a chance," he replied, "the Colts'll wallop them!"

The Jets and Broadway Joe Namath disagreed, 16-7.

Since the merger of the American Football League with the National Football League in 1966 and the subsequent division of the combine into two thirteen-club conferences, such officials as Tommy Bell, a ranking Kentucky lawyer during the week, Norm Schachter, a Los Angeles school system executive, Joe Connell, Jim Tunney, Lou Palazzi, and Stan Javie have carried on the Sunday Zebras' brand of excellence. Norm Schachter was not only a great referee, he is co-editor of the NFL Rulebook and compiles all of the rules tests.

Since 1925, only five years after professional football came into formal being, it has lived under a code of written rules. Entrusted with compiling the code was a scrawny little man, Hugh "Shorty" Ray. It was he who devised the modern method of a permanent crew of officials, working together each Sunday and demanding written reports from them He conducted rules interpretation and in 1925 formed a national organization of officials. Ray produced a football code for national high school athletic associations in 1929 which to this day is the basis for every football rule book ever written. "Shorty" Ray is enshrined in Pro Football's Hall of Fame in Canton, Ohio.

The NFL rules, refined by more than fifty years of experience and use, have been recodified and modernized from time to time, the most recent of which was done by Norm Schachter, who retired after Super Bowl X in which Pittsburgh defeated Dallas, 21-17, on January 18, 1976. Schachter was my crew chief when I joined the Zebras in the 1964 season.

All of the men I've mentioned and more were officiating pioneers who laid well the foundations for honesty and integrity upon which a statue of the Sunday Zebra could be erected. All enjoyed, but with their own variations, the slam-bang, head-knocking football of those early days.

The slam-bang, head-knocking growth of private enterprise in America has been mirrored by the phenomenal growth of professional football, and the reasons for continued and successful growth are the same for both football and business in general. It has been said that, "an institution is the long shadow of one man."

I would change that to say that "a lasting institution is the long shadow of many talented, dedicated and hard-working men and women who pursued a great dream, and were willing to pay the price for success."

In football those men include George Halas, George Preston Marshall, Art Rooney, Jim Thorpe, Red Grange, Bert Bell, Sid Luckman, Vince Lombardi, Pete Rozelle and many more. It is impossible to name all of them. But, it is possible to look at some common traits among this group of men from a wide variety of backgrounds who contributed so much to the growth of this game.

Knute Rockne knew what was required in a man for him to succeed. His six basic requirements for players can also be applied to the officials or to anyone else.

1. Brains — resiliency of mind. Resourcefulness. Power of analysis.
2. Spark — the emotional urge that lifts a man out of the commonplace.
3. Hard work — no man ever succeeded without it.

4. Proper point of view — to play fairly, to respect the rights of opponents and rules of the game.
5. Sense of responsibility — chores pay dividends, and clearing the path for a teammate comes under the heading of chores.
6. Mental and moral courage.

These qualities are what makes leaders of men. Off the playing field and in the hard world of business they are equally vital. Develop them and apply them to your own career. The results may astound you.

If you possibly can, tour Professional Football's Hall of Fame in Canton, Ohio. See George Halas' notebook from the 1930's, where he kept the records of income from ticket sales, concessions, etc. Look at the worn shoulder pads of Jim Thorpe and you can almost feel the enthusiasm that is a part of any new venture struggling to keep its flickering flame alive. Think of the constant dedication that went into pro football to maintain that life. Like mouth-to-mouth resuscitation, it can only be successful if those breathing life into it have the dedication, knowledge and creative thinking to make it succeed. This is not Pollyanna stuff! Whether we talk about the Ford Motor Company, pro football or one insurance salesman, knowledge, dedication, creative thinking, enthusiasm and hard work pay off.

I sub-leased office space from a real estate broker in my home town some ten years ago. He leased *four times* as much space as he could use because, as he said, "In two years I'll need all of it!" And he did!

Dedication to excellence is not easy, but a business that is populated with men and women who have this dedication to excellence cannot fail.

Vince Lombardi said, "I want forty men who believe they can win a national championship. If they are not here, I'll find them!"

Statistics don't win championships! Teams win championships and championship teams are built and maintained carefully by top coaching and management.

Yes, it started in Canton, Ohio on September 17, 1920, in a garage and now it is in practically every home in America at least once a week! It just grew and grew — but it had a lot of help.

CHAPTER SIX

MY DEBUT . . . AND MORE

My first league game as an NFL Zebra was a memorable one for me. It occurred in Green Bay on opening day, September, 1964, and was memorable because, for the first time in pro football, a rare offensive play was successfully completed and I was in the thick of it!

The Packers were playing the world-champion Chicago Bears. It was a cool day with a brisk north wind insisting that it, too, intended to get into the game. There were less than thirty seconds left to play in the first half and the Bears had the ball deep in their own territory. A punt was called and the Bears would have to kick out of their own end zone.

Back in the Packers' secondary loomed number 22, Elijah Pitts, playing safety. The ball was booted and soared aloft. Pitts on his own 48-yard line raised one hand fully extended above his head, the signal for a "fair catch." As soon as that signal is given there are three promises made. A receiver says, "I promise if I catch the ball, I won't run with it."

The kicking team then returns the courtesy by

saying, "We promise if you do catch it we won't tackle you."

Then there's a third promise, this one from the officials. We say, "We promise that if any of you birds breaks your promises, we're going to throw the flag!"

Pitts caught the ball on his own 48-yard line and kept his promise. I signaled time out, looked at my watch and saw there were only four seconds left in the half. At that moment a voice from the Green Bay side declared, "We want a free kick!"

I learned later that the owner of that voice was Jerry Kramer. He had been studying the rule book a couple of nights before and had come across that rule. He was right and we were then obliged to line the Packers up on their own 48-yard line. The Bears were lined up ten yards away at their own 42. This done, I went to my position under the goal post. Norm Schachter, head of our five-man crew placed himself behind Paul Hornung, who was to kick for Green Bay. Paul nailed the ball and it sailed for the goal post, but then it began to falter and it appeared that it would fall short. At that moment the wind got into the game. It picked up briskly, caught the ball and carried it over the cross-bar by inches! Three points!

The only time that play had ever been successfully completed in the history of professional football — and I was privileged to call it in my first game as a National Football League Official. What a thing to remember!

I shot both arms into the air with a vigorous "good" signal and fired my gun to end the half. Immediately a rather incensed fan in a grey jacket vaulted the low rail separating the playing field from the stands, his beady eyes riveted on me.

At that time our dressing room was located at the north end of the stadium — right near the hot dog stand. (It's always nice to be near the food.) Since we had to go through the crowd of fans to get to our dressing room, the Green Bay police department had a man assigned to us as we came off the field. This guy came running up to me and yelled, "You son-of-a-bitch, you're always figuring out some new way to beat the Bears." Needless to say he was a Bear fan, he did not like the field goal and he did not know the rule. Nevertheless, I said nothing as I edged closer to the friendly policeman and continued on my way to the dressing room. In a situation like that, you're better off as an official to keep your big mouth shut.

That was the first time that play had been successfully completed and it has only been repeated once since. Interestingly, the other time occurred in another Green Bay-Chicago Bears game. Again, it happened in Green Bay in 1968. Max Percival kicked the ball for the Bears after a Chicago fair catch and made a 48-yard field goal. Bob Frederic, the referee on our present crew, was one of the officials in that game. The play has been tried a few other times since then, but never successfully.

I will always remember how Green Bay was professionally ready to grasp the opportunity when it presented itself. There was no time wasted sitting around discussing the situation. A decision had to be made and someone had to make it. That's leadership. There is an old Arab proverb that suggests, "When you are an anvil, be patient; when a hammer, strike!"

Of course, this old proverb assumes that you and I know what to strike, when to strike and how to use the hammer before the opportunity ever arises, and this was exactly the case in Green Bay. Someone knew the rule and was ready. Paul Hornung was a good kicker and the wind was at their backs. Moreover, the percentages for scoring with an unmolested field goal attempt were far better than any other way.

Seizing the initiative might be labeled, "Now-or-never thinking." Procrastination — putting things off — deciding to wait too long is often disastrous in selling, in managing and in life itself. Our time is too valuable to waste, just like the time left in the first half of that football game. When the clock said four seconds, the immediate question was, "How can we use that four seconds to our best advantage?"

There were no tomorrows on that play and believe me, there is no tomorrow where putting good habits to work is concerned. We owe this to ourselves, our companies, our families, and most of all to our God, who gave us our talents to develop to their fullest extent.

Indecisiveness is the death trap of officials. In 1970, Bob Finley was the referee of our crew when we worked a game in the inevitable snow of Buffalo. It seems like it always snows when I officiate a game in Buffalo, the home of God's Frozen People!!

The Bills were playing the Baltimore Colts in the stadium's winter wonderland. It was snowing hard when the stadium crew removed the tarp from the field shortly before the kickoff. It was a wasted effort, for in a matter of minutes the field was solid white. No side lines, no goal lines, nothing in the way of markings, except the flags fluttering above the snow at the corners of the end zone and the goal lines.

Things got so bad during the game that Finley had to call a "time-out." Calling the coaches together, he said, "We're not going to be able to measure any first downs and the side officials are going to have to line up between the flags and make out-of-bounds decisions based on what they believe is right." With that understood, the game proceeded.

Never do I remember a game where so many arbitrary decisions were made with such a minimum of help, accompanied by such a minimum of controversy. The head linesman placed the stakes where, to the best of his knowledge, the ball was. Then when the action brought the ball close to a first down, the referee made a decision. Either it was, or it wasn't.

We had a play on the goal line — right near where the chair lift should have been! By this time the snow was deep and there were piles of it a few feet from the side line.

Buffalo erupted with a running play to my side and I hung in there, watching them come, trying to sight between the goal line flag behind me and the one across the field. I should have moved quicker. The ball carrier got hit by several Baltimore tacklers, right at the goal line and about seven hundred pounds of meat hit me and upended me into a snow bank. Now the question was, did all of the ball get out of the end zone? If it didn't, it was a safety!

By the time I dug myself out and got back on my feet, the play was over and there was a big pile of football players out of bounds at the goal line. I had no idea whether it was a safety or not, but right there on the half-yard line stood our referee, Bob Finley, feet planted firmly and yelling, "Give me a damn ball!" He had seen me get dumped and had to make a quick decision. "No safety!" he roared, "Ball dead on the half-yard line!"

There are times when we have to make a quick decision to assist another official who, for one reason or another didn't, or couldn't, see the play. Helping others is an American trait. Many of us believe it is our prime reason for being on Earth. By helping others we also help ourselves. Alexis de Tocqueville, a French statesman and writer 150 years ago commented, "These Americans are a peculiar people. If, in a local community, a citizen becomes aware of a human need which is not being met, he discusses the situation with his neighbors. Suddenly, a committee comes into existence. The committee thereupon begins to operate on behalf of the need and a new community function is established. It is like watching a miracle, because these citizens perform this act without a single reference to any bureaucracy, or any official agency."

There is a story about the executive who died and found himself in heaven. At the pearly gates, St. Peter met him and said, "We have a lot of executives up here, some successful and some unsuccessful. We keep them in separate places and perhaps you would be interested in visiting each group."

The man allowed that he would and so St. Peter took him to see the unsuccessful group first. It was lunch time and the visitor noticed that these executives were a skinny, scrawny lot. "Why are they so thin?" he asked.

"You'll see," smiled St. Peter.

Then as the men prepared to eat, the visitor saw that they each had a large spoon strapped to one arm, reaching from the armpit to beyond the hand. They were unable to bend their elbows, or their wrists, so no matter how hard they tried, they were unable to get a bit of food.

"Now," said St. Peter, "Come with me where the successful executives are."

They went to another dining room and there they saw a group of happy healthy executives and again, each with a long spoon strapped to one arm. When they began to eat, however, they paired off and fed each other.

"You see?" said St. Peter. "Each time they help each other, they help themselves." The one sure way in life to get what we want is to spend our time helping others get what they want.

This, of course, is also the story of football. O. J. Simpson, the explosive "Juice" of the Bills and the '49ers, gave a gold bracelet with a solid gold football on it to each of his offensive linemen at Buffalo. He did this in appreciation and acknowledgement of their up-front blocking, when he broke Jim Brown's old rushing record of 1863 yards and gained 2003 yards rushing in the 1973 season. That was the only time any runner has exceeded 2000 yards in rushing in a single season — but he didn't do it alone.

For most of my years wearing a striped shirt, I have been a line judge and I have worked numerous games involving Buffalo. I can't remember how many times I've seen O. J. Simpson start out on a countless number of his record-making runs, but I have rarely seen him finish one! That was not my job. My job was to see to it that there was no one offside when the ball was snapped. After that, my responsibilities included following the wide receiver, either end or back, on my side of the field and looking for rule infractions that might occur behind the back of the umpire, who was watching the linesmen directly in front of him.

I have the same regard for a superior passer. I have seen thousands of pass plays begin, but rarely do I see them finish (except for the short passes on my side), because my eyes are glued to that area of the field which is my responsibility. It is the same with all my co-workers in the game. Each of us has his assigned duties. For example, the referee knows everything there is to know about what happens to the quarterback. We call him a "babysitter" for the quarterback. But, in doing so he never knows if a pass is complete, incomplete or intercepted. The other officials have to tell him what happened when the play is over. Can you imagine what chaos and mayhem would develop if, when Tony Dorsett started a run, all official eyes turned to him while the other twenty-one players were ignored? We'd have to put out a call for a platoon of paramedics. The human zebra is exactly like the animal zebra. He doesn't have eyes in the back of his head — he can't look everywhere at once.

It is rare when an argument between an official and player is anything but vocal, and even when one does start it is curtailed quickly. Confrontations between players are also becoming rare and those which do occur are usually meaningless. Often the two player-combatants have spent all their frustrations and hostility with a single blow each, but that gives the would-be peacemakers on the bench a chance to join the fray. These peacemakers can be an official's worst problem. Their very presence suggests their active participation in a squabble they really want to help stop.

I am often asked what an official such as I, weighing 172 pounds, standing 5 feet 10 inches and 57 years of age, does when confronted by an irate giant who is 28, weighs 265 and towers 6 feet 5. I always give the same answer. "I look him right square in the navel, and say very little."

Call it whatever you wish: respect for authority, discipline, or sportsmanship. It is something that makes it possible for a group of middle-aged men who are past their athletic prime to keep as many as 80 of the biggest, strongest and fastest young men in the nation under control for a full three hours of professional football, a sport that is replete with physical contact and an emotional intensity hard to describe.

Just as in life, football has its code; but in contrast with life, the football code is enforced with the four F's of good officiating — FIRM, FAST, FRIENDLY and FAIR. These four F's are as important in management as is product knowledge, market awareness, personal relations and so on.

Cavett Robert, an authority on human engineering and personal development, advises, "Unless I can get together with a person physically, mentally and also emotionally, regardless of what else I may accomplish I shall not move him to action. These are the three dimensions which lead to action. All three must exist if our end is to be accomplished."

When Moses was given the Ten Commandments, the Lord did not say, "Here are ten suggestions. You do not steal unless you are in dire need, and it is suggested that you not kill except in times of danger." These commandments are blunt and to the point: thou shall not steal; thou shall not kill.

The football code is every bit as blunt and to the point. Thou shall not clip, says one restriction. Thou shall not treat a foe with unnecessary roughness, cautions another. And like the Biblical and legal codes, football rules list punishments for any infractions. In Biblical phrasing, the penalty would read, "If thou clippest thine opponent, thou shalt have a 15-yard penalty." Discipline that is firm, fast, friendly and fair is a vital part of the game and is an essential element in successful managerial pursuits, as well as in life. I firmly believe that all people function best in an atmosphere of sensible rules which are sensibly enforced. Without limits we wouldn't have a meaningful game and without limits I don't believe we can have a meaningful life.

Midway in the 1976 campaign, I officiated the Monday night game involving Los Angeles and San Francisco. The Rams, ultimately the champions of the Western Division in the National Football Conference, were to win with relative ease. Apparently, the 49ers did not know that they were doomed to defeat and played enough inspired football to win 16-0.

During the game, a big defensive player for the Rams showed his frustration by hitting a San Francisco player on the helmet with his open hand after the ball had been blown dead following yet another 49er gain. He turned to see if the infraction had been spotted by an official just as I dropped the yellow flag at his feet.

"What's that for?" he snarled with all the frustration of a woodpecker in a petrified forest.

"You are not going to like this particularly," I replied, as I hurried to report the foul to the referee, "but the flag is for unnecessary roughness and the penalty will be 15 yards!"

I was correct! He did not like it particularly and began a tirade of abuse against me, my mother and the rest of the Holst family. Finally, I called a halt and told him the penalty would stand and that if he did not quiet down, I would also charge him with unsportsmanslike conduct and penalize him another 15 yards and an early shower as a reward! He was absolutely mum the remainder of the game.

Often, some of the action seen on the field is not what the spectators believe it to be. Some years ago, I officiated a game in which few, if any, penalties had been called in the first two quarters. As the players raced to their dressing rooms for the intermission two huge rookie linemen, one from each team, squared off in the middle of the field and began exchanging blows that appeared to be as lethal as any thrown by Muhammed Ali, Jack Dempsy or Joe Louis in a heavyweight title bout.

The crowd rose to its feet as one person and cheered them on. I was the official closest to the fighters and ran toward them yelling, "Hey, knock it off! Knock it off!"

When I got closer to them, I could see the blows were missing by fractions of an inch, and that the men were smiling, really enjoying themselves. It turned out that the two had been roommates in college, teammates on a championship team and often worked off some of their excess energy by shadow boxing. This game was the first time they had seen each other since graduation and what (to them at least) was more fitting than a round of non-violent boxing? One of them grinned and said, "We're not mad, Ref, we're just having some fun!" Just the same, I became a hero for breaking up the fight.

After my first season, I was working on the sidelines in civilian clothes at the NFL championship game in which Stan Javie, a no-nonsense guy and senior official in the NFL, was the back judge. The NFL championship was at stake and the Cleveland Browns being hosted by the Green Bay Packers, then coached by the volatile Vince Lombardi, were defending their title of the previous year. It was a lousy day — with very wet snow and temperatures in the low 30's. The field became a mudhole for the madness of the world championship of pro football.

Near the end of the game the Packers had just added another touchdown en route to their 23-11 victory when Dick Modzelewski, a brawny tackle for the Browns (and emotionally very high for the game) did his number. Ripping his helmet off late in the fourth quarter he threw the helmet at the official's feet, clenched his hands into fists and raised his arms to the heavens. It looked like he was reading Javie off — but good!!

To the surprise of the 50,777 fans, and especially to the amazement of his fellow officials who knew the Javie temperament, the veteran official listened to the player and then walked away without saying a word.

Of course the first thing we officials wanted to know from Javie when we reached the dressing room after the game was, "What was Modzelewski bleating about when he charged at you?"

"He wasn't mad at anything," replied Javie, "except the situation in which the Browns now found themselves when the Packers scored again. All he screamed was, 'Damn it, Stan! Now we'll never be able to catch them!' "

So things are not always as they appear to be. The Zebras are often taken to task by the fans for some of the calls they make. However, what is seen from the stands is not always what has actually taken place on the playing field. The official making the call may have an entirely different perspective and he *has* to be right!

Of course the first thing we officials wanted to know from Javie when we reached the dressing room after the game was, "What was Modzelewski bleating about when he charged at you?"

"He wasn't mad at anything," replied Javie, "except the situation in which the Browns now found themselves when the Packers scored again. All he screamed was, 'Damn it, Stan! Now we'll never be able to catch them!' "

So things are not always as they appear to be.

The Zebras are often taken to task by the fans for some of the calls they make. However, what is seen from the stands is not always what has actually taken place on the playing field. The official making the call may have an entirely different perspective and he *has* to be right!

Consider with me the possibilities of the "instant replay" concept in evaluating job performance on both a short-term and cumulative basis. An NFL official is evaluated four times each week. Once is by an observer who is present at the game and who rates each on a series of items. The ratings range from a high of seven to a low of zero. These items include judgement, knowledge of the rules, position and others. The observer's ratings are then mailed to the NFL office after the game.

On Tuesday or Wednesday Supervisor of Officials Art McNally and his assistants rate each Zebra from the game films. The game film is cut into five rolls. One roll is for kicks, two for home team offense and two for home team defense. We are then rated by both coaches. The following Saturday when the officials check in at the hotel the day prior to the Sunday game, these five rolls of film of the previous game are waiting.

After a good dinner it's movie time — not an "R" rated flick — just the game films. Seven men are cooped up in a hotel room with a projector furnished by the home team. One wall of the room serves as the screen and they commence watching films of their own performances and studying the play by play sheet that comes with the film. On that sheet, the league office marks all plays where there are questionable calls, or where their positions could be improved.

These sessions are dominated by the whir of the projector, punctuated by remarks like, "Run that back again!" or "OK!" or "Art, you weren't deep enough for that punt!" or "Good call!" or "Way to go out there!"

We are our own harshest critics — in the seclusion of that hotel room anything goes. After the film, or sometimes before we showed it, Bob Frederic, our referee, would go over the comments he got in a weekly report from the league office. You can be sure that this always triggered a lively discussion.

Objective managerial evaluation, followed by objective self-evaluation, is an excellent way to improve any kind of team performance and I feel the advent of weekly movies for NFL crews, which got its start about ten years ago, has done more to bring consistency and hence better officiating than any other single thing during my fifteen years in the league.

So you see, we strive constantly for excellence. After all, the official Zebra motto is, "To err is human — to forgive is not league policy."

All of the foregoing, of course, happens after you have become an NFL official. Arriving at that status is almost as rugged as getting through the pearly gates. You begin at high school and college games and you are scouted, just like players are. The observer who grades the officials during a game on Sunday may have stopped along the way to look at a college official on Friday night or Saturday. Their job? Find talented young officials for the professional ranks.

In 1967 our son, Jeff, played tackle on the Peoria Richwoods high school team. I was to work a game on Sunday but on Friday night we went to a game in East Peoria to watch Richwoods play. As my wife and I, along with the parents of the quarterback, came into the stadium, I saw the familiar figure of Charlie Berry with his coat collar up to protect himself from a miserable cold rain. Charlie was an American League umpire for years, as well as an NFL official. By 1967 he was retired and working as one of our league observers. I yelled, "Charlie Berry, what are you doing here?" He said, "I'm here looking at an official, Art. What are you doing?" I told him, "I'm here to watch my boy play and try to keep from freezing!" He said, "Do you know a young official named Jorgensen?" I said that I didn't — and I didn't then. But in 1968 Dick Jorgensen, now an accomplished referee, came into the league as a line judge. Charlie Berry had come all the way from the East Coast to central Illinois to check out Dick.

Some of the young officials may be eliminated from consideration after a single look. Others may be followed for two or three years, but once they're put on the list of prospects, the real investigation begins. Not only does the NFL screen its prospects on their knowledge of the rules and their conduct on the field, but it also has a security department, consisting of many ex-FBI agents, which delves into the non-football aspects of the candidate's life. Is he financially stable? Who are his friends? Is he a family man? What is his off-the-field occupation? Psychological testing is also a part of the evaluation process before a man becomes a member of the

NFL officiating staff.

If the prospect gets a clean bill of character on all these questions, does he get a snow-white gown complete with halo and wings? Not quite. Instead, he is issued a Zebra shirt and other garments which make up his officiating wardrobe and a contract that calls for payment of $325 a scheduled game plus expenses for his first two years. If he is selected for special contests, such as the playoff games and Super Bowl, his pay can climb to $3,000 a game. However, seldom does his NFL pay for a season climb above $17,000. The top pay for a regular season game is $800 plus expenses beginning with his eleventh season in pro ball.

During the summer, when other sports lovers are busy following the baseball races, the NFL official spends at least one long weekend at a rules clinic, where written and oral tests are given. If that isn't enough, he is punched and poked through a physical examination that is on a par with those given to marine recruits at a boot camp.

This vigilance and concern has paid off. Never, to my knowledge, has an official even been rumored to be involved in shady dealings.

It is worth the price.

CHAPTER SEVEN

FOOTBALL FIELDS AIN'T FOR GRAZING

Not hardly!! There's too much action out there to allow a Zebra to graze. Another thing — all football games begin with a tie score, 0-0. Regardless of how good or bad a team is, when that first kickoff starts everyone's juices flowing, the score is still 0-0. It's a fact, and no matter what the sports writers write, the television commentators say, or what Jimmy "The Greek" predicts, it's still anybody's ball game in the NFL.

I emphasize this because one of the most dangerous pitfalls in officiating is to relax and think, perhaps subconsciously, "This one'll be easy! Team A will kick hell outta' Team B!" Wrong! You can never take anything for granted — and this, quite naturally, follows in business as well.

If you are a salesman and have a prospect you feel is a cinch, look out! Having that attitude decreases your enthusiasm and as your interest lags, so does that of the prospect. You and I must concentrate on the job at hand. You must constantly stimulate your client's interest by proving how your product not only fills a need, but fills it better than anything else. Concentrate all your thoughts on the product and what it is going to do for your client. That's how sales are made! Concentration! You can't win without it! You can get everything you want by helping others get what they want.

Concentration is probably the most important key to top-notch officiating. From the time we walk on the field, five minutes before the kickoff, until we return to the dressing room at the end of the game, the crew of officials must have 100 per cent concentration, not only on every play, but on everything, even the dead ball period between plays.

Concentration begins on Saturday night. It's a work night. The first thing concentrated on is food. The whole crew enjoys a good dinner. Field Judge Bob Wortman, eats all the rolls in sight. He's always hungry enough to eat a skunk! One official on our crew was a vegetarian and sometimes it was difficult to find enough herbs and grassy stuff to fill him. The rest eat a normal dinner and not one is bashful in the knife and fork league! It's an ice cream eating crew. This is especially true of Lou Palazzi who has an astounding record of twenty-eight years in the NFL. One point worthy of note is the fact that the drinking of alcoholic beverages is strictly forbidden from the time we leave home on Saturday until we're on the plane after the Sunday game. Absolutely no exceptions!

I usually slept very well the night before a game. But before I hit the sack, or while flying to the game, I did the weekly test that would be gone over when we were all together the next day during our Sunday morning meeting. I also studied a list of items which I had put together before the season — things I wanted to do to help the crew do a better job during the season. It's surprising how many times something we reviewed in the test Norm Schachter writes each week, or that I had on my own list, occurs in a game.

I believe there's a lot of merit in check lists — not only for airplane pilots, but for NFL officials as well. As a matter of fact, a check list is important to anyone who wants to be a pro!

I knew a young executive once who kept a business diary, filled with everything he did — every decision he made, complete with details, his own check list. When I asked him why he went to all that trouble, he replied, "I used to be deathly afraid of making mistakes — dodging decision-making as much as I could. Then my boss called me in one day and asked me why I lacked aggressiveness. I told him of my fear of making mistakes and he said, 'Never be afraid of making mistakes. If you don't make mistakes, you never learn anything!'

"So now I'm more forceful and I'm getting someplace — and the reason I keep this diary so faithfully is to ensure I don't make the same mistake twice!"

Sunday morning we all rolled out of bed and went to early mass. That's because we had three Catholics on our crew. We piled into our rented car and started looking for the nearest Catholic church. The hotels have mass times and the addresses of churches listed in their lobbies, but sometimes the Catholic church is hard to find. I learned that the easiest way is to just look for the big BINGO sign.

When Tony Veteri and I were together on the same crew, he always lighted three candles after mass. One Sunday, I asked him, "Tony, what are the candles for?"

He replied, "One's for my wife, Rosie; the second one is to help me do a good job on the game, and the third candle is a prayer that all bad things that happen today will happen on your side of the field."

So help me, that very day I had a screwy, loose ball, questionable-possession play right in front of me, and the proverbial roof fell in! After the smoke cleared I trotted across the field to Tony during a TV time-out and growled, "That damn candle you lit worked!" There's an awful lot to be said for church.

People often ask me why I don't go to my own church on these Sunday football mornings. Folks, I don't even know a Presbyterian who is up at 8 a.m. on Sunday, let alone in church. We Presbyterians don't open before 9:30 a.m.! The Presbyterian business doesn't get good at all until 11 a.m. One thing is sure; it's the safest time to drive the freeway in San Francisco and L.A.! The Catholics are the only ones on the roads.

After mass comes the breakfast ritual. I say "ritual" because it's always the same. Palazzi, our umpire, has 40% Bran Flakes every Sunday because as he says, "You gotta' stay loose!"

Personally, I eat like a ranch hand: cereal and milk, two eggs, bacon, toast, fruit and coffee. Zebras have to be at the playing field at 11:15 a.m. for a 1 p.m. kickoff, so it's no lunch! That was okay with me because, as you have noted, I'm a big breakfast man, anyway.

After breakfast it's back to work. We would all gather in Referee Bob Frederic's room for about an hour and go over Norm Schachter's weekly test. It usually covers one rule and consists of one page of true and false questions plus two pages of play situations. How about trying your hand at it? Maybe you're ready for a Zebra shirt yourself! Here goes. Answer the following questions true or false. The correct answers are at the end of the chapter, and if you were a working official, they'd better all be right!

GENERAL QUESTIONS

TRUE-FALSE

_____ 1. After a fair catch signal the opportunity for the receiver to make a catch ends when a kick is muffed.

_____ 2. A try for point attempt is unsuccessful if an eligible receiver catches a second forward pass for a score.

_____ 3. It is legal to bat a ball towards an opponent's goal line.

_____ 4. It is a 10-yard penalty for lifting a runner to his feet by his teammate.

_____ 5. A palpably unfair act by the defensive team may result in a touchdown for the offense.

_____ 6. An illegal crackback block is a 15-yard penalty.

_____ 7. Tripping is always a 15-yard penalty unless it is half distance.

_____ 8. It is a touchback when a backward pass by A1 on the A3 yard line is batted over the end line by B1.

_____ 9. Any field goal attempt which touches the ground before it passes through the goal posts cannot be successful.

_____ 10. B1 may contact eligible receiver A1 once on the scrimmage line and once three yards beyond line.

_____ 11. Clipping is a 10-yard penalty if it occurs three yards either side of the scrimmage line.

_____ 12. It is encroaching if a player crosses his line and contacts an opponent.

_____ 13. If a tight end takes the place of a backfield man, he must report his change of position to the referee.

_____ 14. A legal forward pass is incomplete if it hits the offensive crossbar or goal post.

_____ 15. It is a touchback if a fourth down forward pass from inside the B20 is incomplete in the end zone.

_____ 16. A forward pass from behind the scrimmage line may be caught by a T-quarterback.

_____ 17. When a scrimmage kick is blocked, any touching behind the line by an offensive player is legal, and he may recover and advance.

_____ 18. There is no such thing as fair-catch interference in the end zone.

_____ 19. On a point after touchdown, if any foul by the defense would ordinarily result in a safety, the point scores for the offensive team.

_____ 20. Eligible receivers who are lined up within 2 yards of their tackles on the line of scrimmage may be blocked below the waist at the line or behind scrimmage line.

_____ 21. The first World Championship game played indoors was Super Bowl XII in the New Orleans Superdome on Jan. 15, 1978.

Well, how did you do? Are you ready, rules wise, to hop on down to the ball park and don a striped shirt? Not so fast! Before going, there are a few more things to do. One official is assigned by the referee the week before to go over one rule in detail. He leads the discussion in this area. Whatever the rule is, there is in-depth discussion concerning it. When the subject is exhausted the Zebras check out of the hotel and head for an appointment with the unknown — the intricate and unexpected things that will begin happening in just a few short hours.

I'm so sold on these tests that I believe the business world would profit immensely from similar tests. They could be on product knowledge, sales techniques, management procedures or whatever. These exercises could go a long way to improve a business or enhance a professional performance in any field.

Pilots take a "check" ride with their own human

"instant replay" looking over their shoulder, checking their every move. Surgeons are scrutinized, carefully, by other surgeons to ensure that their competency remains high. I want the pilot who flies me or the surgeon who operates on my gizzard, to be perfect the first time — and then get better! The same goes for officiating.

Let's look at an example. Remember, in track, the four-minute-mile barrier track? Many learned men said the human body could not tolerate the physical demands required to break the four-minute-mile. Some even went as far as to warn that the human heart would burst. Then Roger Bannister blazed down the track, and the four-minute-mile barrier was shattered forever! Two weeks later, Landy broke four minutes. Since then, countless runners have done it and now a sub-four-minute mile is run in virtually every major race. But remember, it all begins with advance preparation. That's why Saturday nights and Sunday mornings are times of preparation — to get minds and bodies ready to work the best game possible on Sunday.

Question: Are you ready to do your best every hour of every day? If you want to achieve total self respect and self pride, you will not allow yourself to be a mediocre human being.

A top-notch professional in any field does things that his or her public never sees or knows about. Let's take an NFL officiating crew as an example. They are required to be in the dressing room an hour and forty-five minutes before kickoff and on the field thirty minutes prior to game time, so the seven leave the hotel and usually drive a rented car to the stadium or taxi the distance. Once in the dressing room, it doesn't take too long to don uniforms; the extra time is devoted to pre-game duties which must be done before going out on the field. An hour or so before kickoff the home team will bring in 24 new balls, inflated to 13 pounds of pressure. The first thing done is removing with a damp towel the powdery yellow stain left on each ball after the manufacturing process. As this is being done by two officials, the referee rechecks the inflation of all the balls with an air gauge which he carries.

Six new balls are used each quarter and one pre-game duty is to instruct the four ball boys. "Instruct?" you ask. "What's to instruct on flipping a ball to an official?" Well, let me tell you, some of the ball boys get overanxious and zing the ball just as you are signaling. I have been hit in the face a dozen times by footballs thrown accurately at my face by overzealous ball boys. A Wilson NFL football with 13 pounds of pressure hits hard, Folks, and it smarts when you get hit right in the puss by a football!

Another duty is to trot over to the TV control truck and set a watch to network time, ascertain the time of kickoff, length of half-time and time allowed for player introduction. This is done when the Zebras first get to the stadium, usually before donning the striped shirt, as sometimes the Zebras must go through the fans to get to the truck.

The TV control truck, or really trucks, are two huge semi-trailers. The maze of wires, phones, monitors, switches and head sets seem to put "Mission Control" in Houston on a minor scale. Getting the game out to the fans at home via television is a complex challenge and requires the same kind of teamwork required in the game itself, if not more so. Then it's into the dressing rooms of both teams to inform the coaches of the correct time, time of kickoff, length of the half and any peculiarities of the game clock. Occasionally repeater clocks in the stadium may be a second or two off in relation to the official clock. If so, the coaches must be told.

Each dressing room has a personality all its own. Some are quiet with almost no conversation — others have a more businesslike atmosphere and still others have loud music booming from speakers around the room. Sometimes I was kidded about, among other things, my glasses. One coach looked at me right after I got them and said, "Well, I'll be damned, over 200 million people in this country and we can't find officials who can see without glasses!" One of the tough linebackers was needling me before a game in 1978 and I said something like, "I'll see you on the field!" He said, "Okay, Ref, but I won't say anything to you out there. One question though," he went on, "there's no penalty for thinking, is there?" I said, "No, of course not!" He said, "Good, cause I think you're a lousy official!!"

The official clock is now the field clock and the wrist watch worn by the line judge, which is furnished by the league, is used as a back-up, as well as to make corrections in the event of a timing error. When I came into the NFL in 1964, the back judge (there were only five officials then) kept the official time on his wrist. The field clock became official just a few years ago.

The loss of time is as serious to a football team as it is to any individual. Indeed, perhaps more so.

Let's face it — the one area wherein we are all created equal is in the amount of time we have at our disposal each day. How we use it is largely up to us. How productive we are — what we accomplish with our time — depends on our priorities. You would be amazed at how much more could be accomplished if men and women planned their time as a football team does. Do *you* have a game plan for your day?

A constant awareness of time is of critical importance to both teams, because "death" for one team, or "sudden death" for both teams, in the event of a tie, is only sixty minutes of playing time away. Because this time frame is so absolute, the coaches and players work for hours, practicing how to make the most of that time.

As the official primarily responsible for the correct timing of the game, the line judge must be thoroughly familiar with all the timing rules and ensure that the clock operator is starting and stopping the clock according to those rules. This means that clear signals from every member of the officiating crew are of vital importance. One of the last things I said to our crew before we left the dressing room was, "Everybody — good signals!"

Football fields are higher in the middle to allow for easier drainage during a rain. This condition, added to the size of the players, makes it difficult to see signals from the officials on the opposite side of the field. That's the reason we all "echo" the signal of the official who called the play.

I don't know who Murphy is, but isn't it Murphy's Law that warns, "Everything that can go wrong — will go wrong." That sure must go for clocks that malfunction! I think I'd be smart to have Murphy's Law tattooed on my wrist, to remind me of all the clock problems I've had over the years. I refer especially to the stadium clocks — those sophisticated, electronically-operated "Jonahs" that flash pictures, sketch cartoons, advertise, cook breakfast and bring instant replay to the fans. Somehow, a few times each year, the wires get friendly with each other, or Murphy himself climbs into the maze of transistors and lights, and screws up the game clock. If we cannot correct it immediately, the line judge becomes the official timer with his Heuer Game Timer watch. The procedure is then to notify the coaches and captains that time will now be kept on the field.

I remember a critical game back in 1972, when I was with Bernie Ulman's crew. Bernie, who is now an observer for the league, runs a big sporting goods store in the suburbs of Baltimore. Anyway, we had the San Francisco 49ers and the Minnesota Vikings on a Saturday national-TV game in the last week of the season. Dick Nolan's 49ers needed the game to wrap up a division championship. They were down by four points with about five minutes left in the game when the field clock began to skip seconds. I called time out and we notified Bud Grant of the Vikings and Coach Nolan that I would now have the official time. I recall how calm Dick Nolan was when I told him. He merely said something like, "Okay! Just keep my captain informed."

John Brodie had just replaced Spurrier as quarterback for the 49ers and was the offensive captain. I trotted over to him, informed him of the situation and we resumed play. San Francisco gave up the ball on downs, but no matter. They held Minnesota and forced a punt, only to have defensive holding called, which, at that time, returned the ball to the Vikings at the spot where it was snapped for the punt. First down! (That rule has now been changed, and in its present form the 49ers would have retained possession with a "post possession" offensive holding penalty.)

However, the ball went back to Minnesota. Again San Francisco held and again Minnesota punted, with time left in the game now down to about two minutes. Brodie, a fine quarterback and one of the calmest players under pressure that I have ever seen, brought the 49ers down the field and called his third and last time-out, with under a minute left in the game. I jogged over to him during the time-out and said, "Remember, I've got the official time!"

He smiled and replied, "That's fine — just keep me advised!"

When play resumed there were 29 seconds left in the game, fourth down and inside Minnesota's ten-yard line. Brodie took the ball and rolled to my side. His receiver was a third-string player who had not caught a pass in regular season all year. As the young receiver ran his pattern, Brodie pounded toward me, calmly chewing his gum and searching for the opening that would mean a ball game and a championship. Suddenly, this fine, alert quarterback motioned with his left hand for the young receiver to change his direction. He did. Brodie threw on the run and the rest is history. The young man caught his only pass of the year for the winning touchdown.

As I signalled the touchdown, Brodie glanced at me and smiled, as if to say, "Just another normal day at the office!" The point here is that the talent to throw the ball was very important — but proper use of time was vital! Incidentally, John Brodie is now an accomplished commentator on NBC-TV during NFL games.

After blowing ourselves through two quarters of hard-played football, we'd return to the dressing room for a brief half-time respite. The dressing room is locked and guarded and one might think the Hope diamond was hidden there. No one gets into the room except the officials — no coaches, no players, no members of the press — although we normally invited the four members of the head linesman's chain crew. Sandwiches, juices, milk and coffee were available. The menu changes at Baltimore where they serve crab cakes, and at Houston where there's always a huge slab of Texas roast beef and cheese to make Dagwood-type sandwiches.

It's easier to relax between halves when the weather conditions are normal. The most difficult weather condition to cope with is heat. For a time in mid-August of 1977, we thought it was going to finish us off completely. Dallas and Baltimore were having at it in Dallas and the temperature was brutal. Midway into the third quarter, Umpire Ralph Morcroft beckoned me over from my line judge position. When I trotted up to him, he mumbled, "This heat is getting to me. I'm dizzy and I think I'm going to keel over!" Now, I didn't want him to be sick because I'd move to umpire — and I did *not* want that! "Ralph, you look great! Hang in there!"

At that moment the brilliant young quarterback of the Colts, Bert Jones, walked past and overheard Morcroft's remark. "Mr. Umpire," he said, "if you're suffering from the heat, try some of this. It always helps me!" With that, he handed Morcroft a small packet of snuff, which he had carried onto the field hidden in his stocking. Morcroft put a pinch of it in his mouth and forgot all about the heat. He spent the rest of the game trying to get rid of the taste.

During these pre-season games, especially in the South and on artificial turf, the temperatures can climb well above 120 degrees on the field. Of course, the domed stadiums are air conditioned and heat is not a problem.

If you think you've heard enough about the problems of the official, bear with me a little longer. Let me tell you about "stickum." That's the goo receivers and running backs rub on their hands. Receivers like Cliff Branch will keep a generous supply of this light brown sticky substance on the insides of their socks and will reach down between plays to dab a little more on their hands. I swear, some day during a game, Branch will have his hands held by an opponent, a pass will hit his chest and splat! It'll stay there quivering, but immobile.

On the other hand, the quarterbacks want a clean ball, so we throw the sticky one out and replace it with a clean one. So the ball boys must keep the balls wiped clean at all times. A simple thing like ball boys who do their jobs right and keep their heads really contributes to the smoothness of the game.

Occasionally we happen upon a "leaker" ball. In 1973, our crew worked a Pittsburgh-Oakland game in Oakland. This game is always a donnybrook, and that particular day, in a very close game, the Steelers were going for a second-half field goal. I tossed the center a fresh ball and after taking it in his hands he turned to our umpire, Lou Palazzi, and asked for a new ball. Lou, in turn, asked me.

"I just gave him one!" I said, but the center persisted. Reluctantly, I got another ball and made the exchange. After examining the original ball more carefully, I discovered it was that rare "leaker" and was going soft. The sensitive hands of the Pittsburgh center were right!

In addition to being "ball inspectors," officials must be bookkeepers, too! Before the game starts, officials have game cards to make out. They keep a white game card, and after the game transfer the information to a larger yellow card that goes to the league office. This card includes game number, date, temperature, teams, final score, fouls called, when called, type of foul, whether accepted or declined, the number of the fouling players, the quarter in which it was called and the number of officials who called any particular foul. A photocopy of my Super Bowl XII game card is shown in the picture section of this book.

In addition, I note the time the game started. All officials enter the time of the game, final score and any unsportsmanslike conduct information or unusual situations, like clock problems, etc. The referee will then forward the yellow cards with a summary of the game to the NFL office via air mail at the close of the game. These are compared against game films and, in this way, accurate records are kept.

I used to get a kick out of twitting the fans when they would occasionally ask me, "What are you writing about out there?" I'd tell them, "Margie likes to hear from me once in awhile, so I write her a card during the game." That went along okay until one night, after a speech I had just concluded, a lady asked me the same question. Again I answered in the same tongue-in-cheek manner, and so help me, she believed it! She said, "I think you should pay more attention to the game!"

One more detail that must be taken care of before the opening kickoff concerns the kicking tees. These are used by the kickers to position the ball for kickoffs. These tees may only be used on a kickoff following a touchdown, or a field goal, and at the opening of each half. Kickoffs (or free kicks, as they are properly called) following a safety, or fair catch must be made *without* a tee. If desired, a punt can also be used as a free kick, but only following a safety. Because kickers vary in their preferences of kicking tees, all officials carry different sizes of tees. The head linesman and line judge each carry two-inch tees, the back and field judges carry three-inch tees, and the referee and umpire each carry a one-inch tee.

Before the game, the home team equipment man pays a friendly call on the kickers and inquires what size tee each prefers. With this information, he then obtains two tees from the officials and returns them to us after the game.

Finally, the timer delivers a gun and shells to me so that I can play the Lone Ranger at the end of each quarter. There was a time when each line judge carried his own gun, but airline security put a stop to that. I remember I worked a Hall of Fame game in Canton, Ohio, where they showed up with a .22 caliber revolver and .32 caliber shells! Murphy at work again!

I chuckle as I remember when Frank Glover, now a head linesman, entered the league. His first game was a pre-season contest in Philadelphia. Frank was a line judge then and had to shoot the gun. As a rookie, he was naturally excited about his first game and proceeded to shoot it near end of the first quarter, with one minute left on the clock. Ed Marion, a veteran head linesman and now president of our NFL Officials Association, also worked the game. Ed has a great sense of humor, and he placated the benches with some comment like, "Your clock is off!"

That might work once, but not twice. In the second quarter, Frank pulled his weapon and fired it at the two-minute warning. Marion's classic comment to Glover at the end of the first half was, "Frank! You're officiating in a National Football League game and not playing the goddam sheriff in a western movie!"

Ah, a sense of humor sure helps.

GENERAL QUESTIONS — ANSWERS

1. FALSE
2. TRUE
3. FALSE - Except for a pass in flight.
4. TRUE - You can never help your teammate to his feet or push or pull him if he is a runner with the ball.

5. TRUE - After a conference by the officiating crew.
6. TRUE
7. FALSE - It is a 10-yard penalty.
8. FALSE - It is a SAFETY.
9. TRUE
10. FALSE - He may contact the receiver only once in the first 5 yards . . . unless the quarterback runs out of the pocket (beyond tight end).
11. FALSE - Clipping is a 15-yard penalty, *but* it is not a penalty at all if within 3 yards of the line of scrimmage between the offensive tackles during initial line play.
12. TRUE
13. FALSE
14. TRUE
15. FALSE
16. FALSE - But he CAN catch it legally if the pass is first touched by the defense or an eligible teammate.
17. TRUE
18. FALSE
19. TRUE
20. TRUE
21. FALSE - The first world championship game played indoors was played in the Chicago Stadium in 1932 between the Chicago Bears and the Portsmouth, Ohio, Spartans. A blizzard roared through Chicago on game day so into the Stadium it went. The size of the arena allowed only an

80-yard field that came right up to the walls. The goal posts were moved to the goal lines and in-bounds lines or hashmarks were drawn 10 yards inbounds for safety reasons. These innovations became rules changes the following season. Who won this strange game? The Bears — 9-0!!

CHAPTER EIGHT

MURPHY'S LAW AGAIN

Did I say we were out of the dressing room yet? Not so. Before our crew appears on the field, we have, perhaps, twenty minutes in the dressing room alone. Our pre-game duties have been completed, and now the back judge and field judge announce the names and numbers of the offensive and defensive captains. We officials note this information on our game cards. This procedure is extremely important, since only the captains may call "time-out" and they save time-outs like misers hoard gold!

After a final chat with the other officials concerning whatever peculiarities of the field or ball park, I review the clock information. This entire procedure is finally capped off with one of us admonishing, "Everybody, good luck!"

If nothing has gone wrong so far, we've been lucky. Unfortunately, we're not out on the field yet, and that's where Murphy is lying in wait to invoke his evil law, "Everything that can go wrong — will go wrong!" With this grim shadow looming over us, Bob Wortman, our field judge, reminds us of the importance of this game. "Gentlemen, this game is the biggest one of the year for those two teams. Let's do a bang-up job!"

Bob then holds out the game ball to be used for the kickoff and we all place our hands over it. Bob Frederic offers something like, "Good ball game, Men!" and then I asked, in a prayer, that we give the teams a good job and that no one would be seriously hurt. If this all sounds like the ritual of the Royal Order of Zebras, it is, and we're very serious about it. I'm not quite sure how or why I happened to be the one to start offering the prayer. It was just one of those things that occurred shortly after we came together as a crew. I know that among the seven of us there was a general feeling of thankfulness to our Lord that we were granted the privilege of having this responsibility. We all felt we needed His help to do the job right in a game where, as officials, we never knew what would happen next. All we did know was that anything could happen — and we'd better be ready.

This is uppermost in the minds as Zebras leave the dressing room and walk through the tunnel toward the field. At the last moment everyone shakes hands and wishes good luck. I made sure everybody had gum if they wanted it.

Sid Semon was the "rookie" in our crew. He's a product of California, where he serves as a teacher and golf coach. Sid was in his first year, and as a "rookie" he was given all kinds of little duties — simple chores like picking up the projector at the hotel and delivering it to the home team dressing room when we arrived at the park on game day. He also mailed the film back to the league office, and at our Saturday night meeting he was the great provider of candy for the crew. Incidentally, each of the fellows on the crew is known for some extra special item he carries in his bag. Lou Palazzi has a spare pair of striped baseball socks and extra whistles. I had gum for everyone, extra pencils and so on.

So it's gum for all and on to the field to await the introductions of the teams and to stand by for the coin flip. As we waited for the kickoff, this was the time my heart pounded the loudest. I'm sure the players and coaches feel the same emotion.

I shall never forget the excitement and tension of my first game in the NFL. The time was August, 1964. I was the back judge on a five-man crew to work the Minnesota -New York Giant, pre-season game in Minnesota. "Red" Pace, now retired was the referee. "Red", a tall, garrulous ex-Navy man, had a rather strained relationship with Norm Van Brocklin, coach of the Vikings. At the time, "Red" was raising a small herd of Black Angus cattle, among which was a very nasty-tempered bull, "Norman," which didn't improve the bull's disposition one bit!

As we entered the field, I asked Ed Marion to point out Coach Van Brocklin for me, as I hadn't the slightest idea what he looked like. Marion jerked his thumb in the direction of two fellows chatting and said, "He's the guy with the short hair talking to the guy in the blue blazer."

With that, I dashed off, eager to do my first on-the-field job — to give Norm Van Brocklin the correct TV time. What I didn't know was that the man in the blue blazer was a TV sportscaster from New York and they weren't simply involved in idle conversation, but were engrossed in a live interview which was being telecast. If I had seen the camera, I might have guessed what was going on, but the damn thing was set way back and they were using a zoom lens.

So into the middle of the interview jogs Art Holst, number 33, unknown rookie back judge in the NFL. "Coach," I said, "I'm Art Holst, the back judge for tonight's game!"

Van Brocklin sized me up with one glance and muttered something like, "Oh, a new fella."

"That's right, Coach," I replied, trying not to jog in place. "The correct TV time is 7:34!"

Van Brocklin chuckled, "Thanks," he replied, "You've just made the best call you're ever gonna make!"

With Murphy's law working already, I knew I was in for a long night. Nevertheless, I proceeded bravely to commit my second bobble. I hadn't the slightest idea what Francis Tarkenton looked like, nor did I know his number. "Coach," I continued, "what's the name and number of your captain, please?"

He shot me an incredulous look, then with a wry smile he said, with pauses punctuating each syllable, "Number E-LEV-EN . . . TAR-KEN-TON!"

That was when I noticed Marion, who had set me up to stick my nose into the interview, standing twenty-five yards away with three other officials, all laughing like baboons at the antics of the new rookie. I had been had! However, one must rise above such horseplay.

On the field, each official performs his pre-game duties. I recheck with the clock operator to ensure the field clock is okay. The side judge gives the ball boys their instructions. The head linesman meets with the chain crew and the box man, the fellow who handles the pole that displays the down number. They then check the length of the chain to ensure it is exactly ten yards long. We once worked a game where one link of the chain had to be removed to make it precisely ten yards long.

The umpire is in charge of all equipment and must inspect all tapings and casts worn by the players. A cast may be worn, but must be properly covered with foam padding. Obviously, without padding, a cast would make a formidable weapon. The umpire also checks the kicker's shoes to see that they are legal. The kicking shoe must be of a standard manufacture and must not be altered by adding laces to the toe or putting lead in the sole. Prior to this rule, some players appeared crippled as they dragged a weighted kicking shoe out onto the field.

The back judge and field judge are responsible for inspecting the field and the area around it. They must satisfy themselves that the field is properly marked and the benches located in the right place. They must also see that the corner flags are properly placed, that both goal posts are adequately padded and that nothing unusual exists that would constitute a hazard to the players, or that might interfere with the game itself.

You wouldn't believe the oddball things that turn up during what seem to be routine inspections. In 1964, the late Bill Downes was refereeing a game in Wrigley Field, Chicago, when his field judge discovered a huge camera mounted near the top of one of the goal post's uprights. Bill sought out the photographer and informed him that this could not be allowed and that the camera would have to come down. The photographer protested, wailing, "Think of the terrific shots I'll get from there!"

Downes, then a feisty five-foot-six-inch Irishman who ran Chicago's three airports, snapped back, "I don't give a damn about your pictures! Get the damn thing down from there before we kick off!"

Who would think to put in a rule prohibiting cameras on the goal posts? I tell you, you can write policy manuals from now until the end of time, and sooner or later Murphy will getcha! Things are bound to happen that will demand common sense decisions from those in authority. That's one of the reasons they are given authority. Hesitation or vacillation is often a cause of executive failure. Sometimes even the old army adage applies, "Do something — even if it's wrong!"

While this is not a book about baseball, I am reminded of an incident in that popular sport that involves decision-making. Casey Stengel, the famous manager of the Brooklyn Dodgers back in the '30's, always took quite a razzing from the Brooklyn fans. One day, a particularly vociferous fan was giving Stengel the business throughout the game.

In the first inning, when Brooklyn had a man on first, the fan hollered to Casey, "Tell the bum to sacrifice bunt!" Instead, Stengel signaled for the man on first to steal second. He did and made it.

In the fourth inning, Brooklyn had the bases loaded with their power hitter coming up to bat. The grandstand strategist again shouted to Stengel, "Tell the bum to belt it outa the park!" But Casey ignored the clown and signaled the batter to wait it out. Sure enough, the pitcher blew up, the batter walked and a run was forced in.

Then in the eighth, the Dodgers came to bat with a six-run lead and the first man doubled. When the second hitter came to bat, Casey turned to the box-seat genius and shouted, "All right, Wise Guy, what do I do now?" "Fer cryin' out loud!" the heckler hollered back. "I got you this far, yuh bum! Now do your own thinkin'!"

Another case for decision-making. In 1976, Minnesota played the Detroit Lions at the beautiful new, plastic-topped dome stadium in Pontiac, Michigan. It's a great place to watch a football game, but the traffic problem is something else! The traffic flows from two expressways onto only two exit ramps and you can really get trapped.

The other officials and I stayed at a motel near the airport and checked out early that Sunday morning. Our first stop was a restaurant near the stadium, where we had pre-arranged a private room for breakfast and our usual crew conference. Everything went as expected. Lou had his 40% Bran Flakes; Wortman ate all the rolls, and I had my usual farm hand breakfast. We finished up and wandered over to the dressing room well before 11:30 a.m. for a 1:05 p.m. kickoff.

I might have known things were going too well. When I went to the Vikings dressing room at noon to give coach Bud Grant the timing details, the place was empty. No Vikings. Well, perhaps just a few minutes late, I thought, so off I went to see Rick Forzano, the head coach of Detroit. When I returned to the Viking dressing room at 12:15, still no Vikings. By 12:30 p.m. I began to sweat. That damn Murphy and his wretched law were rearing up again. Now my thoughts were darkened with the big question, "What if?"

Have you ever had to face a "what if" situation? This is a question that all good salesmen, business executives and, indeed, even families should consider more often than they do. "What if" sells life insurance, fire extinguishers, car repairs, stocks and bonds and you name it. Think about it.

Well, here we were with a "what if" situation. At 12:45, the "what if" seemed to be a reality. The Vikings had still not arrived. Finally, at 12:50 p.m., they hurried in, victims of a traffic tie-up. By that time, we six officials had discussed this unusual, unprecedented and, eventually, rule-changing situation. We finally arrived at a decision. We would give Minnesota ten minutes to warm up after the last Viking player hit the field, dressed for the game. This decision was confirmed with league authorities in the press box and with the CBS-TV network. The network was filling precious time during the delay, and time is all they have to sell.

It became my lot to inform both coaches about the time situation. Referee Bob Frederic joined me as I headed for the Minnesota dressing room to see Coach Grant. He was at his locker dressing for the game when I approached and said, "Coach, the time is 12:51!" Without a smile, he looked at his watch and replied, "That's funny. I've got 12:15."

Frederic and I looked at each other blankly. Now there had just been an interesting article in Sports Illustrated magazine about Bud Grant's off-the-field addiction to hunting and fishing and it had a picture of him fly-casting a stream somewhere in Minnesota. So, equally serious, I shook my watch and declared, "This damn thing hasn't been running right since I got it wet the last time I went fishing."

Grant just grinned and asked, "What are you going to do?" Bob told him his team would have ten minutes to warm up after the last player arrived on the field, then we'd flip the coin. Whatever the outcome, the Vikings would get a fifteen-yard penalty. His answer was a calm, "Whatever you fellows say is all right with me."

So far, so good. Now I had to inform Coach Forzano of the Lions what the procedure would be. I found him on the field being interviewed, so I waited at the bench area near the stands for him to finish. The fans were edgy and kept shouting, "Are you going to forfeit?" and other similar remarks. Of course we weren't going to do that, and when Forzano finished his interview, I went over to him and told him what was going to happen. I'll never forget his answer. "Art," he said, "I want to win this game as much, or more, than any game in my life. But they have some tremendous athletes, and if I were in Coach Grant's shoes, I'd appreciate an extra ten minutes to warm up. It's fine with me if you can do it."

I will never forget the good sportsmanship displayed by both Bud Grant and Rick Forzano in a very difficult and unprecedented situation. Obviously, with the television commitments and other considerations, we were unable to grant more time to the Vikings and we finally kicked off at 1:27 p.m., 22 minutes late. The Vikings went on to win a thriller, 10-9. This, of course, led to the rules change which now penalizes the team arriving late fifteen yards, plus loss of the choice for both halves.

Unexpected situations demand careful thought, creative thinking, common sense and the courage to make a firm decision.

Back in 1967 we were scheduled to officiate a game in Yankee Stadium, between the New York Giants and the Detroit Lions. Jim Tunney, who was the referee in Super Bowls VI and XI and who was to do another repeat in Super Bowl XII, was in his first year as a referee. About 45 minutes before the opening kickoff, the television producer entered the dressing room and asked to see Jim. When Jim was pointed out, the producer approached him and, very pleased with himself, said, "We're going to do something different today. We'd like to put a microphone under your shirt with a remote transmitter, so we can tape record all the field conversation."

Jim asked the producer if he had league approval and when the answer was negative, Jim politely refused. Everything went especially smoothly during the game, with a surprising lack of controversy and four-letter words. That bothered me. I began to think of Murphy's law again. Then, in the fourth quarter, it happened! Tunney called a face mask foul against a Detroit lineman as he tackled the quarterback. The defensive captain for Detroit was the great all-pro tackle, Alex Karras, who came running up to Tunney snarling loud expletives and protesting the call.

After Alex started referring, ungraciously, to Jim's family background, I stepped in and said, "It was a good call, Alex."

Karras whirled on me and snapped, "What the hell do you know about it?" Before I could answer, another Detroit player ran up to Karras and cautioned, "Alex, Alex, the microphone!"

Karras then turned to his teammate and roared, "To hell with the microphone! To hell with the officials, and to hell with you, too!"

Of course, the TV control room was up for grabs, for the little added fillip they had devised had backfired on them. It seems that, after Tunney had refused to wear the microphone, the TV people had gone to the Detroit dressing room and obtained permission to place the remote mike under Karras' shoulder pads. This, most certainly, accounted for the smooth day we had up to that point.

I have learned to expect the unexpected, even before the game. Everything you can possibly imagine can happen — and probably will.

You don't believe me? Well, let's talk about Burl Toler's pants. Burl was the first black official in the NFL, you'll recall. He entered the league in 1965 and we were roommates his first two years.

The "Lost Pants Caper" happened in Los Angeles. We were all there to do a Sunday game and Burl's last ritual before leaving the hotel was to check his bag to see if his lovely wife, Mel, had packed everything. At the moment, I was on the bed, reading the rule book and I heard Burl inquire, "Artie, did you hide my pants?"

Well now, not being a collector of pants, particularly men's, I laughed and replied, "Not me!"

Then I looked up and saw him going frantically through his suitcase. "Come on, Artie," he said. "Where are my pants?"

By the worried look in his eye, I knew it was no joke. I said, "Honest, Burl, I don't have your pants!"

Here we were, ready to leave for the Los Angeles Coliseum, and we had a pants-less head linesman. Just by chance, it happened that one of the officials, off that week, lived in Los Angeles, so we called his home. He was going to take a busman's holiday and come to the game, so we prevailed upon him to bring along a pair of his white knickers. Trouble was, Burl is about six-feet-five and this guy was about five-feet-eleven. Toler's waistline was trim, so they fit well in that area, but he sure had a helluva time keeping those knickers below his knees.

That's problem solving. Any professional, salesman, actor, doctor, lawyer, athlete, and yes, even a football official, has problems that the public isn't even remotely aware of. The mark of a real pro is his ability to meet these unexpected, behind-the-scenes crises and *do* something about them. If you and I expect our professional lives to move along a gold-plated road to success, riches, and glory, we are headed for trouble and unhappiness. The trick is to remain calm and cheerful when everything seems to be going wrong. Then, when things are going right again, we will enjoy more, create more and accomplish more. Add to that the fact that you will also learn to avoid that particular pitfall again, and you'll find that the entire exercise was worth the effort.

There are many benefits to be derived from problem solving, not the least of which is what the practice does to improve our self-image. We begin to see ourselves as capable of meeting the unexpected, in a positive and professional manner. The more we respond to these unexpected and behind-the-scenes problems in a professional manner, the better equipped we become to handle the next one. Burl Toler packs his own bag now — and I'll bet his wife is glad he does.

Tension is another problem to be dealt with. With the players, coaches and officials, it begins building in the dressing room and doesn't end until the game is over. In business, it's a daily companion. Tension, anxiety, pressure. Call it what you will! It can either destroy us or excite us to the point where our performance is actually enhanced. I enjoy the tingle I get from tension and I am eager to get the final preparations over with. These last details involve the television commercial and the coin toss.

Usually Frederic is beside the television contact man because as the commercial ends, he'll start for the center of the field and signal the back judge and field judge to bring out the captains for the coin flip. This little ceremony may sound routine and uninteresting, but that's not always the case. Even in this simple exercise, strategy is employed.

During my first season with Norm Schachter's crew, we worked a game in Yankee stadium. Andy Robustelli was the greying defensive captain for the Giants. The Giants, being the home team, allowed the visitors the opportunity of calling the toss. They did and lost. Now it was the Giants' choice. They could receive, kick or choose a goal. Schachter looked at Robustelli inquiringly. "What do you want, Andy?" he asked.

Robustelli replied, "We'll take the ball down there!" and he indicated one end of the field, thereby stealing all the choices. The other captain started to say, "Yeah, we'll kick from here," when Norm interrupted him with a smile and turned back to Robustelli. "Andy," he said, "you can have the ball or the goal, but not both!"

With that Robustelli grinned and replied, "Okay, Norm, we'll take the ball."

Now the other captain thinks there's oil down at the end of the field where Robustelli had pointed and triumphantly declared, "We want that goal!"

One of the advantages of artificial turf is that the silver dollars most referees flip will land flat. With natural turf, the coin can occasionally come to rest on edge, supported between blades of grass. This requires a second flip of the coin.

Most of the conversation between the players at the time of the coin toss is brief, but friendly. Both teams are keyed up for the game, and a brief handshake and a "How yuh doin'?" is usually it. Sometimes, a couple of the opposing captains will be off-the-field friends and will exchange a few extra-personal greetings.

The tension before the game infects everyone involved and the coaches are certainly not immune. In my first two years with the league, I was a back judge and had to obtain the names and numbers of the captains from their respective coaches. In an opening pre-season game at Green Bay, I went to Packer Coach Vince Lombardi on the field, thirty minutes before the game, and asked, "Who are your captains, Coach?"

Now that seems like a simple question — about like asking your children, "Who's buried in Grant's tomb?" or "What kind of fruit is grown on orange trees?" But that particular night the tension, plus all the details Lombardi undoubtedly had on his mind, made him draw a blank.

He hesitated, then looked away and roared, "Isn't that awful? I can't even remember my own captains! Phil!" Phil Bengtson, Lombardi's top assistant trotted up and Lombardi queried, "Who are my captains?"

Bengtson replied, "Eighty-seven, Davis, and seventy-six, Skoronski!"

"That's right," Lombardi echoed, "eighty-seven, Davis, and seventy-six, Skoronski!"

I knew this before I came up to him, but it wasn't my place to remind him.

Pressure does strange things to people, to all of us. A good example of this is the amateur speaker who must address an audience. Suddenly, the palpitations commence; the palms become moist; the words tumble forth from an unnatural voice. This all happens because of our emotions. Emotions can make our tear ducts flow, cause the heart to pound rapidly and cause us to forget basic, well-known things when under pressure. The constant repetition of good habits in selling, management, officiating or any area of human relations helps us to do the right thing when we are under pressure.

Rudyard Kipling once said, "What we do when we don't have to determines what we will be when we can no longer help it." Think about that. It's a sharp bit of observation and tells us a little something about the challenge of living. In the area of professional officiating, it provides some understanding of why it takes so many hours, days and years of high school and college officiating to make a pro. That's why it takes all those hours, days and years of a player hitting the blocking sled, tackling dummies and practicing the various zone defense — so that when the pressure is really on, the reaction is right.

The practice of good habits must be pursued constantly in every endeavor we follow if we expect to excel in that field. Remember, as the famous Hall of Fame quarterback and now head coach at Green Bay, Bart Starr, has so often said, "Perfection is impossible, but excellence is not!"

Before we leave the subject of the coin toss, just one quick visit with Alex Karras again. In a Detroit game in 1965, Alex and John Gordy were the captains for Detroit. Karras had been suspended for a year by Commissioner Pete Rozelle for betting on his own team. Detroit was the visiting team and as we gathered for the coin toss, Schachter turned to Karras and inquired, "Are you going to call the toss?" With a straight face, Alex backed off and said, "Not me! Let John call it. I don't gamble!"

The coin toss is now scheduled three minutes before the opening kickoff and when it is completed, the National Anthem is played. Never have I stood on a football field for our National Anthem without goose bumps traversing my spine in every direction. The privilege of living in the greatest nation of God's green earth is a blessing we should give thanks for, every waking moment. In spite of all America's faults, its men and women have more opportunity to live up to their full potential than the citizens of any other nation on the face of the globe.

I am twice blessed, for I also have the privilege of being a part of what I consider to be the greatest sporting event on earth. Football is a vehicle for individual as well as team play. Together, they symbolize what our founding fathers intended when they wrote a declaration of independence from human bondage and in the same instrument declared our dependence on God Almighty as the underlying foundation of our liberty. They boldly declared to the world our rights to "life, liberty and the *pursuit* of happiness," yet to do all this within the law and accept our individual share of the team effort of a nation. That's what the National Anthem means to me.

As the last strains of the National Anthem die out, we move to our assigned positions. I'm situated on the receiver's 15-yard-line, just across from the head linesman. The referee is in the middle of the receiver's end zone and the back judge is at the receiver's free-kick line, which is the kicking team's 45. The field judge has the ball at the kicker's 35, where he'll tell the kicker to raise his hand when ready, but not to kick until the referee blows his whistle. The side judge is opposite the field judge and the umpire is behind the kicker.

A quick, final silent prayer that no one gets hurt and that something we do that day will glorify God's kingdom. With that, my hand goes up to signal the referee that all is ready on my side. As all of the officials raise their hands to signal that all is ready in their respective areas, too, Referee Bob Frederic blows his whistle and the kicker's shoe pops squarely into the ball.

All of the preparation is over — now it's a football game!

CHAPTER NINE

THE GAME ... BROUGHT TO YOU BY ...

It's an immensely popular game; the audience numbers in the millions, and the purchase of TV time to reach those millions with commercial messages is almost as competitive among advertising agencies as the sport is itself among teams. Whether we like it or not, NFL games are going to be sending commercial pitches your way for everything from laxatives to luxury automobiles for a long time to come.

It has been said that a man sitting in front of a television set watching NFL football for more than five consecutive hours can be declared legally dead! I've heard a story about a wife who, after five months of solid weekend TV football viewing by her husband (not to mention Monday nights) said, "He never notices me anymore. I'm so desperate, I finally had to go out and buy a new nightie made of astro-turf before his eyes blinked."

I don't suppose there's any truth in that tale, but it is true that Super Bowl XII attracted 102,010,000 viewers in the United States alone, plus countless millions in foreign countries. It was one of the largest television audiences in history. It is just that kind of audience impact that makes the football spectacle a prime target for advertisers. This is dramatically highlighted by the latest television contract which industry sources consider the largest television package ever negotiated. All of the major television networks are involved and the contracts cover four years beginning in 1978.

Obviously, the TV networks intend to recover this substantial outlay of cash plus a healthy profit by selling commercial messages of every description. This electronic huckstering is contrived to influence you, the fan, to replace that outdated car you're driving, switch deodorants and drink a different beer, because it will make you macho, or eat at the fast food restaurant that shall be nameless here. All of these inducements follow a time out or a touchdown, as you take time out to visit the "john."

What might come as a surprise to you is the fact that we, the officials, have the shared responsibility to ensure that you, indeed, get the opportunity to see and hear these appeals to your taste and pocketbook. Part of our pre-game duties include meeting with the television producer and the sideline contact men to work out the details so that you do not miss either the commercial message or any part of the football game.

Let me emphasize right here that we do not interrupt the flow or momentum of the game to insert a commercial. If there is no score in the first few minutes of the quarter, we wait until the second change of possession to give the first commercial opening to the TV network. Prior to that, the contact man on the sidelines has signaled the referee by crossing both arms on his chest. This indicates that he wants a commercial break at the very next opportunity.

The referee acknowledges this request by pointing to the ground. This means "I read you, Buddy, and we'll give it to you at the next change of possession, provided it does not take the impetus away from a ball club."

For example, the officials would not grant the commercial if the change of possession was due to an intercepted pass that was run back well into the other team's half of the field. In that case, we would wait until later for the commercial.

Momentum is vital to a football team, and so it is to a salesman, or to a business. If things are going great and suddenly the inventory goes to zero, or a supplier doesn't get the materials or product delivered on time, the competiton can seize the opportunity to recoup. And here comes the big 'what if' again. What if the rhythm is broken, the impetus lost? Have you an alternate plan? Do you consider the vicissitudes of business, of life? Do you include, in your daily musings, the art of "alternate thinking?" You should. It can provide a positive approach to a sticky situation and restore the impetus that was lost.

But back to the game — and the sponsor. When we get an opportunity to break for a commercial — let's say it's a punt, dead on the receiver's 24-yard line — Bob Frederic, the referee, would signal time out and point to both teams. This doesn't mean that both teams called time out. What it does mean is that CBS, NBC or ABC is going to start getting their millions back. Now you are going to be told that if you would just start using a certain deodorant, your success in business would improve. What's more, those people who've been crossing the street as you approach will now rush to greet you. Why? Just to whiff your new-found fragrance. Who knows, even your love life might improve. Not a bad promise, if you swallow it. On second thought — don't swallow it, just splash a little on your face.

After this plea for your deodorant dollars begins, the TV contact man on the sidelines places one hand over his heart area. No, the National Anthem isn't playing again. It simply means the network is on a commercial and don't resume the game yet. While all this is going on, another little scene may take place. A player against whom I have just called pass interference, may come up and say something like, "Pardon me" or words to that effect. I'll answer his query or listen to his plea, but always with an eye on that sideline TV guy.

At ten seconds before the commercial ends he drops his arm, and with that the field judge, Bob Wortman, blows his whistle and signals the referee. Referee Bob Frederic will then blow his whistle and thrust his right arm skyward. This is the "ready for play" signal. When Frederic's arm goes up, Wortman punches his 30-second stop watch and the 30-second field clock starts, allowing the offense only 30 seconds to complete their huddle, line up, shift, set and snap the ball. I have been in this league for fifteen years and if I may say this without appearing to be egotistical, our crew has never missed a single commercial!

Our job is to allow four or five commercials each

quarter, in addition to those which come between quarters and during halftime. To understand the importance of this procedure, you must bear in mind that on Super Bowl XII, when Dallas defeated Denver, the advertiser paid $175,000 for only 30 seconds of television time. So let's face it. Without the sponsor, the game would not be available through television. I think we need to be reminded of this fact from time to time for, in a free enterprise system, sales dollars keep this big machine we call America rolling, and advertising is a vital cog in the gears.

Important as the commercials are, however, the biggest challenge for TV, by far, is to cover the game so effectively that you will receive the best camera work possible. I, personally, think the TV pros have done a fantastic job. CBS had thirty-one cameras on Super Bowl XIV to capture the action. The cameramen were extremely alert to the flow of the game, as they fixed on the action which their cameras funneled back into a master control truck. There in the truck at a mind-boggling console, receiving the pictures, the director and his assistants decided which shot to use — and you must remember they had absolutely no idea what was going to happen next. I wouldn't even hazard a guess as to the miles of cable running throughout a stadium to make this coverage possible. It is really remarkable!

With the TV coverage left in very capable hands, all participants of the contest stand by, trembling, waiting for the whistle that will start the game. It comes, finally, and we hear, simultaneously, the "thunk" of the kicker's shoe meeting the ball and the roar of the crowd.

The instant the football is in the air, twenty-two men and a ball, known geometrically as an oblate spheroid, become the subjects of the seven Zebras' total concentration for the next two-and-a-half to three hours. The kick that starts the game is classified as a "free kick" and is far different from a "scrimmage kick." For example, a "free kick" is just that, meaning that, after the ball goes ten yards or is touched by one of the receivers, either team can recover and keep the ball. A "scrimmage kick" recovered beyond the line of scrimmage by the kicking team will still belong to the receivers unless the receivers touched it first.

One past season, we had an opening day game when the deep man for the receiving team — a rookie — either didn't know the rule or simply forgot, and as the kickoff ball rolled into the end zone, he turned and started to walk away. He was thinking, "touchback," as it would have been on a punt. Meanwhile, galloping down the field came the kicking team, not unlike Merrill Lynch's herd of bulls. They were simply slaveringly bullish on recovering that ball in the end zone for what would be a touchdown for the kicking team.

At the same time, a player on the receiving team sprinting up, yelled, "Fall on the ball, you dummy! Fall on it!" At the last second, the deep man woke up, turned quickly, and dived onto the ball. The moment was saved for the receivers and they took a touchback and possession on their own 20-yard line. But it was only the frantic cry of the deep man's teammate that denied the opposition a cheap six points and possibly seven.

One of the differences between the "free kick" and a "scrimmage kick" is the restriction imposed on any member of the kicking team who goes out of bounds. If, during a "free kick," a kicking team player so much as steps on a sideline, he cannot even touch the ball until it has been possessed by the receivers. If the same thing happens on a punt, he is restricted from touching the ball only until it has been *touched* by the receivers. So imagine yourself an official, with that ball coming down the field, the detail of that rule and many others must be going through your mind. Want another? If the free kick goes out of bounds before it is *possessed* by the receivers, and is untouched, or last touched by the kickers, the flag appears and it is a mandatory five-yard penalty against the kickers — and this penalty cannot be refused.

How can this rule possibly bring problems? It sounds so simple. The intense rivalry between Cleveland and Cincinnati is quite commonly known. I have worked these two Ohio teams several times when they were pitted together. Back in 1975, I was with Bernie Ulman's crew in Cleveland for the Bengal-Brown game. Cleveland was trailing at the half in a very touchy ball game, and during the half-time interval we officials discussed how we should keep our concentration on *every* play — to be six professionals during every second out there. As the second half was about to begin, we trotted out onto the field determined to prove that we were professionals.

Cleveland kicked off and the ball headed toward me at the 15-yard line, where I was standing on the Browns' side of the field. The ball hit inbounds at about the 14-yard line and angled toward the sideline. A simple out-of-bounds kick, I thought as I grabbed the weight on my flag that hangs over my belt. But, suddenly, at the nine-yard line, the ball took one of those funny bounces and kept bouncing about six inches inbounds, parallel to the sidelines. I was sure it would go out of bounds on the next bounce, but no. It hit on the four and bounced up in the air again, this time actually angling a little farther onto the field. Now here came the thundering herd, the kicking team in Cleveland uniforms, running like scalded dogs, determined to get that ball inbounds, which they could then keep.

The Cincinnati kick return man was galvanized into action from his deep position centered on the goal line. Over he came, a real speed burner! He leaped as the ball took that last bounce and landed six inches out of bounds on his left foot. He then reached back in and caught the ball, which was still inbounds by a yard and planted his right foot a good half yard inbounds.

"What the hell is this?" I thought. My mind drew a blank! I seemed numb, the mental computer wasn't programmed right! I ran to the spot at the two-yard line and signaled a time out. That I knew was right!

Now Bernie Ulman ran over and asked, "What have you got?"

I stepped toward him just as things began to sort out in my mind and my mental computer cranked out the answer. "It's a free kick out of bounds! It's a five-yard penalty and kick it again!"

Ulman smiled and chided, "Arthur, why don't you throw your flag?"

Zoom! Up went the flag about five seconds too late and with it, the roof fell in. Forrest Gregg, Cleveland's excellent coach and a fine man, was over to us so fast he could have been an Olympic sprinter. Naturally, he wanted Cincinnati stuck back there on their two-yard line.

I said, "Coach, it was a free kick, out of bounds! The Bengal man was out of bounds *before* he touched the ball!"

"That ball was a yard inbounds!" he countered.

"I know," I replied, "but it's still out of bounds if it touches a player who is out of bounds!"

I'll never forget his answer. He said, "I'll bet you a thousand bucks you're wrong!"

"No, Coach," I replied, "I won't take your bet, but I'm right!"

There was no question about it. The call was right! Unfortunately, however, the mechanics were horrible. It didn't *look* right and that was the clinker! As professionals, we not only have to *be* right, we have to *look* right. If Zebras are hesitant, the public reaction is that the officials are wrong or, at best, confused. It is for that reason that Zebras spend a major portion of the pre-game meeting each week on what we call mechanics. They constantly strive for the smooth togetherness which makes an NFL officiating crew look right, as well as be right. Indeed, even the pre-season, four-day clinics, which are mandatory for all officials, are largely devoted to proper mechanics.

It's the same way in every walk of life. The requirements of professionalism concern not only *what* we know, but how we put that knowledge to use, what kind of timing we have, where we are, how we look and how we sound. All of these things combined go into the making of a top professional in any field — as well as a professional in the day-to-day activities of life.

A good creed we might all follow is simply: we must have knowledge without superiority; confidence without arrogance; respect without prejudice, and humor without hurt.

But, we digress. Back to the playing field and the so-called suicide squads. These consist of the kickoff and punting teams, the kickers and receivers. Here is where speed builds up the most before the inevitable collision of body against body. Suicide squads? I can't think of a better name. But apart from the bruising, bone-breaking activities of this phase of the game, this is also where the element of surprise is often used.

I was the line judge in the 1974 Minnesota-Dallas championship game, where surprise was used to its greatest advantage. I might add that I was to receive two surprises that day, the first one occurring just before the second half was to begin. Norm Schachter was refereeing, and we had been in the dressing room for our half-time rest, fuel and pit stop.

As we assumed our positions on the field for the second-half kickoff, I noticed some small, light brown, egg-shaped nuggets on the field. I jogged over to see what they were and was really perplexed until I remembered that the half-time show was a circus. I hadn't seen the show, but I quickly put two and two together and got goats. Some goats had been part of the halftime show and had forgotten their social graces.

I ran over to Schachter and said, "Before we kick off, I need a shovel!"

Schachter looked at me like I was some kind of nut. "Here we are," he said, "ready to kick off for the second half of a championship game, with millions of TV fans watching, and you want a shovel!"

"I know," I replied, "but either we get a shovel, or we're gonna have goat manure on the uniforms."

Schachter grinned and summoned a groundskeeper with a shovel. So there we were, Norm Schachter, Art Holst and millions of fans, both in the stands and watching on television, witnessing the transformation of a goat outhouse into a clean football field.

Well, the circus wasn't over yet. On the kickoff to Dallas, we received our second surprise. The Dallas deep man caught the ball and ran toward the head linesman's side of the field. Then suddenly, he handed the ball backward (he must hand it backward on a play not from scrimmage) to "Hollywood" Henderson, the Dallas linebacker. Now Henderson, though he's a linebacker, is also very fast. He came whistling across the field like an express train, heading right for me. Then, quickly, he turned up-field, about two yards inbounds and went all the way for a touchdown. I don't think anyone laid a hand on him.

This is the kind of action on kickoffs that demands sharp eyes on the part of the three officials in the deep zone. The referee, the head linesman and the line judge must be extremely alert to see that if the ball is handed off, it is handed off backward. If the ball is handed off forward, it is ruled dead, unless the ball is muffed and intercepted by an opponent while it is still in the air.

A forward hand-off on a free kick is considered an illegal pass, for which the penalty is five yards from the spot where it occurred. If the ball is muffed and hits the ground, the official blows his whistle and the ball is ruled dead. Only if the defense intercepts the ball in the air is the play allowed to continue. Do you wonder that I pray before the kickoff? Well, actually, there's more to prayer than that.

Let me repeat some of the words of world-famous scientist, Dr. Alexis Carrel. Dr. Carrel, author of *Man, The Unknown,* and for many years head of the Rockefeller Institute, said, "Prayer is the most powerful form of energy one can generate. The influence of prayer on the human mind and body is as demonstrable as that of secreting glands. Its results can be measured by increased physical buoyancy, greater intellectual vigor, moral stamina and a deeper understanding of the realities underlying human relationships. Prayer is as real as terrestrial gravity. As a physician, I have seen men, after all therapy has failed, lifted out of disease and melancholy by the serene effort of prayer. It is the only power in the world that seems to overcome the so-called 'laws of nature.' The occasions on which prayer has dramatically done this have been termed 'miracles.' But, a constant, quieter miracle takes place, hourly, in the hearts of men and women who have discovered that prayer supplies them with a steady flow of sustaining power in their daily lives."

That's why I pray.

One of the other wild kickoff plays is the shortie, or as it is commonly called, the on-side kick. It's a hairy play and creates some real tough calls for the back judge, side judge, umpire and field judge. The ball must go ten yards or be touched by the receivers before it goes the required ten yards. Usually, we are alert to it, because if a team scores with little time left in the game and they are still behind, the short kickoff is probable. If that short kickoff does not go ten yards before it is touched by a member of the kicking team, it is ruled a foul. The flag is thrown and the penalty, if accepted, would be to rekick the ball from the 30-yard line instead of the 35.

That short kickoff is really something. When you have all those helmeted mastodons attempting to capture an elusive football, it's a bigger "hey rube" than trying to catch a greased pig at a county fair. The resultant melee is one of the reasons most National Football League officials don't carry their whistles in their mouths. It is embarrassing, in fact downright humiliating, (not to mention catastrophic) to blow that whistle and then find that the ball is still loose.

One of the little subtleties of the rules prohibits the kicking team from running with the ball after a recovered kick. Naturally, they would prefer to do this. A case in point. We worked a game several years ago between New Orleans and Minnesota in Tulane stadium (also known as the Sugar Bowl each year on January first). The Vikings surprised everyone, including the officials, with a short kick to start the second half. The ball took a high bounce over the first line of New Orleans' receiving unit. In swooped a Viking player, scooped up the ball and hightailed it into the end zone for what he thought was a touchdown. I immediately ran to the spot where he grabbed the ball, planted my foot, blew my whistle and pointed, "First down — Minnesota!"

The would-be touchdown hero charged back to me from the end zone and yelped, "What are you doing, Man? I made a touchdown!"

I replied, "The only thing you made was tracks! The ball is dead, right here!"

Remember, the kicking team cannot advance a kick until it has been possessed by the receivers. The only exception is a scrimmage kick, (punt, or attempted field goal) that has been blocked and is recovered by the kicking team behind the line of scrimmage. Then and only then can the kicking team advance a kick while it is still a kick.

Free kicks provide some of the most interesting plays in football. One play which is very rarely used is the one that allows the team making a fair catch the option of putting the ball in play with a free kick. The kick, if chosen, is made from the mark of the catch. The big difference in a free kick occurring after a fair catch is that if the ball goes through the goal posts it is a field goal and three points go up on the scoreboard.

I'm sure you'll agree with me that a plus in viewing the wild action of NFL football on television is instant replay. Contrary to what many people might think, I like instant replay. Admittedly, it puts Zebras under the gun, but it gives you, the fan, the opportunity to enjoy the game more and to understand more fully the sophisticated teamwork game that football really is. It also proves to you that we, the officials, are indeed *always right!* We knew it all the time, but you needed a little help!

In some of the pre-season games of 1978, the NFL tested the use of instant replay to help officials. What do I think about that, you ask? Well, first of all, I'm in favor of anything that will bring better officiating to the game. 1978 was also the year seven officials, instead of six, gave better coverage to the action. However, if instant replay is to be used as an officiating aid, several questions come to mind.

First, how expensive is it? Second, (really a part of first) how many cameras are needed, situated where, to get the right angle? Who has the power to change an official's decision? How much time does it take to review questionable plays? And, finally, the most critical question of all: is what is seen on the instant replay really *right?*

I was involved in a play in the Miami-San Diego game near the end of the 1977 season that decided a division championship. San Diego threw a little screen pass thrown forward, which I felt was juggled by the receiver for three steps. He was hit in the middle of the third step and the ball slithered loose. A Dolphin defender picked it up and ran for an apparent touchdown, but, unfortunately for him, I had already ruled it an incomplete pass. If the ball had been possessed, then fumbled, it would, indeed, have been the touchdown that would have put Miami in the playoffs.

The instant replay showed he apparently had possession for three steps. So did the game film — but a few days later, NFL films came up with a shot taken from behind my left shoulder with a zoom lens focused right on the receiver's hands. Results? This excellent, slow-motion shot showed he never had possession. The instant replay missed that one, but how do you boo the instant replay three days later?

I could have used instant replay to prove a call in one pre-season game in Green Bay. Packer Boyd Dowler caught a pass at the sideline and it appeared to be a completed pass. Unfortunately for Green Bay, however, it didn't look that way to me. As Dowler's feet came down, his left foot just touched the sideline, while his other foot landed a good two feet inbounds, but I was right there and yelled, "No! Incomplete pass! Out of bounds!"

Well, Dowler turned to me and began screaming! I said, "Gimme the football!"

He refused, putting it behind his back and yelling, "Look at my foot! There's no white on my shoe!"

I yelled back, "I'm not interested in your foot! You're out of bounds! Gimme the ball!" He wouldn't give it to me and I had to yell at him again, "Dowler, give me that football!" Well, this time he reluctantly handed the ball to me.

Coach Lombardi, who had been a good 15 yards down the field and with no way of seeing the play as I saw it, came running over to me, roaring, "Art, goddammit! You missed it! You missed it! You missed it in this pre-season game and you'll miss it in a championship game and cost us a championship! And I won't have it! Phil!" he yelled, "Why can't we have good officiating?" and he continued ranting and raving.

As we were walking off the field at the half, I was wondering to myself, how in the world could

Lombardi complain about that call when it was so close, and I was right on top of it? And as we walked off the field, Lombardi came alongside of me and, as if nothing ever happened inquired, "How's everything, Art?"

"Fine, coach," I replied, in complete wonderment.

"Good!" he added, "Nice to have you here in Green Bay," and that was the end of that conversation.

Well, I was puzzled then, but I have since figured it out, and I'm sure I'm right. What Lombardi was really telling me was, "I'm not upset with you. I didn't really mean what I said." Being the psychologist he was, he was simply showing his player, Boyd Dowler, that he was actually backing him up.

As for the call itself, there was no question about it. Dowler stepped on the line. He only nipped it, but that was enough. Instant replay on the field would have settled the matter at once, even to Dowler's satisfaction.

Position, not only of the body, but of the head, where the eyes are focused, at a given time, during a given play is all-important. In fact, a portion of our ratings are based on where the head of an official is pointing. In the use of instant replay as an aid to officiating, camera position is only one facet. Its effectiveness will also depend on where it is pointed and what it is focused upon. Also, don't forget that the human eye sees in *three* dimensions, while the camera sees in only two.

What do you think about electronic Zebras, without stripes?

CHAPTER TEN

TRENCH WARFARE

Over the years, an expression has evolved in football that likens the line play to the desperate trench action of warfare. In professional football, the men who play in the offensive and defensive lines average about six-feet-four inches in height, and go about 250 to 260 pounds in weight. When you have that kind of power and weight colliding, it's awesome.

I have often been asked about the brutal physical contact on the field. It is really difficult to describe. Unquestionably, a one-word summation of the activity would be *violent!* I think that's the thing I remember most vividly about my transition from officiating college football to professional football, although college players are no sweet peas either.

I am reminded of the story about Bob Zuppke, who coached at the University of Illinois for many years, some time ago. Zup always taught his boys to give it everything they had when they were out on the field. One afternoon, at practice, he went over the fundamentals of tackling. A few minutes later, during a scrimmage, one of the linemen zoomed through the air and nailed the ball carrier.

The tackler, pretty pleased with himself, looked up at Coach Zuppke and inquired, "How was that, Coach? Were you watching?"

"Son," Zuppke replied, "I never watch tackles! I *listen* for them!"

In the professional trenches, whenever you don't hear the explosive pop of the pads filling the air, you can be sure not much is going on. When I first saw and heard the contact between these very big, very fast, and very talented football players, I was sure that it registered about 7.8 on the Richter scale. Yet, in any of the games in which I participated, we have never had a serious head injury. There have been many leg and arm injuries, particularly to the knee, but I cannot remember a serious head injury in a game in which I was one of the officials. Granted, occasionally a player will get his bell rung, but that's only a little momentary music. This lack of serious head injuries is a tribute to the excellent equipment used in football today. The helmet would come out very well in a collision with a truck. The padding inside the helmet holds the head, like an egg, encased in a cushioned cocoon of very hard plastic.

The face mask is another fine safety accouterment, for it has cut down on many injuries to the face. Broken jaws still happen, but not frequently. Today, it is not unusual to find a veteran football player with all of his own teeth. This was not the case thirty years ago.

The face mask, however, does have a negative factor. It provides a perfect handle to grasp in attempting to drag an elusive halfback to earth. It can also be very dangerous because of the mechanical advantage it provides, so grasping the face mask is a "no, no," a foul, and the word in the rule book is grasping. Simply placing the hand across the face mask is *not* a foul, however. Moreover, it is not a foul if the tackler grasps the edge of the helmet. We often hear about "no calls" from the sideline, because a team feels its man has been tackled by the face mask when, actually, the defender grabbed the edge of a helmet. The face mask foul nets a five-yard penalty and a first down (if committed by the defense) and fifteen yards if the foul is flagrant.

Face masks are a necessary item of protection, in spite of the misuse they are sometimes subjected to. Just as vital are the other protective pads the player wears, so to do his job effectively and safely, a player must dress for the task at hand. Many of the players in the NFL are successful businessmen off the field, but they leave their business suits at home or in the dressing room on Sunday and don the special gear appropriate to the job at hand.

For your information, the following is a list of items a player in the NFL must wear. He must wear a helmet. However, the face mask is optional. He must wear a shirt with numbers of a prescribed size and with the same numbers on the front as on the back. He must wear a helmet with a chin strap on it. He must also wear shoulder pads, hip pads, thigh pads and knee pads. Stockings and shoes are required, *except* for kicking. Tearaway jerseys are illegal and no altering of the knee area of the pants is allowed. The face mask is not required but most players feel it's a great idea to have one. This safety equipment is now required by rule since 1979.

Do we, in our business life, dress for the job at hand? How we look plays an important part in how we come across to other people. Imagine a professional football player, playing the game in a business suit. Ridiculous, right? You'd think he was a little flaky. But in the business world, many times a man or a woman is dressed in a manner totally inappropriate for the job.

A prime example of "looking the part" is the airline pilot. Wouldn't your toes curl if you saw a guy in greasy blue jeans, work shoes or sandals and a three-day growth of beard, seat himself behind the controls of a modern jetliner? I don't know what you'd do, but I'd get off! Now! On the other hand, the professional with the neat haircut, wearing the cap with trim visor, the shirt, tie and uniform with the four stripes on each sleeve, exudes a competence that puts one and all at ease. He may not be a better pilot, but his appearance tells me, "I'm capable of getting this 300-ton plane off the ground at night, flying 2,000 miles and finding Los Angeles in a fog."

You see, we gain confidence in his appearance. This, of course, does not guarantee that your luggage won't end up in Las Vegas, but the point is you are safely on the ground when you find out you lost in the game of luggage roulette.

But let's get back to that other game: the hard, bruising contest of professional football. I have previously mentioned that contact on the field is fierce, but it bears repeating. We had a game in Pittsburgh back in 1977 where Terry Bradshaw got hit by a charging Dallas lineman, just as he released the ball for a pass. He was hit so hard that he actually popped right out of one of his shoes. It was not a foul, but what a jolt he took! Surprisingly, he was not injured and stayed in the game to help the Steelers defeat Dallas 28-12.

I think the psychological foundation upon which this game is built goes back to the basic desire of a human being to acquire and own property. Think about it. This is what our game is all about. I kick the ball to you and you attempt to get it into my yard and play. The right of property ownership we enjoy, as Americans, goes back to our founding fathers' recognition of this basic human desire. The right of acquisition and ownership of property is fundamental in our way of life and the salesman or woman who does not appeal to this human trait is not doing a professional selling job at all. Selling, after all, is the science of helping people acquire and own that which they need and would like to have, if they just knew about it.

There is pride in ownership. Remember how proud you felt when you bought your first new car or that dream home? Vince Lombardi used to say, "Pride is what makes the Packers what we are. This team is built on pride!"

The battle for possession of the ground between the goal lines is intense and, ofttimes, bitter. But there is a great satisfaction in the struggle itself. Things that are difficult to achieve leave us with a great glow of accomplishment. Things that come too easily arrive with the zest removed.

There is no easy way to advance the ball. The quarterback must grind it out, play after play. Sacking the quarterback is every defensive lineman's dream. A player once told me,

"Whenever we have steak at our house, I don't charbroil it. I just brand it with the letters Q.B.!" They're still talking and writing about the Monday night game our crew worked in Los Angeles. The year was 1976 and Tommy Hart of the San Francisco 49ers sacked James Harris, the quarterback for the Los Angeles Rams, six times during that game.

The job of the offensive lineman is to protect his territory, to protect that parcel of land on which the quarterback is standing. To get at the ball carrier, passer, or ball itself, the defensive lineman is allowed to push or pull the offensive lineman opposite him out of the way. Now, just imagine a player six-feet-five inches tall, 265 pounds, who can lift over 400 pounds, having the right to grab you and pull you to the ground in his efforts to get at your teammate. On the other hand, you, as the offensive lineman, are prohibited from grabbing him.

Beginning in 1978, the offensive lineman was allowed to use his open hands to push the defensive man, provided he keeps his hands within the framework of the defensive man's body. This is a major change in the rules, as it has always been illegal for the offensive player to have his hands open. However, grabbing by the offense, tackling or hooking will still be called offensive holding.

While these men are exceptionally large, they are also exceptionally mobile and quick. Some of the moves they make are hard to believe. I once saw Doug Atkins of the Bears leap clear over a blocker and tackle the quarterback. Another time, when the referee got too close to the passer, a big defensive end took the blocker, the passer and the referee

This is Latrobe, Pennsylvania, but Arnold Palmer isn't on hand. Latrobe had the first professional football team, which made its debut in 1895 and defeated the Jeannette, Pennsylvania team by 12-0.

"Slow Whistle" was tramped into the snow of Fort Pitt Park, Pittsburgh, before the Houston-Pittsburgh championship game in 1979 as a reminder to the Zebras. Good thing, too. There were a record number of fumbles — all called right!

Super Bowl XII Crew — January 15, 1978 (Dallas 27, Denver 10). Left to right — kneeling: RAY DOUGLAS, back judge; ART HOLST, line judge and author of this book; CAL LEPORE, alternate; TONY VETERI, head linesman. Standing, left to right: NICK SKORICH, assistant supervisor of officials; FRANK SINKOVITZ, alternate; JIM TUNNEY, referee; BOB WORTMAN, field judge; ART McNALLY, supervisor of officials; JACK READER, assistant supervisor of officials.

Each official carries a game card and records the fouls he calls and other pertinent information as the game progresses. This is my game card for Super Bowl XII.

ZEKE BRATKOWSKI'S touchdown pass to MAX McGEE enables the Packers to beat the Baltimore Colts in Milwaukee in 1965. Author ART HOLST is the Zebra watching the play. The man with the white gloves is the sideline contact man for CBS.

Referee BOB FREDERIC adjusts his microphone in Soldiers Field, Chicago during a time out in a Bears-Detroit game. I stand by giving encouragement as BILL SWANSON, the back judge, comes up from behind. If you look closely, you can see the Heuer Game Timer watch on my left wrist. Also, you can see Swanny's and my bean bags sticking out of our belts and the weight on my penalty flag at the belt line nearer my right hand.

Repeat after me: "Football is fun! Football is fun! Football is fun!" Not all officiating is done upright; some is done from the ground as Umpire LOU PALAZZI would testify following the Tampa Bay-Atlanta game in 1978. Tampa's DEWEY SELMON, #61, decks Lou along with the ball carrier while his brother, LEE ROY SELMON, #63, looks on approvingly. It smarts, Folks!

WALTER PAYTON, #34, of the Chicago Bears returns to the huddle following a play in the Bears-Detroit game in 1978. The familiar Zebra, wearing #33 is Author HOLST.

in one big armload. The referee looked like the meat in a Zebra-burger!

Alex Karras was an all-pro defensive tackle for many years at Detroit, but he didn't look like one. With his poor eyesight, jowly face and his ample midsection, he seemed more like Friar Tuck, but when the play started, one saw a different Alex. I was surprised when I saw him in a 1964 pre-season game with Baltimore. The man had the quickness and the reflexes of a cat. He was very strong and had a competitive drive second to none. Keeping him out of the offensive backfield was as tough as moving a family of polar bears across the Sahara Desert on skate boards.

Because the defensive linemen are so intent on getting at the quarterback, many of the referees will shout after the ball leaves the passer's hand, in order to prevent a "roughing the passer" foul. Tommy Bell, number seven, a great referee from Kentucky who is now retired, used to bellow out in his distinctive southern drawl, "The ball is gone!"

In the pits, where these big linemen battle for their piece of real estate, the umpire is in the middle of the play and ofttimes doubles as a peacemaker. Lou Palazzi, the umpire on our crew, is really talented at this. Lou, with his almost unbelievable twenty-eight years in the league as an official, can come up with the right words at the right time to cool things down. I recall a Detroit game when Mike Lucci, the very tough line-backer for Detroit, got into a verbal duel with one of the opponents. Lou jumped in and broke it up and then, as Mike turned away, Palazzi, a fellow Italian, called to Lucci in Italian. Lucci turned with a surprised expression and Lou exchanged a few words with Mike in their native tongue. All was peaceful thereafter. I've often wondered what he said. Surprisingly, Lou is really a quiet man, but he has the talent of saying the right thing at the right time.

Actually, the amount of talk between players and officials is minimal, and for a good reason. Football is a very complex game and the players must have their heads in the ball game at all times. The more time they waste jawing with officials, the more likely they are to miss a signal or assignment. The signal the quarterback calls in the huddle gives direction to his team. Nothing works better in keeping a man or a woman striving toward a goal than having a specific plan or play to follow. Off the playing field, in the work-a-day world, nothing is more frustrating than to see talented people living out their lives in an uncharted sea of generalities.

It's not easy, but no one ever said life was going to be easy for the professional in any field. Failure is almost a guarantee to those who expect success to come easy.

Bob Zuppke, that great University of Illinois football coach, long ago said, "Footballs take funny bounces!"

Well, so does life, and a positive mental attitude toward life's "funny bounces" helps us to greater success. A good mental attitude that looks at problems as opportunities seems to foster an accelerated percentage of success.

Charles Kettering, the renowned inventor at General Motors, once said, "Don't bring me your good news! Bring me your problems! Good news tires me!"

Problems officiating? We've got 'em! When Norm Schachter and his crew worked the Green Bay - Dallas world championship game in 1967, the temperature was twenty-two below zero! Norm blew his whistle to signal the kickoff, and from then on the whistles were strangely quiet. It was so cold, every whistle froze up! Norm has said, and with a great degree of accuracy, that the entire game was officiated primarily by talking to the players through chattering teeth. That was the football game when Hall of Fame Quarterback Bart Starr of the Packers ran a quarterback sneak over Jerry Kramer's block, with seconds left in the game, and scored the touchdown which beat Dallas on that frozen field. No, it just isn't easy.

The struggle for excellence which takes place in the trenches of professional football is matched by the performances of backfield men and on the sidelines, where coaches are constantly making decisions — and yes, among the Zebras as well.

When I broke into the National Football League, as an official in 1964, there were only five men in a crew. The line judge position did not exist. I officiated in the Hall of Fame game at Canton, Ohio on July 27th, 1977, where, for the first time in the history of the game, seven officials were used. The following year, 1978, seven officials would work all NFL games. Strange as it may seem, this is not a record for the most officials ever to be on a field for a game. In Super Bowl I, there were twelve officials on the field. The explanation is that six actually worked the game, while the other six were held as alternates for each position. Half of the twelve were from the American Football League and the other half from the National Football League.

The seventh official is called a side judge. He is positioned on the same side of the field as the head linesman, just opposite the back judge. This gives us better coverage, particularly on pass plays to the head linesman's side. One of the features which has made professional football ever more popular has been its ability to change. The owners and coaches have been willing to try new ideas to make it a better game for the fans.

This is true in any enterprise. The old maxim, "If you stand still, you're really going backward," is true. It can be likened to Einstein's theory of relativity when applied to the business world. You may be standing still, doing the same old thing, in the same old way, but when the front runners go by, in relation to them, you're going backward! It's as simple as that!

You see, a lot of people don't want to change. Most of us are satisfied with that rut once in a while, but some people want it all the time. Someone once said that the only difference between a rut and a grave is the length! An ad in the personal column of a newspaper read, "68-year-old man who smokes and drinks, wants to meet 68-year-old woman who smokes and drinks. Object: smoking and drinking!" You see? He didn't want to change, and what's more, he didn't want to be associated with anybody who wanted to change.

Leadership demands the flexibility of thinking that allows us to use those creative talents God gave us. Doing it better, faster and more economically should be a constant goal. Cross-pollinating ideas, as we cross-pollinate corn, is not limited to the laboratory. It can be done on a football field, in the kitchen or on a sales call. One of the most creative ideas I have heard in recent years of selling came from a salesman whose calls were such that his first contact was the key man's secretary. In spite of his ingenuity, smile and great charm, he was unable to get in to see the top man. Before leaving, however, he noted the secretary's name, and later at the airport, he put a quarter in the automatic "gambling machine" that sells air travel life insurance. The machine bets you $7500 against your quarter that you will arrive at your destination alive. Pretty good odds.

Now our ingenious salesman used his creative talents. Whose name do you think he inserted on the policy as beneficiary? If your answer is the name of the big prospect's secretary, you're right! He mailed her a copy of the life insurance contract and included this note. "Dear Ms. Jones, it was nice meeting you and I hope this flight is a safe one, as I am looking forward to seeing your boss the next time I'm in town. If I picked the wrong plane, enjoy the $7500!"

Guess who got in to see Mr. Top Man the next time?

Are you willing to be creative to get out of the rut you're in? The game of football cannot afford ruts. It must constantly provide excitement for the fans. If existing rules inhibit this necessary ingredient, they are either changed or new ones are written. There must be more opportunity for scoring, for that's the way ruts are eliminated.

In 1978, one rule was changed to permit double

touching of a forward pass by the offensive team. Prior to that time, double touching of a forward pass by two eligible receivers was a foul, but the penalty was only loss of the down, just like an incomplete pass. Now, with the new rule change, after an eligible pass receiver touches a forward pass, any other eligible member of the passing team may catch the ball. An action such as this was formerly a penalty and resulted in the loss of the down. You can see how this new rule has provided more opportunity for excitement and scoring. One further note, the offensive man cannot deliberately bat the ball forward to a teammate.

Back in 1967, I worked a game in New York. The Giant quarterback was Fran Tarkenton, who threw a pass that touched a potential receiver. The ball then accidentally hit an offensive lineman on the line of the helmet, behind the line of scrimmage. I threw the flag and this big guy turned and growled, "What did I do?"

I said, "You touched a forward pass and that's illegal!"

"Hell!" he yelled, "I was just standing there!"

"Well," said I, "You should have stood somewhere else!" Of course, everybody's gotta be someplace, but this guy was in the wrong place at the wrong time. The penalty? Just loss of the down since the touching was both unintentional and behind the line of scrimmage.

Lest I forget, I must admit there are occasions where we *know* we are right, when actually we are wrong! I have in mind the case of Jim Marshall, number 40, the great and durable defensive end of the Minnesota Vikings. It was October 25th, 1964, and the Vikings were playing the San Francisco 49ers in San Francisco. A pass from 49er quarterback George Mira was completed and then it was fumbled. Marshall, reacting instinctively, hurdled the player nearest him, snared the fumble and galloped for the goal line, 60 yards away. There was only one problem. He took off the wrong way. As he thundered down the field, his teammates were screaming hysterically from the sidelines, imploring him to turn around. But the wind was with him; he was making marvelous time, and no one was going to deny him this touchdown. He crossed the goal line, elated with the touchdown he thought he had scored, only to be told by an extremely grateful 49er that he had, in fact scored two points for San Francisco on a safety. That one wrong-way touchdown effort of Marshall's did not affect his spirit or his will to win. With Jim's help, the Vikings went on to win the game 27-22. Jim has started and played in an unbelievable and record-holding 250 consecutive NFL games prior to the start of the 1978 season. Each game in 1978 became a new record for this durable and fine football player, and at the close of the 1979 season he will have started 291 consecutive NFL games. What a record!!

While trench warfare is exceptionally grinding on linemen, the playing life of a kicker is less punishing by contrast. Kickers last longer and for an obvious reason. They are not subjected to the physical punishment of a guard or tackle. Marshall took this kind of punishment for years and amassed an amazing record for a lineman. The fact that he committed a grievous mistake did not damage his positive spirit, for, through his playing thereafter, he demonstrated that a mistake will only affect a person as much as he allows it to.

To some people, failure is a brand that they carry for the rest of their lives. It's like a 40-ton load that keeps crushing them to earth. To others, failure isn't failure at all; it's merely a step toward success — but only if they refuse to stop.

One of the most unusual plays I was ever involved in happened in Yankee Stadium in 1966. Norm Schachter was the referee for a game between the New York Giants and the Dallas Cowboys. It was a tough game and the Giants had yet to score. Finally, they fought the ball down to the Dallas six-yard line with fourth down coming up. They elected to try for a field goal and in came field goal kicker, Charlie Gogolak. Charlie and his brother, Pete, were Hungarian soccer players who came to America to go to college and then play football. These soccer-style kickers kick the ball with the instep side of the foot. Charlie was a right-footer kicker and a pretty good one. So, when they lined up for the snap, everyone, including the officials, was certain it would be a routine field goal. It wasn't!

At the kick, Bob Lilly, the great all-pro tackle for Dallas, broke through the line and took the ball square in the chest, blocking it. The ball bounced back to Gogolak, who was by now surrounded by a herd of elephant-sized Dallas players, pursuing the bouncing football. Just as Lilly regained his balance and went for the ball, Gogolak, a soccer kicker, proficient with either foot, reached out left-footed and kicked the ball right out from under

Lilly's arms and over the crossbar! The fans went wild and, for an instant, the officials were stunned. But, quickly, Schachter dropped his flag. "Illegal kick!" he cried.

Pandemonium engulfed the stadium, because the scorekeeper had already put three points on the board. Now, since the ball went through the end zone, it was a simple declination of the penalty and Dallas' ball on the 20 for a touchback. Don Meredith, the Dallas quarterback and offensive captain, trotted on to the field and approached Schachter, "What is this, Norm?" he inquired. "I don't understand the ruling."

Schachter grinned and said, "Touchback! Don't ask questions, just get the ball in play! You came out smelling like a rose!"

Now the question arises: when can you kick a ball in professional football? The answer is simple. Anytime you have possession of the ball. You can catch the other man's kick and kick it back — an action that is called a "return kick." You can run the ball past the line of scrimmage and punt it, or drop-kick it, or even place-kick it. You could catch a pass, run with the ball for ten yards and then kick it. There are sufficient legal ways to kick it, but if you kick the ball deliberately, when it's a loose ball, it's a foul and that team is awarded a ten-yard penalty (15 yards back when that play happened). The only time you can kick a loose ball is when you kick it accidentally. That is not a foul.

I think this story points out several things that relate to professionalism in any field. Although he violated a rule, Charlie Gogolak used his best judgement under circumstances that demanded an immediate decision, if his team were to score. Being a kicker with a background in soccer, he was proficient with both feet. He didn't try to be any other kind of a player. He didn't try to pass or run because he wasn't a passer or a runner. He was a kicker, so he reached out *left*-footed and kicked that ball over the crossbar. The point is, he did something. He just didn't stand around and watch his opponents scramble for the ball when his first attempt at a field goal was thwarted.

Now let's consider the reaction of Norm Schachter. I was right next to him and was able to see the expression on his face. I'm sure that Norm threw that flag purely on instinct. Here was where experience paid off. His years as a referee told him, "Aha, something is wrong here!" Out came the flag and you could almost hear the gears clicking together in Norm's head as the screwy play ended. Experience isn't the only teacher, however. It's a good teacher, but not the best one.

Then you ask, what is the best teacher? O.P.E. is the best teacher. Other People's Experience! It is the fastest, least expensive and least dangerous way to learn. The Approved Rulings, or A.R.'s, in our rule book come from O.P.E. The questions — all one hundred and eighty of them — for our annual test come from O.P.E. They come from cards that are made up by Norm Schachter of plays which actually occurred over the years.

Public libraries are full of books based on O.P.E. This is the professional shortcut to success. The salesperson or management executive who attends meetings to listen and ask intelligent questions is profiting by O.P.E. Putting into practice this new knowledge, that portion which is relevant to them, will move them up the professional ladder faster than those who don't or won't.

There is a basic personality difference between defensive and offensive football players. For an example, an offensive captain may come up to an official and say, "Sir, could I ask a question?"

On the other hand, the defensive captain might show a different mood by addressing the official thusly, "Awright, Banana-nose! What the hell are you looking at?"

Now, of course, all defensive captains don't talk that way. Some are very mild-mannered individuals whose size and violent play belie their calm and well-controlled emotions. Willie Davis, number 87, the renowned defensive end and captain for Vince Lombardi's Packers, is a good example of a man with well-controlled emotions. He is an intelligent man who always had his eye on a business future when his playing days were over. He is now a highly successful business man.

How are the players selected for different positions? Bart Starr relates how Lombardi picked them: "Lombardi had a brick wall built at one end of the practice field and had the men run at it, full speed, heads down. Those who hit and bounced back, he made offensive linemen. Those who hit the wall and knocked a brick or two out of it, he made defensive linemen. Those who burst through the wall, he made fullbacks, and those who ran up to the wall, stopped and then ran around it, he made quarterbacks!"

Actually there are different qualities looked for in a football player. Size and speed are important, but temperament is not neglected, for nuances of temperament seem to go with different positions. One must consider that offensive linemen know what they are going to do on every play. For example: when the guard hears the quarterback call for a 49 sweep, he knows he is going to pull out and get ahead of the ball carrier to block the opposing linebacker.

Offensive football players are athletes who enjoy putting pre-planned plays into action. On the other hand, defensive football players, by the nature of their positions, must be reaction-type people. The offense decides if it's a run or a pass and the defense must react to it.

A good example: I remember a play "Deacon" Jones made during his last career season as a defensive end for the Los Angeles Rams. This exceptionally large and agile athlete still retained those amazingly fast reactions even then near the end of his career. As he rushed full tilt at the quarterback, an offensive blocker crouched in the blocking position, knees bent slightly, elbows flexed, ready to meet the charging Jones. Almost upon him, "Deacon," with one great leap, hurdled the blocker and nearly demolished the quarterback. I know this was not pre-planned at all. It was an instinctive reaction by a great defensive player.

In their scouting programs, NFL personnel use a variety of measurements to attempt to evaluate who will make the best football player at what position. However, there are two things that are next to impossible to predict. They are desire and the ability to perform under the pressure of a game.

The same can be said for business. You and I

have seen young men and women with all the talent, training and appearance to take the world by storm, but they don't. Then along comes a guy or a gal with just average talent at best and a very ordinary appearance. But what he or she lacks is more than made up for in that burning desire to succeed. He or she possesses that mental attitude that says, "I will make every sacrifice to make it to the top." And they do!

A good example of the lack of that gung-ho determination, or simply a lack of knowledge of one's craft, can be clearly illustrated by an incident that occurred in a game I worked in 1972. One player fit the above pattern while another, his teammate, demonstrated a determination which was laudable, albeit fruitless. I was on Bernie Ulman's crew and we had a game in Denver, between the Broncos and the Kansas City Chiefs.

Early in the game, Kansas City threw a little screen pass my way. The receiver caught the ball cleanly, ran a few steps and got hit, hard! A real shot! The ball popped loose, rolled on the ground and a Denver man fell on it. Now, you must understand that in pro football he can get up and run with it if he is not touched by an opponent while down. Well, I guess the Denver man liked that spot on the field, for he just lay there. A teammate came running up and yelled, "Get up!" Nothing happened. He tried again. "Get up, you dumb son-of-a-bitch!" he yelled. And with that he began pulling the prone player to his feet.

That would never do. "Helping the runner" is a foul, seldom seen, but it was good for a 15-yard penalty. Now the penalty has been reduced to ten yards. So, I threw the flag as the Denver man ran the ball back another 12 yards. After the whistle, I reported the foul to Bernie, who walked off the 15 yards from the spot of the foul. Just then, Coach John Ralston came running up, "Art! What's that penalty for?" he asked.

"Helping the runner!" I replied.

He looked at me incredulously and pleaded, "Helping the runner? Helping the runner? How deep did you have to dig to find that one?"

But it was a foul, and it was very plain later on the films.

Later in the game, Denver punted. The Kansas City receiver muffed the kick and immediately there occurred the inevitable scramble of several big men after one capricious football. The back judge, Ben Tompkins, was closest to the play, but none of us could see who had the damn ball! I'm sure you will agree that this is, of course, very important. It's fundamental in officiating to know where the ball is all of the time, yet you'd be surprised to know how difficult it is to know where the ball is some of the time. You feel awfully silly when someone asks the simple question, "Where is the ball?" You don't know and all you can do is shrug your shoulders. It's like being asked, "Where's the steering wheel on your car?" And you just can't come up with the right answer.

Anyway, I ran up and stomped my foot down, because I knew the ball was dead at the pile of players; not in the trenches now, but thrashing around in an imaginary shell hole. Then suddenly, 25 yards away, in the end zone, was a Denver player, gleefully holding something over his head.

You guessed it, it was the elusive ball. By that time, Bernie Ulman had come running up and asked a very embarrassing question, "How did that guy get the ball into the end zone?" The answer he received from his back judge, line judge and field judge consisted of three blank looks. He said later that we looked like a tree full of owls.

Then Bernie came up with a real creative idea. He summoned the innocent ball boy who has charge of the extra footballs on the sideline. "Did you give him the ball?" he asked the wide-eyed youth. The ball boy denied any implication in the "lost ball caper," pleading "not guilty, by reason of ignorance of the whole matter!"

What a quandary! Well, what were the things that we knew? We knew that Denver kicked the ball. (That wasn't too tough!) We knew that the receivers touched it first, but never possessed it. We knew that the kickers ended up with the ball in the end zone, but we also knew that the kickers could not, legally, advance the kicked ball from beyond the line of scrimmage unless it had first been possessed by the receivers. The only thing we didn't know was how the football got from the bottom of a pile on the 25-yard line and into the end zone.

It was decision time in the mile-high city, so we declared the ball boy innocent and gave the ball to Denver at the spot of the big pile up. We made the right decision. Are you surprised? Later, the film showed that a Denver man at the bottom of the pile *did* recover the ball. But as he lay at the edge of the pile, flattened by this mass of humanity on top of him, a teammate slipped up, took the ball from him, hid it in front of himself and sauntered nonchalantly into the end zone. Actually, all he had done was take a dead ball over the goal line, but we gave him an "A" for effort and creativity. Determination!

Self-confidence is a requisite for a good official, but sometimes too much of it can get him into trouble. In 1966 I worked a pre-season game in Green Bay, between the Packers and the Pittsburgh Steelers. With a few seconds left to play in the first half, the Steelers had the ball down near Green Bay's 30-yard line. The quarterback threw a pass to a Pittsburgh receiver in the end zone, but it was too short. Then up loomed Herb Adderley, the all-pro defensive back for the Packers, to make an easy interception. The Steeler man raced up to Herb before the ball got there and grabbed him. I threw the flag at the two-yard line for offensive interference. Adderley caught the ball and the defensive man whirled him around, back into the end zone, and the ball went loose.

I signaled, "Incomplete pass!" Herm Rohrig, our field judge and now supervisor of officials for the Big Ten Conference, came running up and suggested, "Art, wasn't that an interception?"

I was adamant. I refused Herm's help, forgetting about O.P.E. and teamwork and all the rest. Full of confidence which had now moved into the stubborn and foolish zone, I repeated, "No! It's an incomplete pass!" I had blown it!

Lombardi stormed! Italian lightning flashed! Roman thunder engulfed the stadium as the coach of the world-champion Packers roared his comments about my incompetency. This call, of course, gave the ball back to Pittsburgh at the 30, fourth down. You guessed it! Pittsburgh kicked a field goal as the half ended.

As we walked off the field, Lombardi came up and said, "You gave them three points they didn't deserve!"

He was right! There were six officials out there and when help was offered, a good official should, at least, have considered taking it.

We can draw a parallel to this in a business or professional career of any kind. No salesperson or doctor or lawyer can go it alone all the time and live up to what God expects of him, or what he should expect of himself.

We learn, in officiating football, that when you're in a tough spot and don't know for sure, look for help. The Lord said, "Seek and ye shall find. Ask and it shall be granted unto you." The first words in those two sentences are, "Seek" and "Ask." That puts the burden squarely on the individual.

CHAPTER ELEVEN

CAMP CHARLEY-HORSE

What else can you call training camp? Here is where the body and mind are put in shape; where knots are kneaded out of tortured muscles, and the mind is honed to a fine edge. There's no ducking it! Training camp is a must! All professional football players and officials, as well, must get ready to meet the tremendous challenge of the season ahead. This means training camp for the players and the school of self-discipline for the officials.

When a young player is drafted into the National Football League, his life as a professional football player begins with a very rigid physical examination. The official, too, must pass a rigid annual physical, one that includes a very close look at his weight. I have weighed within two or three pounds of 172 pounds ever since I came into professional football. We officials are not only weighed by our own doctors at our annual June physical, but we are weighed again during our four-day rules clinic in July. A third weigh-in takes place during the middle of the season. Lugging a few extra pounds around that field can be like trying to officiate a football game with a brick in each hand!

It has always seemed to me that good physical conditioning should not be confined to the world of sports. For any person to work at his or her peak efficiency, good physical condition is vital. Why then, shouldn't a man or woman in any other field of endeavor keep his or her body as fit as possible? When I travel throughout this country to speak before many different organizations, I am appalled at the appearance of many middle-aged folks who, in the prime of life, are carrying thirty or forty pounds of excess flab on their frames twenty-four hours a day. It is amazing how people are so careful to feed their dogs a good diet, but are totally neglectful of themselves. Just a little care in food selection, just a few minutes of strenuous exercise a day can add years to one's life, but more importantly, life to one's years.

A rookie or veteran reporting to his NFL camp, should be in pretty fair shape coming in, for when he gets there, the real hard work begins. He must now look forward to six to eight weeks of living away from family and friends. Living conditions are Spartan, usually in a stark dormitory on some college campus. Moreover, he is expected to obey a rigid schedule of mental and physical preparation. Here is where his skills will be measured against the skills of others. He will also face the decision of whether or not he will be selected as a member of the elite guard that will carry the banner of that team into the real battles of the regular NFL season.

The pressure on all of the players is tremendous, but especially so on the rookie. He had formerly been a premiere college player, but now he will be facing his equal or better every day!

The typical day in training camp begins early. Breakfast is at 7:30 a.m., followed by the usual taping and running. Then come calisthenics, weight lifting, one-on-one and two-on-one drills, pass drills and so on and on. Whatever time is left must be devoted to the study of the play book. This is the bible of a pro football camp and is the constant companion of a budding pro football player. The actual schedule varies from training camp to training camp.

But what about the officials? Is there any comparison between the players' preparatory training and that of the Zebras? Not quite. But the officials may even have it more difficult. I don't mean in the physical effort or the isolation, but in self-discipline. There is isolation of a sort, in that Zebras are actively pursuing normal careers and have no one to motivate them but themselves. They are the only ones responsible for getting the "old machine" in shape in order to do a first-class officiating job in football when the season starts. In my own case, I made three trips a week to the Bergan High School gym in Peoria, Illinois, to lift weights with my legs and then, added bicycling to that.

When the weather is inclement, I use the stationary bike at home in my study and read or watch television as I pump my legs into shape. Physical work, emotional strain and intellectual pursuit are the prices we pay for success in any endeavor. Persistence is the key word.

President Calvin Coolidge said it best, "Nothing in the world can take the place of persistence.

Talent will not. Nothing is more common than the unsuccessful man with talent. Genius will not; unrewarded genius is almost a proverb. Education will not; the world is full of educated derelicts. Persistence and determination alone are omnipotent. The slogan 'press on' has solved, and always will solve, the problems of the human race.''

Getting ready for a new season, as an official or a player, demands the persistence and determination that separates the pros from the "also rans." The same can be said for competitors in any other field. Anyone who has reached the top in his field, be he actor, doctor, engineer, salesman or business executive, has paid a price for success. His fans, patients or clients may never realize what it took to get there, but it was a lonely, obstacle-littered road and to reach the goal, it had to be traveled.

There are no big crowds along the street, cheering me as I pump my bike from High Point subdivision along Mount Hawley Road to Edgewild and back. The only interested parties are those in the passing automobiles trying hard not to hit me, and the dogs that constantly find my legs appetizing. The interest of the crowd quickened when I walked out on to that field for the first August pre-season game. The fan expected me to be ready and he didn't give a damn what it took to do it! He doesn't applaud me for it, nor should he. Neither, as our manual says, does he applaud for ice in his coke, hot coffee or a dry seat. But he will raise hell if any of these things are missing, including capable officiating.

All-Pro, Hall of Fame Receiver Raymond Berry, who was Johnny Unitas' favorite target while

Unitas was throwing passes for the Baltimore Colts, is an excellent example. I shall never forget the first time I saw Berry. It was in 1964, a pre-season game in Detroit. Berry made two or three of those patented side-line catches where he caught the ball, then rotated his body in the air and tapped his toes, both feet, inbounds. Both feet must hit inbounds to make a caught pass complete. If the receiver is carried or knocked out of bounds, and in the official's judgment he could have come down inbounds, it is still ruled complete.

Raymond Berry was not the fastest of receivers and what's more, he had to wear glasses. What then, you ask, made him so great? The answer? Persistence and determination. He was paid to catch passes and almost anything he touched he caught. He had magnificent concentration as he went for a ball. No matter that a linebacker or cornerback was racing toward him to literally fold him up, as his body was extended to catch the ball, his concentration never wavered. He could be counted on for the big play, but most people have no idea what training and sacrifice it took to make this possible.

Back home in Texas he started early. Every spring he'd plant two posts in the ground and stretch a heavy rope taut between them at about shoulder height from the ground. Then this great receiver would run toward the rope and leap for a pass thrown over the rope to him by a local boy. Hour after hour of this punishing practice put together the coordination and mental toughness necessary to catch a football, no matter what the competition did. And all of this was done weeks before training camp even opened.

There is a private world of the professional, a private world that thirsts for excellence, a private world that believes no matter how well a job is being done, it can and will be done better.

So every July big men, fast men, great throwers, skilled receivers and elusive running backs toil to get ready in twenty-four professional football camps. Sixty to eighty men in each camp sweat and strain, fall and rise again, determined to win a position on an NFL team. And while they give their all under the watchful eyes of skilled coaches and those of sports writers reporting on their every move, ninety-eight other men across the country are preparing to lay their talents on the line as members of officiating crews, who will keep the contest a game and not a riot.

As training camp persists, the evaluation and screening process continues. Movies are filmed of practice action and coaches spend late-night hours agonizing from these enlightening screening sessions over whom they will put on waivers or cut as the regular season approaches.

The pre-season games, which are a part of the whole picture, provide opportunities for coaches to see young players perform under game conditions. And the supervisor of officials and his staff get to study the performances of new officials and veterans as well. I am certain that observing officials during these pre-season games helps the office people to decide which seven men will make up a specific crew.

I believe this is important in all work situations. We must be so well prepared that we will feel the inner confidence in our job ability which tells us there is no one else present who can do the job better. As a professional speaker (when I wear my other hat), at the moment I am introduced to the audience, you can bet that I have at least double the material in my mind that I will need for the allotted time. But preparation takes work.

All football players must prepare themselves for the demands of the game. Some players seem to be naturals for their positions. Others have to work, work, work, to achieve success. Bart Starr, Green Bay's Hall of Fame quarterback and now head coach of the Packers, was plagued by injuries during his playing career at Alabama. When he was drafted in the seventeenth round by Green Bay, he set out with great determination to turn himself into a professional quarterback. With the help of his wife, Cherry, he took a bunch of footballs out every day in the early summer and threw pass after pass, while Cherry retrieved the balls. He might have been cut from the team without this extra effort; but when the dust settled, he managed to make the squad at Green Bay as a third string quarterback. But he didn't discontinue practicing his skills as a passer and ball handler. Then a new coach came to Green Bay. He had been the assistant coach with the New York Giants and, of course, his name was Vincent Thomas Lombardi. The rest is well-known sports history.

Bart Starr, the often-injured quarterback from Alabama, had been preparing, mentally and physically, for this chance and he rewrote the record book in leading the Packers to three consecutive world titles. Luck? Remember what

Charles Kettering said, "Luck is what happens when opportunity meets the prepared mind!"

Of course, practice alone doesn't guarantee success. I know a lot of golfers who shoot 110. They practice six hours a week, but they practice bad habits, so they don't improve. Intelligent practice and good planning go hand in hand. You've got to have a plan and when opportunity knocks, use it!

On a small road near Edinburgh, Scotland, a slight automobile accident occurred and several of the victims were lying in the road. MacPherson, of the locals, was walking past and stopped to speak to one of the unfortunates lying in the road. "Has the mon from the insurance company come aroon' yet?" he asked.

"No!" came the answer.

"Ah weel," said MacPherson, "I'll just lie doon aside ye then."

MacPherson had a plan, and when the opportunity came along, he used it! I see and talk to many sales people who, unfortunately, do not have the breadth and depth of knowledge they need to produce a top sales presentation. All business executives or salespersons should have some form of "pre-season" or "pre-game" preparation so that they may enjoy that abundance of good, solid material with which to work, if needed.

You notice that I said, "if needed." In any single football game, we never get to use all, nor even nearly all, of the material or mechanics that we have boned up on for so long. But an official has to know it all because he never knows when that little snippet of almost obscure information will mean the difference in a game or a championship.

On a late Sunday afternoon in 1970, the Kansas City Chiefs, under Coach Hank Stram, were playing John Madden's Oakland Raiders. The game was being televised nationally on NBC, and the bitter rivalry was even more pronounced that day because both teams had a shot at the division championship. Late in the fourth quarter of a continuously close game, Kansas City led by three points and had possession of the ball near midfield. It was third down and about eight or nine yards to go when the Chiefs' quarterback, Len Dawson, faked to the halfback, going left and then boot-legged the ball himself around right end. He ran down to about the Oakland 30-yard line with just under two minutes left in the game and this first down would have practically iced the game for Kansas City.

Then the unexpected happened! Dawson tripped over his own teammate and fell to the ground. Immediately, the handle-bar mustachioed, defensive lineman for Oakland, Ben Davidson, dived helmet first into Dawson's ribs. Head Linesman Cal LePore quickly threw the flag. Helmet first into an opponent is "spearing" and is rewarded with a 15-yard penalty. As Davidson bounced to his feet, Otis Taylor, number 89 of Kansas City, forgot his manners and attempted to rearrange Davidson's mustache! Davidson, of course, did not feel the need to have his mustache trimmed by a Kansas City forearm, so he protested quite vigorously and physically to Taylor. The fight was on! Twenty minutes worth!

After the game when I returned home, my wife commented, "You're sure not a fighter, Artie!

When the fight was on the 20, you were at the 30! When the fight got to the 30, you were back at the 20!"

I said, "You're right, Honey! I'm a lover, not a fighter!"

After the fight cleared, the referee, Bob Finley started to run off 15 yards against Oakland. I was on the opposite side from where it all happened and everything appeared right at the time. Then up trotted another official, who declared, "Hey, there were two fouls! One was on Oakland and one was on Kansas City!"

Holy mackerel! Now we had a problem! The chains and down box had been removed. Finley called to me and asked, "Where was the ball?"

That seems like a simple question — just like, "What's your last name, Holst?"

I was baffled! All I could say was, "It was third down, Bob, and now you know all I know!"

Casting a baleful eye at me, he whirled and sped for the press box phone between the benches and dialed the press box. He might just as well have tried "Dial-A-Prayer," for the press box couldn't help him either. Finley, undeterred, sped back across the field to the TV contact man on the sideline and asked him. The TV fellow, in turn, called the statistician in the press box. As we waited, the horde of fans was growling and threatening. If this had been the coliseum in ancient Rome and someone had given the thumbs down signal, six Zebras would have been devoured by lions.

Naturally, I was becoming concerned! I ran up to Finley and inquired, "Bob, what are you doing?" I shall never forget his answer.

"Art!" he replied, "That first foul was a live ball foul, because Dawson could have gotten up! The second foul was a dead ball foul, so that makes it a double foul and we have to replay the down at the spot of the previous snap!"

Okay, but we still didn't know where the ball was on the previous snap. "Bob," I complained, "we've been standing out here for 20 minutes!"

"So?" he shot back, "I don't care if we have to stand here for an *hour* and 20 minutes! We're gonna' get it right!"

I have always admired him for that and for knowing that one obscure sentence in the rule book states that if there is a double foul, one a live ball foul and one a dead ball foul, the teams replay the down at the previous spot. You see, you never know when that one bit of extra knowledge will be the very thing that will save a sale, keep a customer or make all the difference in a football game.

Well, the word finally came down from the statistician and we put the ball down near the 50-yard line and repeated the third down. The Chiefs didn't make it and had to punt. Then Oakland brought the ball back upfield to about Kansas City's 42-yard line, where the ageless George Blanda kicked the game-tying field goal, with eight seconds left.

Fifty thousand screaming fans at the game and millions watching on TV *knew* we were wrong, but actually we were right! There were still four or five seconds left on the clock and after Blanda's field goal, Kansas City had acquired two, not one, but two, 15-yard penalties due to some of their players' uncomplimentary remarks to Mr. Finley. Now, Oakland was kicking off from Kansas City's 30-yard line! Unbelievable! I edged up to Finley and said, "Bob, I've never seen a kickoff this close to the receiver's goal line!"

"I've got news for you," he replied, "neither have I!"

Well, right after the kickoff, the game finally ended and I ran hard for the dugout leading to our dressing room. You may have noticed how we officials make excellent time, running to the dressing rooms after games have ended, particularly when the roof is ready to fall in. On this occasion, I was running full throttle, when one of the chain gang, running behind me, yelled, "Art! Gimme the gun!"

I stopped about twenty feet from the dugout to give it to him and that was my big mistake! As I handed over the gun, someone hit me from the rear with an attempted tackle. I, of course, shook the individual off with my speed and shiftiness. (They don't call me 'Ol' Swivel Hips' for nothing.) As I turned around, I saw two policemen sitting on a prostrate fan — my would-be tackler.

When I got to the dressing room, it was a madhouse! People were pounding on the door, demanding our scalps. I even thought I heard someone call for a rope! The police, who believed that scalping and lynching football officials would not give Kansas City a good image, remained with us in our dressing room to give us protection.

The back judge, Grover Klemmer, number eight, and I both had early flights, so, after filling out our game reports, we left in the company of two policemen who carried our bags for us. They suggested that they walk about twenty paces in front of us. I'm not sure what the strategy was, but I think they wanted to be far enough away so they wouldn't get involved if we were jumped.

Anyway, we walked back out through the dugout and up through the stands with the hysterical fans. Fortunately we were wearing our business suits now and looked like just another couple of fans. One of the irate fans even turned to me and growled, "Damn lousy officials! They stole the game from us!"

Without a moment's hesitation, I replied, "You're sure right!" There was no way I was going to disagree with that man, or risk identifying myself.

The controversy raged in the press for several days until the film was processed and screened. It showed, beyond a doubt, that Dawson had *not* been touched by an opponent before Davidson speared him. We were right, but nobody believed it!

Little did I know at the time that two years later, I was to meet my would-be tackler. I was doing a series of speeches for the Kansas Bankers' Association and at breakfast one morning I happened to tell the story. One of the executives at the table asked if I knew who tackled me. I replied in the negative and he said, "It was a bank president and he will be in your audience next Tuesday night!"

"Well, I'll be damned!" I exclaimed, "I want to meet that bird!"

So the following Tuesday I arrived early for the cocktail hour, but he wasn't there. Later, after the speech, one of the bankers present called the guy at home and told him a friend of his was in town and wanted to buy him a drink. He only lived about ten miles away, so he rushed right over and we were introduced. The bankers explained I was the old friend they had called him about and after we ordered a drink, he said, "Gosh, I can't remember you."

I chuckled and said, "Do you remember the Kansas City-Oakland football game?"

He thought for a few seconds, then started to get up, saying, "You're not the guy I tried to tackle, are you?" I said I sure was and he muttered, "I think I had better leave."

I laughed and said, "Sit down! Let's have a drink!"

He settled slowly back into his chair, smiled and said, "I'm buying this drink. I'll always be grateful to you for not swearing out a warrant on me." I had refused to sign a warrant for his arrest and his name had never made the newspapers.

We had a nice visit and he turned out to be a great guy who had simply lost his head temporarily. He couldn't even remember racing some forty rows down to the field to get at me. That feat made me develop a new respect for the athletic abilities of bank presidents. Later, I autographed one of my record albums and gave it to him.

The inscription noted, "Congratulations! You have great speed! Sincerely, Art Holst."

CHAPTER TWELVE

EVERYONE TALKS ABOUT THE WEATHER, BUT . . .

Wasn't it Samuel Clemens who said, "Everyone talks about the weather, but no one ever does anything about it!"? Well, all I'm going to do is talk about it, too, but I sure wish someone would level it off. Unfortunately, the elements are not always kind to the game of football, nor to those involved in it, and that includes the spectators as well as the players and officials.

I have officiated the game under the most adverse conditions, from one extreme to the other. It is the only game that is played regardless of weather conditions. Baseball games are delayed or postponed because of rain. Basketball and ice hockey are played indoors, under controlled conditions. But football, like the postal service, is undeterred by rain, sleet, snow, swamp or whatever.

I have worked games in heat that can only be compared to Death Valley, in frozen ice fields that evoked scenes of Arctic explorations and in quagmires that could only rival the swamps of the Everglades. This spread of weather conditions occurs because the twenty-eight teams of the NFL are scattered from Seattle to Miami; from San Diego to Boston, and that includes everywhere in between. So everyone involved in the game of football is exposed to all the whims of weather on the field and off.

My mind is cluttered with the memories of games I've worked, wherein the weather would challenge the combined resources of a polar bear, a crocodile and a gila monster. Perhaps the memory that stands out most vividly was the famous "Freeze Bowl," the NFC championship game between Dallas and Green Bay played in Green Bay in December of 1967 — a game I did not work. Temperatures that day were reported as anywhere from fifteen degrees below zero to twenty-two below zero, to colder than a mother-in-law's kiss! No matter how you'd describe it, it was unquestionably colder than the inside of your deep freeze. Now that the scene is properly set, let me bring on the officials. One of the facts that few people consider is that the officials in football games go *both* ways: offense and defense. The players spend half a game in front of the oil-fired space heaters on the sidelines, but the officials are stuck out on that field for the full game.

Now the players have an even better deal, for American ingenuity has reached out to almost completely eliminate the players' discomfort. In 1977 I saw for the first time a product called "The Hot Seat." It's a plastic bench for the sidelines with slots along the front through which hot air is blown to warm the legs. Warm air is also circulated throughout the inside of the bench making the whole thing warm to the derriere. The longer I worked that football game, the more I wanted to be benched.

In that "Freeze Bowl" game, in spite of the warm clothing and the constant physical activity that should have kept the blood circulating merrily, Norm Schachter had one of his heels frostbitten. It was so cold that day that all of the officials' whistles froze! As a matter of record, Joe Connell blew his whistle early in the game, took it out of his mouth and pulled a piece of his lip away with it.

I went to these polar romps as well protected as possible. I carried long underwear, a heavy turtleneck black shirt, three pairs of socks, insulated underwear — top and bottom, white knit headband for my ears, and a plastic rain jacket to wear under my striped shirt. Also, as I mentioned in an earlier chapter, I carried little plastic sandwich bags to wear between layers of socks for added warmth. Once for a game in Green Bay I was given a pair of electric socks with batteries; but they made my legs look like I had tumors, so I removed them.

It's surprising how quickly you forget the discomforts of bad weather when the game begins. Although I did not work the "Freeze Bowl" in Green Bay, I have worked three other games with temperatures around zero. That opening whistle starts your juices flowing and your blood tingling as you gallop into the wild melee of colliding football players.

I worked the playoff game between Minnesota and Dallas in December of 1975. This was the unforgettable game that ended disgracefully, when "Turk" Terzian, our field judge, was struck on the head by a whiskey bottle thrown from the stands by some mental minus mark.

The temperature at the time of kickoff that day was hovering around eight above zero and I entered the field with gloves, earmuffs and all the heavy underwear I could pack under my shirt and pants. Actually, I put the earmuffs away before we came on the field and by the end of the first quarter I had put my gloves in my back pocket. By the time the half rolled around, I was warm enough to shed the plastic jacket which I had put on under my shirt. Then Dallas' last-minute "Hail Mary" pass from Staubach to Drew Pearson warmed the stadium to a fevered pitch and precipitated the bottle throwing.

There is no question in my mind that the intensity of concentration can produce an almost hypnotic state, insulating one against the cold. After a few minutes of play, all discomfort from the frigid temperature dissipates. I hasten to add, however, that on that particular day the wind was not blowing and the sun was shining, so we were not exposed to a bitter chill factor which, of course, makes a big difference.

One of the coldest games I ever worked occurred in Buffalo, the year O. J. Simpson broke Jim Brown's rushing record. The Bills were hosting New England and the temperature had dropped to only thirty-three degrees, but there was a gusty wind and the air was filled with blowing, wet snow. Before the game got underway the field was covered with a heavy carpet of white, so the ground crew came on the field to do their thing. They drove small trucks with giant circular brooms mounted in front. These brooms became clogged with snow immediately and wouldn't work, so they had to be retired for the day. But as they say, the show must go on. And it did.

In an almost unbelievable performance by a great athlete, O. J. Simpson rushed for over 200 yards that day. His longest run was a 77-yarder early in the third quarter. I'm sure that O. J.'s intensity of involvement in the game and his contribution to it overcame the physical problem of staying on his feet. It was in this particular game that the famous photo of Tommy Hensley, number 19, our umpire, was taken, with snow shovel in hand, as he attempted to clean the yard lines off. Actually, he had organized a whole crew of men with snow shovels to clean sidelines and yard lines between plans. After that photo of Tommy came out in the newspaper, several cities offered to hire him as commissioner of snow removal.

I might relate here a little episode in that game that gives some insight into the kind of man O. J. Simpson really is. It happened in the first half. Here he was, with the eyes of the sports world on him, heading for Jim Brown's record and determined to hit that 2,000 yard mark. The footing was impossible for the wet snow covering the Astroturf made it only comparable to a slushy, ice skating rink. The teams slugged it out for the first quarter; then suddenly, in the second quarter, O. J. broke around my side for a gain of nearly 17 yards. But it was not to be, for just as the ball was snapped, I threw the flag for an off-side against Buffalo.

Need I say there was an uproar in the entire

stadium? Seventy-five thousand fans and the entire Buffalo team wanted my hide! I ran to Bernie Ulman and stated, "Bernie, I've got off-side, Buffalo!"

As Bernie walked off the five yards against Buffalo, I turned and picked up my flag. Just then, O. J. came trotting by. He gave me a smile and said, "Don't let them kid you, Ref. You're doing a great job."

It was amazing. O. J., who had the most to lose, kept his cool better than anyone else. Undaunted, he finished the first half with under 50 yards gained, but in the third quarter he ripped off that unbelievable 77-yard run and went on to a 200-yard plus game. All that on a day when the field was difficult to walk on, let alone run.

But, oh, the weather. By the end of the third quarter, I was so cold that I couldn't get my hands to function properly. I was trying to get one of them into my pocket to get the gun out, but it was impossible. I turned to Ben Tompkins, our back judge, and yelled, "Ben, I can't get the gun out of my pocket! Can you help me?"

Ben is from Fort Worth, Texas, and as he stood there with his arms folded, he looked like the Abominable Snowman. "Help you?" he chattered through lips that were turning blue. "I'm frozen stiff myself!" I don't believe I have ever been colder.

Well, maybe one other time. It was in Baltimore in 1969, when the Colts played the Detroit Lions. Don Shula, the Colts' coach, had not yet departed Baltimore for Miami. It was a miserable, cold day with the temperature playing around at the freezing mark and slushy, wet snow lousing up the field. Our referee was Bud Brubaker and the game was tied in the third quarter when Baltimore punted to Detroit. Now pay attention 'cause we're gonna check you on this! The Lion safety man signaled a "fair catch" down around his own five-yard line. A "fair catch" signal in pro ball is one arm fully extended above the head with the palm open.

The Detroit safety signaled properly, but he had no intention of catching the ball. All he wanted to do was slow down the on-rushing Baltimore Colts. So, at the last moment, he lowered his hand and moved quickly to his right, away from the ball. But the ball took one of those crazy bounces, hit him in the left hip and bounced into the end zone where Baltimore, the kicking team, fell on it.

Call it quick, now! What was it? Touchdown, Baltimore? Wrong! It was a touchback and the field judge, Frank Luzar, called it immediately. He extended one arm to the side, parallel to the ground, and moved it up and down from the side of his leg in the touchback signal.

The Baltimore fans went wild! So did the team! They wanted a touchdown, but there was no way they were going to get it! A scrimmage kick, (punt, drop-kick, place-kick or return kick) that crosses the goal line, from the impetus of the kick, was a touchback, no matter who touched it, nor how many times it was touched. We were an unpopular herd of Zebras, for Baltimore had the ball in Detroit's end zone and the game was in Baltimore. The touchback call was about as welcome as an Israeli tank on an Arab farm!

The fans started throwing snowballs at Luzar,

but he was in the middle of the field; not even Tom Seaver could have hit him! All the balls were falling short! Right around my head! We couldn't get the game started again because the noise from the mob drowned out the Lions signals.

Finally, Coach Shula called Stan Javie, the back judge, over to ask him about the call. Stan explained the ruling patiently as I listened. The fans became especially rowdy now, as they thought Coach Shula was chewing us out. Sixty thousand of them snarling and screaming their frustration. The game was delayed for about twenty minutes because of the din and finally a big lineman from Baltimore, teeth chattering from the cold, said to me, "Ref, penalize us 15 yards and maybe they'll quiet down!"

"I can't do that!" I replied, "There's no rule allowing us to penalize the fans! However," I continued, "you can cuss me out and I'll stick you for fifteen for unsportsmanlike conduct!"

He said, "Hell, I'm not mad at you! I'm just freezing to death!"

By the time the twenty minutes were up, we were all frozen — players and officials.

At the airport later on the way home, I ran into Jerry Kramer and a producer from CBS. Jerry had been the color man for the game and we were all together on the same flight to Chicago. Jerry spotted me at the gate for the flight and said, "You guys blew that punt call!" I told him to have patience and I'd explain it later on the plane. After we were in the air, I took out my rule book, found the exact play, as an approved ruling, circled it with my red pencil and gave it to Jerry to read. He was smoking a big cigar and every time he'd read the play he'd shake his head, send up big smoke clouds and mumble.

At length Jerry said, "Art, I played this game for thirteen years and never knew that rule!"

"Jerry," I replied, "They pay us for the tough ones!"

That's true! The payoff in life comes from being prepared to do the tough ones when they come along, and do them right! That call in Baltimore was really a standard call for a football official, and even though it doesn't happen too often, the rule was clear. Any *scrimmage* kick which crossed the opponent's goal line from the impetus of the kick was a touchback — unless the receivers picked up the ball and ran with it. Even then it could have been a touchback, unless the receivers fumbled it, advanced it into the field of play, or fouled in the end zone. Incidentally, the rule has been changed, and if that play happened now, it would be Baltimore's ball, first down and goal at the spot where Detroit touched it.

Officiating a game in a field of ooze is also tough for an official, but tougher, quite naturally, for a player. The linemen must have good footing for leverage; the quarterback risks fumbles with a sloppy ball, and the running backs are vulnerable on a muddy field when they are forced to make quick changes of direction, if they are to advance the ball. There was one running back in my memory, however, who didn't seem to be bothered by field conditions.

I officiated a game at Chicago in December of 1965, between the San Francisco 49ers and the

Chicago Bears. The Bears had an incomparable rookie halfback named Gale Sayers. It was one of those cold, rainy, sloppy December afternoons, but history would be made that day. Sayers, the Kansas Comet, or "Magic," as he was nicknamed by his roommate and good friend, the late Brian Piccolo; would run for six touchdowns in that one game and electrify not only the fans at Wrigley Field, but the entire sports world as well.

As the game progressed, Gale pirouetted and darted for five exciting touchdowns and the sixth was coming up. This one was a beauty to watch — an 80-yard punt return that had the fans goggle-eyed. Jon Arnett was the other safety man for Chicago and I was the back judge. Gale took the punt, and sure footed in that muck, danced to his right to avoid the first tackler and sped upfield. While eluding other tacklers, one 49er did get to him, hitting him low and knocking him into the air. But this absolutely superb athlete regained his balance in the air and came down on one foot.

Now another 49er was roaring in to finish the job on Gale and I grabbed my whistle in anticipation of the tackle. But Sayers was a wraith. Completely and immediately in control of his entire body when he touched the ground, he pivoted on his left foot in that slippery mud and was gone. His would-be tackler embraced an armload of air and Sayers wasn't touched from that spot to the goal line. A Gale truly blew in Chicago on that day, and history was made.

There is an interesting sidelight to that great run. As Sayers passed the 49ers' 25-yard line, he looked back. Assuring himself that no one could catch him, he slowed down from there to the goal line. The following year, at our officials' clinic, Mark Duncan, then supervisor of officials and today an executive with the Seattle Seahawks, showed the films of this run in slow motion. Of course, in slow motion you couldn't tell that Sayers had slowed down, but from the 25-yard line on into the goal line, everyone was treated to a shot of the back judge gaining on the great Gale Sayers! It got a big laugh!

Another Bears great, whose true greatness lies before him, is Walter Payton. Sloppy, slippery fields, arctic temperatures and the unbearable heat of pre-season, do not hamper his skill and determination. He proved this in New York Stadium in the final game of the 1977 season on a field of grey slush against the New York Giants. With only 42 seconds left of a sudden death overtime, Payton was to set up the final play that would break a 9-9 tie.

With the Bears threatening on the Giants 25-yard line, the obvious play would have been a Bob Thomas field goal attempt. But the weather had been fighting Thomas throughout the game. The slushy field conditions had caused him to botch three previous field goal attempts. It would be better to get the ball in closer, so Quarterback Bob Avellini called a short, swing pass to Payton.

At the snap, Payton danced out on the treacherous slush, grabbed the pass and headed for the goal line. Larry Mallory, the Giants' free safety, entered the scene determined to gobble him up, but Payton dazzled him with his sure footwork, left him clutching air and reached the 11-yard line before he was brought down. Then, with seconds left on the clock, Thomas trotted out on the field and kicked the winning field goal that would put the Bears in the playoffs.

Obstacles? There were none for Payton. He had the goal in sight and the weather, field conditions and Giant tacklers could not dent his determination.

All professionals have to be prepared to wrestle with bad weather situations. This applies to business as well as football. Preparation requires attention to the details that can be vital when that unusual situation presents itself, and you can be sure it always will. Other people's professions may appear to the outside to be easily performed, but the people at the top pay an extra price to achieve that status, a price not understood by their public (or customers) or not even, necessarily, by their colleagues.

But getting back to the weather and its feud with pro football. We must not neglect artificial turf. This stuff does not get muddy, but it does get wet. One August night I worked a wet pre-season Minnesota — St. Louis Cardinals game where we had two inches of rain during the second half. As you might know, a wet field produces a wet football and a wet football invites a lot of fumbles, so when we are faced with a sloppy field, we must be more than careful about blowing our whistles.

During that particular game, the rain kept running off my cap and down my glasses. The players were slipping and skidding in all directions and when the ball went loose, it was like chasing a greased pig. It was something to see! The impact of a hard tackle would not only jar the ball loose, but it would unleash a shower of water from the tacklee!

One of the problems on a wet field is when the ball squirts out of a carrier's grasp *after* his forward progress is stopped. What happens often is that a ball carrier is hit and driven backwards, but just after his backward movement begins, the ball pops out. That's a dead ball! Now if the defense falls on the ball, the official must take it away from them and give it back to the offense. This act has a tendency to tatter your image as an official, in the eyes of the defensive team.

I remember a pre-season game in Washington a few years ago, where it rained so hard the drains couldn't carry the water away fast enough. Bernie Ulman told me he had to wade through water, hip deep, to get to the dressing room. That game was played on natural turf and the field became a quaqmire in a matter of minutes. This creates a problem of differentiating between the offense and the defense. One team may start with red shirts and the other with white, but in a matter of minutes they are all one color: brilliant mud! The only exceptions are the quarterbacks. They may possibly stay half-way clean, if the pass protection is good. Yes, mud creates the multiple problems of who has the ball, who recovered the fumble and who did what to whom.

One thing is certain, weather is one of the things we can't control. But what we can do, as professionals, is function at our best level by being properly equipped mentally and physically to do the job in spite of the elements working against us. One thing about football: it asks men to do more than they think they can do, regardless of the obstacles thrown in their way. Scientists who have studied the human body say we don't do half as much as we're capable of. I believe that, but I also believe that if we are to overcome what appear to be insurmountable obstacles, we must have recognizable, obtainable goals.

>As I pause to think of something
>That sets some men apart,
>It seems to me that goals in life
>Must be the place to start.
>Imagine playing football
>On an unmarked field of green,
>Not a goal line to be sought,
>Not a goal post to be seen.
>It would be an aimless battle,
>Were there nothing to be gained,
>Not a single thing to strive for,
>Not a score to be attained.
>We must have purpose in our lives,
>For the flame that warms the soul
>Is an everlasting vision.
>Every man must have his goal.

by Art Holst

CHAPTER THIRTEEN

IT'S NO POPULARITY CONTEST

Zebras have rules to enforce. They didn't make them, but it is their job to see that they are obeyed. If one player greets another with a karate chop, he is rewarded with a fifteen-yard penalty. That's what the rules prescribe for striking an opponent. But the offender may scream that he is being shafted, anyway. So, for enforcing the rules, officials are looked upon by the players as a pack of pariahs.

There are 107 pages of rules, reasons if you will, why officials are forced to invoke infractions or penalties. Many of them are judgment calls and, quite naturally, in the eyes of the erring players and their boisterous fans, the Zebras are always wrong. It seems that more and more, officials are under attack on all sides. There has even been criticism in high places that we are unqualified. I quite disagree, as years of experience coupled with constant rules study and testing belie that accusation. But the flak continues to pop, and Zebras continue to take it.

Officials are never applauded as the players are. They are somewhat like Raquel Welch's elbows.

Everybody knows they're there, but nobody cares. Let a Zebra make one close call and he is no longer a nonentity. One time, our crew worked in Green Bay the Sunday following a big controversy. We had no sooner poked our noses out of the runway leading to the field when the whole place came alive with one loud "Boo-oo!" from the stands. I turned to Bernie Ulman who was with me and said, "Listen to that! The game hasn't even started yet. What the hell have we done except get dressed?"

"Arthur," he replied, "that's all that's necessary. After last week, they'd boo Santa Claus, if he was wearing a striped shirt!" The crew in Green Bay the week prior had made a couple of tough calls against the Packers and we were suffering from guilt by association.

As football seasons come and go, hundreds of incidents occurring during games become filed in my memory. They are all ego-shattering. I remember a game in 1965, the first year of the sixth official who functions as line judge. It was a pre-season game and just before it started a player next to me inquired where the new official would stand during the action. Before I could answer, another player sidled up and cracked, "What difference does it make? He won't be able to see anything either!"

I am often asked, "What about officials? Do you wear any kind of protective equipment?" Well, the answer to that is, no, not of any kind. It is our responsibility to stay out of the way. Certainly no player is going to toe dance around you. Indeed, I almost believe that a player gets a little Zebra insignia pasted on the inside of his helmet for every official he wipes out. But even if the players would rather not hit you, there is an element of risk when you are close to the warfare.

Being an umpire carries the highest risk of physical injury of any officiating position. In a game at Tampa Bay in 1977, Lou Palazzi got sandwiched between Dewey Selmon of Tampa and Atlanta Runner Haskel Stanback. (See Picture Section). It reminds one of the story about the umpire who got decked quite roughly and as he was getting to his feet again, a player nearby inquired, "What happened?"

The official muttered, "I got hit from the blind side!"

"Oh," said the player, "right between the eyes, eh?"

Well, Lou did get blind-sided in Tampa and I thought he was really hurt, but he bounced right back to his feet — typical of an ex-lineman. Nevertheless, when we dressed for our next game a week later, I could see that Lou's leg was black from his knee to above his hip.

I had something similar happen to me. It was in December of 1965, my second year in the league. I was working the Minnesota-Packers game in Green Bay. Late in the first half Green Bay had the ball near the Viking goal line. Bart Starr, the Packer's premiere quarterback went to the huddle and called the famous "Green Bay Sweep"; pull the guards, fake to the fullback and give it to Paul Hornung wide around the right side. Here they came! Jerry Kramer, number 64, and "Fuzzy" Thurston, number 63, thundering out of the line like a cavalry charge, looking for someone to knock down. At precisely that moment I committed a personal blunder. Over-eager to be in a position to call the out of bounds or the touchdown, I held too long on the sideline and one of those giants hit me a terrific lick. It was an accident, but I sailed just as far as if it weren't. I did a snap roll through the air, landing about ten feet out of bounds, flat on my can, to the roar of delight from over fifty thousand fans. To make matters worse, I landed right on the fishing weight of my penalty flag in my right rear pants pocket. However, nimble as I was, I did a backward somersault and ended up on my feet. Fortunately, I had seen Hornung go out of bounds, short of the goal, so I could call the play; but I can tell you, that smarts!

To add insult to injury, when the game was over and I had showered and dressed, I came out to one of the exits, my bag in my hand. One of the fans was standing there, blocking my way, "Are you one of the players?" he asked, "Can I have your autograph."

"No," I replied, quite flattered, "I'm not."

"Are you a coach then?" he persisted, "If you are, I'd like your autograph!" and he shoved a program into my hand.

"No," I again replied, "I'm not a coach. I'm one of the officials."

"Aw, hell!" he grumped, "In that case, just your initials will do!"

Good thing it's no popularity contest!

Another time, I was working a game over in Cleveland. It was my first year in the National Football League. Cleveland's fullback was Jim Brown, the legendary all-time rushing leader, with 12,312 yards and 106 touchdowns. Jim is about six-foot two-inches tall, around 235 pounds and he could run the hundred in roughly 9.5 seconds. He was very tough to bring down. Anyway, Cleveland was playing Dallas. On one particular play, Jim came tearing through the line, carrying the ball. A big Dallas middle linebacker in attempting to tackle him, grabbed for anything he could get and it happened to be Jim's face mask. Now that isn't fair, and that's why we're out there. I threw the flag and stopped the clock and reported to the referee, "I got number 55 on the defense, pulling the face mask, personal foul!"

That was a fifteen-yard penalty, and did not improve the disposition of the offender, a big six-foot-three-inch, 240-pound linebacker. Storming up to me, he roared, "What was that for?"

Trying to make light of it, I jokingly said, "Get back in there and play ball, Son, or I'll bite your head off!"

"If you do," he shot back, "you'll have more brains in your stomach than in your head!" What are you gonna' do? He was probably joking. Or was he?

Speaking about a face mask, even an official can be guilty of this misdemeanor. In December of 1965 I worked a game in Chicago, between the Bears and the San Francisco 49ers. San Francisco had the ball in Bear territory and ran a play around my end for a pretty good gain. My hip was sore as a boil from the week before in Green Bay, when I was dumped on the fishing weight in my back pocket and I didn't want to get in the way of those galloping mastodons again. Anyway, as this particular play ended, I stepped in a bit too soon to blow the action dead. Just then a big offensive end blocked Bears Outside Linebacker Mike Reilly. It changed Mike's direction just enough so that he came right at me on that wet turf. I tried to duck out of his way, but couldn't and in that last instant of desperation I grabbed his face mask and down we went. Grabbing Mike's face mask enabled me to pull him to my side and avoid a head-on collision.

Mike leaped to his feet, eyes blazing and grabbed the San Francisco player, "You didn't have to grab my face mask!" he shouted.

I jumped between them and being the peacemaker that I am, crooned, "Easy, Mike, easy. He didn't mean it!"

Right then Bill Schlebaum, our line judge, came running up and helped me to separate the two players. After we had accomplished that, Bill turned to me with a grin and said, "If I could figure out which way to walk off the penalty, I'd have called a foul on you!"

I wish somewhere along the line I could say that we occasionally get some respect; but I am hard pressed to come up with any such incident. Rather, I am reminded of further assaults on our dignity. A case in point: in 1974 we worked a game in Cincinnati where the Bengals were playing the New York Jets. The Jets were behind by four points, with no times out left. The Jets had the ball on Cincinnati's thirty-yard line, and Joe Namath threw a pass to Tight End Rich Caster in the end zone. Now the ball has to pierce the goal line plane to be a touchdown. And Caster, in the end zone, had to reach into the field of play to catch the ball. Just as he did, he got hit from behind and landed on the one yard line. Our head linesman, Tony Veteri, ran up and planted his foot down, six inches in from the goal line.

The tension was mounting. Here were the Jets, six inches short of a touchdown, no times out left and the clock running down. The ball went into play, the Jets stabbing at left tackle, but tossed back for a one-yard-loss. That was it! Time had run out and the divisional championship rode on six inches of space. I was the line judge and had to shoot the gun to denote time had run out. Just after the clock hit zero, a New York guard moved from his three-point stance. That's a false start. The referee threw the flag which would have stopped the clock, would have penalized the Jets, but would have given them that precious one more play that they might have used to beat Cincinnati. There was only one problem; time had run out, but my damn gun jammed!

For the first time in all the years I had been officiating, the gun misfired. Once more "Murphy's law" was at work. So I went tearing across the field, yelling, "No! No! It's all over." Just then, a big Jet tackle reached right around me and picked me up about six inches above the ground. Looking down at me, he said, "Whaddayuh mean the game's over?"

I said, "The game's over! The gun jammed!"

Putting me down, none too gently, the burly tackle told me where I could put the gun. It was a big gun! And that day it was a cold gun! I wasn't about to comply with his wishes!

It's a good thing officials aren't thin skinned for there is no end to the abuse. The story goes that a referee was working a game where one player was wearing a glass eye. He had lost his real eye in a hunting accident some years before. On one play he came charging through the line and someone stuck a thumb in his glass eye. Out it popped and landed in the mud. The Zebra blew time out and the water boy came running out with the water bucket. The player calmly picked up his glass eye, washed it off, and replaced it in the socket.

The official was impressed with this young man's courage and after the game told him so. "Young man," he said, "I'm impressed with your courage and ability in spite of an obvious handicap. You're taking a chance playing with one eye. What if you lost it, too? What would you do then?"

Without a moment's hesitation, he grinned and replied, "No problem. I'd be a referee!"

Another time, I was working an exhibition game in Memphis. I threw my flag at an infraction of the rules and a player cussed at me. "What did you call me?" I snapped.

"Guess!" he said, "You've guessed at everything else today!"

But it doesn't stop there. Everybody gets into the act. Our crew worked a game one year in Cleveland, and on the way to the stadium the morning of the game, we stopped off in a little restaurant for breakfast. The waitress greeted us and took our orders. When she got to me, I ordered my usual big breakfast, "Glass of orange juice, toast, bacon and eggs, coffee and a few kind words."

She smiled at my jocular mien, and left to place the order. When she returned with the plates of food, she said to me, "Will there be anything else?"

"Yes," I replied, sipping my orange juice, "What about those few kind words?"

With that she leaned down to my ear and whispered, "Don't eat the eggs."

Where does it stop? The coaches get in their licks, too. Some years ago I officiated a Shrine pre-season game between the Chicago Bears and the Green Bay Packers in Milwaukee. When we trotted out on the field, there was Coach George Halas of the Chicago Bears down on one end of the field, leaning against a goal post. That was just at the time he had traded for and got new Quarterback Jack Concannon.

I walked up to Halas to give him the T.V. time and said, "Hi, Coach!"

"Hello, Holst," he replied, "How are you?"

Before I could reply, he said, "Holst, I'm not going to be able to help you fellas today."

I laughed at his good humor, but he came right back with, "No, I'm serious. As you know, I always like to help you officials when I can, but right now I've got a new quarterback and I'm gonna' be busy with him. We've put together a new offense and I'm gonna' be very involved with that offense, so you guys are just going to have to get along by yourselves." I think he meant it, too!

Zebras are anonymous and receive practically no fan mail. Hate mail, yes, but no fan mail. An example: Norm Schachter told me of a letter he once received. Its contents are as follows,

"Dear Mr. Schachter:

I watch you every week on television, as you referee the NFL games. I almost feel like I know you, because I've seen your number 56 so often.

I'm writing to tell you what a great job you do as an official. You are always on the play, your signals are great and I have never known you to be wrong. Keep up the good work.

Sincerely,
Joe Fan

P.S. Please excuse the fact that this letter is written in crayon. Where I am, they won't allow us to have any sharp pointy things."

The veteran retired referee and observer, Ron Gibbs, said he received a letter addressed: "World's Worst Football Official, U.S.A."

Ron said, "They found me right away, too. They delivered the letter only one day after it was postmarked!"

Getting back to four letter words and other profanities, when "Buddy" Parker was coaching Detroit back in the '50's, Norm Schachter was working one of the Detroit games. On one play, he made a "roughing the passer" call and the player in question charged him and snarled, "You dumb son-of-a-bitch!"

Well, that's not nice, and Schachter threw the offender out of the game and walked off another fifteen yards. Norm then trotted over to coach Parker, who inquired, "What's that for?"

Schachter replied, "He called me a dumb son-of-a-bitch!"

"I don't blame you for getting upset," Parker smiled, "You're not dumb!"

Getting no respect from fans, players and coaches can be taken even one step further. Officials have some fun with it too. In Minnesota, the management always has names and numbers over cubicles in the officials' dressing room. On October 15, 1978, we were to work the Vikings-Rams game and when I walked into the dressing room, my name was nowhere to be seen. All the other names were in place and there were no empty cubicles (there are only four, so we have to double up). Nobody peeped and neither did I. I walked through to the next room where the showers and toilet were located and there was my name and number — on the floor in front of the John! I tell you — I don't get respect — not even from the crew!

We had eighty-four officials in the NFL for several years, but in 1978 a seventh official was added to each crew. Now the number of officials totals ninety-nine. But back when we only had eighty-four officials, one of the officials I worked with said, "Art, did you know that they've taken a poll and you're ranked as the second best official in the league?"

"Hey, that's great!" I said, beaming, but then getting curious, I asked, "Who's first?"

"Oh," he chortled, "the other eighty-three are tied for first!"

Football has helped me put my life into perspective. It's tough, hard played, highly competitive and the stakes are big. But it is still a game.

This was brought home to me in 1965 in the next-to-last game of the season. Norm Van Brocklin's Minnesota Vikings were then playing the immortal Vince Lombardi's Packers in Green Bay. Norm Schachter was our referee and his quick wit and common sense were never more evident than during the last minute of that crucial game. I say 'crucial' and that's an understatement. The game was vital to Green Bay because they had to win to tie the Baltimore Colts for the conference championship.

With the score 25 to 19 in favor of Green Bay and under a minute to play in this national TV contest, the Vikings had the ball with a first down inside Green Bay's 30-yard line. Tarkenton went back to pass, and down the sideline streaked one of the Minnesota pass receivers. Herb Adderley, number 26, was playing left defensive corner for the Packers. Hall, the Minnesota receiver, flew toward the goal line just a yard or so inbounds with Adderly so close he could have been Hall's shadow! Tarkenton threw, and as the ball descended toward the fleet receiver, he reached out and gave Adderley a gentle shove in the middle of the back at the two-yard line. This caused Herb to break stride just a little and, most important, was a foul. It is offensive pass interference when the receiver shoves the defender out of the way before the ball is touched. I threw the yellow flag as the ball just cleared Adderley's outstretched fingertips and settled into the receiver's arms in the end zone. Pandemonium broke! Adderley whirled and said, "He pushed me!" I said, "There's the flag, Herb," and pointed toward the flag lying peacefully on the turf at the two-yard line.

With that, the Minnesota volcano erupted and the players came charging at me yelling — "Pardon me" or words to that effect. I finally made my way to the vicinity of the 25-yard line where Norm Schachter stood with arms folded and a benign smile on his face.

I came running up to within inches of his face and with the excitement of a second-year official embroiled in his first championship-deciding controversy, I sputtered, "Norm, I've got offensive pass interference on the two-yard line, and the ball was caught in the end zone. It's no touchdown and a 15-yard penalty from the previous spot!"

He looked at me, grinned and said, "Art, take two steps backward and say it again. You're spitting in my face!"

That broke the tension. I grinned, stepped back and said, "Offensive interference, no touchdown and 15 yards from the spot of the previous snap." Amid the rolling thunder from the Minnesota bench, Norm walked off the penalty.

Would you believe that just about twenty seconds later Tarkenton once again threw to the corner on my side? With the clock closing on zero the receiver dived for the low pass at the goal line. He caught it with his forearms just off the ground, but as he did, his shoulder hit the flag shaft and one foot swung around and hit the side line in the end zone. I was standing right outside the side line at the goal line and signaled incomplete pass as I bellowed, "No — incomplete pass!"

Again the "Purple People Eaters" came after me and this time the references to my family background and personal habits became intolerable, so I sent one player to an early shower! Again I had to fight my way to Schachter to report, "Incomplete pass and I ejected a man!" He smiled, and said something like, "OK, Art, but we've only got twenty seconds left in this damn game. Will you please keep the flag in your pants for the rest of the game?"

You couldn't hear yourself think in Green Bay,

as I watched the seconds tick down to zero on my game watch and fired the gun to end the game. The scoreboard still read Green Bay 25—Minnesota 19 as I looked at it and then rushed for the dressing room. As I looked around there was not another official to be seen on the field in Green Bay. They had all gone — whoooosh — to the dressing room and left me alone to the wolves.

I finally made it through the Viking team to our dressing room door and as I opened it, there stood Norm Schachter, that fine referee and my good friend. He started to laugh, shook my hand, and said, "Don't worry about it, Art! Some day we'll look back on this, laugh and say, 'Who was that guy who was with us for a couple of years who made those two calls in Green Bay?'"

But then he said something I shall never forget. In fact, it changed my life! He said, "Art, just remember, eight hundred million Chinese don't even know we played!"

That's perspective! Can we put our lives, both business and personal, in the proper perspective?

Football is a serious business for the teams, the coaches, the officials and the league office. But a sense of humor, the ability to laugh at ourselves and to be able to roll with the punches of disfavor are great assets.

We cannot allow criticism and unpopularity get to us. Our job is to call 'em honestly, as we see 'em, based on our experience and constant study of the rules. We cannot abandon this policy in pursuit of the affection of players and fans. Cavett Robert, in his book on personal development tells of a student in one of his classes at Berkeley, California. They were considering the subject of criticism. The student asked if he might borrow the blackboard for a few minutes.

With permission granted, he went to the board and began putting down figures demonstrating simple addition. He first wrote two and two equal four. Then five and four equal nine. Then six and four equal ten. With one resounding voice, the class of about thirty students said he was wrong. The student at the blackboard put the chalk down slowly, frowned and shook his head. "Twelve times I was right," he began, "and no one complimented me or gave me any sincere appreciation. But make one little mistake and you criticize me, loudly and in unison!" A good analogy.

The American Indians expressed it in another way, "Let me not criticize my brother until I have walked a mile in his moccasins."

Theodore Roosevelt once said, "It is not the critic who counts, nor the man who points out how the strong man stumbled, or where the doer of deeds could have done better. The credit belongs to the man who is actually in the arena; who errs and comes short again and again; who knows the great enthusiasms, the great devotions, and spends himself in a worthy cause; who at the best knows in the end the triumph of high achievement; and who at the worst, if he fails, at least fails by daring greatly so that his place shall never be with those cold and timid souls who know neither victory nor defeat."

You must be your own best friend. Never try to shore up your own confidence by criticizing others, but do it by convincing yourself you are somebody.

Never stop trying; never stop learning. Too many people in sales, business and other endeavors spend a good portion of their time criticizing others and finding excuses for themselves. This is an easy trap for football officials to fall into, for certainly they receive more than their share of public ire. But Zebras must be impervious to the diatribes of the malcontents.

If we spent as much time and effort improving ourselves as we do criticizing others, our lives would be happier and more fulfilling. We can all be somebody, if we think enough about ourselves. People watch television and the movies and gape at the stars. Many of them think, here I am, just an ordinary Joe. Not so! I personally think the Lord wants us all to be stars. I'm sure we can all be stars at something. I think those who can attach stardom to their own lot in life, to do whatever they have chosen to do, and do it well, without worrying about what the other guy is doing, is well ahead of the pack. Somebody has to sweep the floors of life; somebody has to put the nuts and bolts on the motors of the cars that are built, and somebody has to build houses, sell merchandise and so on. When you meet a person who really wants to do his or her job with the very utmost of ability, and has found happiness in doing it, then you've met a star.

My grandmother was an old Swedish lady, a quiet, loving housewife who was a star in her own right. Every Friday morning she was up at 5 a.m., baking rye bread to tantalize my nostrils when I woke up at around 7 or 7:30 a.m. I can tell you, the smell of grandmother's rye bread baking, and the taste of it still can't be beat anywhere. In my book, my grandma was a star-rye bread baker.

Do what you do well. It's as simple as that. We must all earn respect, but we must work at it. To keep going, we must keep growing.

CHAPTER FOURTEEN

ALL THE KING'S MEN

While horse racing may be called "The Sport of Kings," I'd rather like to turn that around where the game of football is concerned and call it "The King of Sports." Therefore, all the personnel involved in it, the players, coaches, managers, owners, trainers, officials and even the water boys are "All The King's Men." I can't include the cheerleaders for obvious reasons, but in recent years, they, too, have been contributing to the whole picture.

Speaking about the cheerleaders, I am reminded of one team which had a line of beauties that fraternized a little too much with the players and the coach didn't like it. Finally fed up, he called in the leader of the girls and told her to keep her girls away from his players. "I'm doing this for their own good!" he growled.

"You don't have to worry about my girls," soothed the leader, tapping her temple with a forefinger, "They're not dumb! They've got it up here!"

"Oh, yeah?" the coach bellowed, "I don't care where they've got it, my men will find it, so keep 'em away!"

You know, one of the things that makes football such fun to play and such fun to watch is that there is no question about the goal line. It's right there where everyone can see it: clear enough for the guy playing the game and clear enough for the fellow watching it from the stands or at home on TV. There is absolutely no question about the goal line and no question about the reward for reaching it.

Now why can't we put that same kind of football clarity into our own goals? Can we set a goal for ourselves, one that is attainable and that we are ready to pay the price for? We must have goals in life, goals we can reach, and we must be able to recognize the opportunities which pop up from time to time that will help us reach them.

The players know this and so do the coaches. That's why their high-precision performances make professional football such a joy to watch. Football is a game of intense concentration and requires a high degree of mental and physical skills; and both mental and physical skills must be honed to a fine edge. So let's examine "All The King's Men" at this point and learn how each player contributes a special skill to the overall team effort. Let's start with the quarterbacks.

This is a very demanding position. It calls for a skilled field general who must possess the ability to call the right play at the right time. He must be a leader the rest of the team can look up to and have confidence in. He must have courage and poise. He must have the ability to throw short, throw long and be able to run with the ball when forced to. He should have determination to stay in the pocket and have the ability to time the pass. Of equal importance, he should have confidence and pride of performance. Finally, even when he possesses all the above qualities he must also be sharp enough to read the opponent's defenses and make the necessary adjustment when calling signals.

Try to keep these things in mind the next time you watch the premiere quarterbacks of the NFL do their thing either at the stadium or on TV. Watch the stars like Roger Stauback of the Dallas Cowboys, Pat Haden of the Rams, the Pittsburgh Steelers' Terry Bradshaw, Bert Jones of the Colts and Bob Griese of the Miami Dolphins. These are the top ones who can always be counted on for slick performances.

What about the running backs? You will find that most teams use three offensive backs, not including the quarterback. Usually, due to the increased emphasis on the passing game, one of the offensive backs will leave his position behind the line and move to the flank. The player most often playing this split position is the one with the most skilled hands for pass catching. However, in today's game, all backs need sure hands because of the number of passes being thrown to the set backs coming out of the backfield!

The halfbacks range from about six feet two inches and weigh from about 200 to 225 pounds. They must also be able to run the 40-yard dash in less than 4.7 seconds. Quite obviously the running backs take a lot of punishment. That's why the coaches look for the big men to fill these positions. I hasten to add, however, that this isn't a hard and fast rule. There are many great ones who are smaller. Robert Newhouse of the Dallas Cowboys is one. He weighs in at 205 and is only five feet ten inches in height. Tony Dorsett, also of the Cowboys, is only five feet eleven inches and weighs 192. San Diego's Lydell Mitchell is only five feet eleven inches and weighs in at 198. Anthony Davis of the Houston Oilers is a five-foot-ten-inch, 190-pound running back. Perhaps the tiniest is Eddie Payton of the Detroit Lions. He measures a mere five feet eight inches and weighs 175. The other extreme is Robin Earl, big Chicago Bear fullback, who towers six feet five inches and punishes the scales with his 242 pounds.

Running backs absorb punishment on almost every play. When they are not running with the ball, they are either blocking, running into the line on a fake or racing out on a pass pattern. In each case they take their lumps. Running backs must have speed, power and good hands for carrying the ball, but above all, they must have great balance. There is no way to train a running back in the art of dodging, twisting and evasive maneuvering. What they do, they do instinctively. A good runner will make full use of his blockers. He must know them so well that he will be able to anticipate how they will react in any given situation.

The offensive linemen in pro football are usually muscular giants with the kind of speed that belies their great size. The guards usually weigh somewhere between 235 and 275 pounds. There are few that are short in stature. Most of them range from six feet to six feet six inches in height. The offensive guard is expected to carry out a number of assignments. He must pass protect, block straight ahead, pull out to lead a sweep, or pull and cut across the field for cross field blocking, but his

The offensive tackle is generally a bigger man than the offensive guard. This is necessary to make it tougher for the defensive player to push or pull him off balance and charge by him to nail the passer. The offensive tackle's size and strength are required for pass protection and straight ahead blocking. If he doesn't have the size, then he'd better have quickness, strength and speed to survive.

The offensive center must, above all else, get the ball to the quarterback or to the holder for the place kick and the punter with great accuracy and be a good blocker. More field goals and points after touchdown have been blown, and more punts fumbled away because of erratic snaps from center. So the center must perform this job neatly before he tries to handle the man on his nose.

Along with accuracy, the offensive center should be quick, have the ability to recover the use of his arms immediately, and be able to move off the line of scrimmage quickly. On most plays his responsibility is to block the man in front of him. So concentration, accuracy and quickness go along with speed and strength to make the ideal center.

The receivers, tight ends and flankers are obviously there to catch the ball, but it isn't all that easy. They must have a natural sense of timing, for that's what most pass patterns are depending upon. They must have great communication with the quarterback, not necessarily verbal communication, but vibrations which tell each what the other is thinking. There must be great understanding between them, for each must know the other so well that they can anticipate each other's next moves in any situation.

Catching the ball is one thing, getting into position to catch it is another. So speed is essential to a good receiver: speed and deceptiveness, the ability to put on a few moves which take the defender out of position.

Moving to the defense, here again, the linemen should have quickness, speed and great strength. They are always big men, some of them hitting 260 to 270 pounds and even more in some cases. The Rams had Lamar Lundy and Deacon Jones, Roger Brown and Merlin Olsen on the line a few years ago. These four giants had an average weight of about 275 pounds. When they ran on the field, it tipped a little! The San Diego Chargers had big Louie Kelcher as defensive tackle, weighing in at 282. The Rams' Roger Brown was around 300 pounds and that was down from over 340 when he played for Detroit. But these athletes were not only big; they were exceptionally fast. Most of them run the 40-yard dash in less than five seconds. They use their tremendous strength to push or pull a blocker to get at the ball carrier or the ball. Their opponent, a tackle, guard or center will weigh from 240 to 260 pounds and will have great strength, too, so they have quite a job moving him around to get at the ball carrier. In one game, Doug Atkins, who played for the Chicago Bears and stood six-feet seven inches, jumped clear over a blocker and literally swallowed the quarterback.

The linebackers must be a very aggressive people. You see them lined up in a defensive formation on or about three yards behind the line of scrimmage.

The linebacker's job is twofold: to stop the run on short yardage situations and to intercept or break up a pass play. He must be skilled at reading keys (the ability to watch an opponent and be able to predict what he is about to do, or what is about to happen, generally). Linebackers must always be where the ball is. Dick Butkus, before he retired from the Chicago Bears, was a tremendous linebacker. He was always around the ball, knew where it was at all times. Jack Ham of the Steelers is like that today — always near the ball on a pass play in his area. Ray Nitschke, formerly with the Green Bay Packers, was another top man in his field. He loved the violent contact, loved to bang people around. There is the old story of Nitschke grabbing Gale Sayers of the Chicago Bears by one leg and Willie Davis had the other one. Seeing this, Nitschke yelled, "Willie, make a wish." The middle linebacker calls the defensive signals, directing his men to where the play is expected to go.

The defensive backs are another different breed. They must be mobile and fast, basketball player types. They are expected to be excellent tacklers and able to get to their man without being faked out, for they are the last players between the ball carrier and the goal. They will do all they can to avoid contact with the offensive blockers, for their job is to stay on their feet until they can bring down the ball carrier. Defensive backs work in tandem on a zone defense and they have to be able to work with each other in covering the pass routes the opposition runs. Now with the new rule that you can only chuck the man within the first five yards and only once within that area, it is imperative for the defensive back to shadow the pass receiver as he comes down the field. Defensive back is one of the most difficult positions to learn to play. It is much easier for a rookie to break in as a running back, which is probably the easiest position to learn.

Finally, there are the special teams or "suicide squads," as the players call them. These are the kicking or kick return teams which play on the kickoffs, runbacks, extra points, punts and field goals. They are usually, but not always, substitute players with great enthusiasm who are fighting to stay on the roster. They are called "suicide squads" because of the many injuries suffered during games. This is partially due to the open field blocking after the ball has been kicked. Players of both teams are running full tilt when contact is made and many knee and leg injuries occur at this time. There are now fewer injuries and less serious injuries on kick plays today because of the new rule which prohibits blocking below the waist. This rule does not apply to running plays and pass plays. These people must be very speedy, able to get down the field fast. They literally throw themselves into the blockers, and play with controlled abandon. They also must learn to stay in their own areas of responsibility. Many a long kickoff return has happened because someone left his "lane."

Two very important members of the special teams are the punter and place kicker. These are the players who put the ball in play for each game, kick the extra point and field goal and punt their team out of trouble. They must have tremendous power in their legs and a good sense of timing. They must be cool-headed and have great concentration. By and large, most punters are tall, lean men. This is not always the case, but generally so. Guys like David Lee from Baltimore, David Beverly of the Green Bay Packers, the amazing Ray Guy of Oakland and many others are long and lean. They have that great whip in their legs.

Contrary to the size of the punter, field goal kickers come in all sizes. There are little fellows like Efren Herrera, who kicks for Seattle and Garo Yepremian of the New Orleans Saints, average size kickers like Roy Gerela, and the long rangy ones like Jan Stenerud of the Kansas City Chiefs. There are a growing number of soccer-style kickers in the game these days. These are the side-winders who approach the ball from the side and kick it soccer-style.

In previous years, the rules stated that no one could be beyond the football on a kickoff except the holder, but now the rule has been changed because of these soccer-style kickers. They place their non-kicking foot slightly in advance of the football before they kick it. So the rule has now been changed to no one's being allowed in advance of the football except the holder and the kicker.

The kicker must have tremendous concentration. He must not be concerned with the opposing players clawing to get at him. He and the holder must decide on a spot to be kicked from and he cannot use a tee for anything but a kickoff. So the ball must be held by one of his teammates if it is a place kick for a field goal, a free kick after a fair catch, or a place kick after a safety. The holder is very important, for he must handle the ball just the way the kicker wants it. Before the snap, he will point his finger right at the spot he and the kicker have selected, take the snap and place the ball right there. The kicker, who has been concentrating on that spot, now sees the ball there and completes the kick.

We now have a rule that brings the ball back to the previous line of scrimmage in the event of a missed field goal, where the ball was snapped outside of the 20-yard line, provided it has not been touched by the receivers in the field of play. I think that rule and the rule that restricts anyone from going downfield on a punt except the two widemen, until after the ball has been kicked, have combined to make the kicker of even greater importance to the game.

The coach is where a team must look for the ultimate success of its efforts. The coach must be a many-faceted individual. He should be a motivator, inspiring his men to desire victory as much as he does. He must demand that his players live up to their capabilities, and not tolerate malingering. He must be a pragmatist, a philosopher, a stickler for details and a man dedicated to excellence. He must be aggressive and demand that same quality of his men. He must be able to communicate and relate to his men, especially his quarterback. He must respect his men and command respect from them. A sense of humor helps in tense situations. He must be an organizer, have the ability to turn a weakness into a strength and know how to play his strengths. He must be a teacher and, above all, a leader. In other words, he must be a damn genius.

I mentioned a sense of humor. This is so important in any endeavor. I remember one incident in Atlanta where a sense of humor relieved some tension before a game. This little scene occurred just after Norm Van Brocklin became head coach of the Falcons in 1968. Back in 1965, he had questioned two of my calls in Green Bay when he was the head coach of the Minnesota Vikings and apparently had not forgotten them. Well, when I came into the dressing room an hour before the game, he was sitting there in a chair and I said, "Hello, Coach!"

He smiled and said, "Hello, Holst!" We then shook hands and he said, "Would you like me to introduce you to the team?"

I looked around at the players, who seemed to be a bit uptight and replied, "No, Coach, that won't be necessary."

"Aw c'mon!" he persisted, "Let me introduce you to the team . . . then maybe you can give them a little speech and tell 'em how you screwed me in Green Bay!"

The players were delighted at that one and the tension seemed to dissipate, but, of course, at my expense.

So, what about the officials? Well, for one thing, they always take a lot of heat for what some fans, coaches and players judge to be bad calls. In an earlier chapter I covered the training, care and feeding of the official and just what his game day is like. Now let's examine the ever-present problem of controversy.

Are pro football officials making more cross-eyed calls, or are instant replay cameras just doing a better job of exposing the few that are made? I feel it is the latter.

Okay. So some mistakes are made. Realistically speaking, how can an occasional error be avoided? Half backs fumble, ends drop passes, defensive men miss tackles and coaches cut players who later become stars with other teams. Our job, as in any other business, is to reduce mistakes to as near zero as possible.

In the last few years the salaries of NFL officials have come into sharper focus, principally because a few coaches have publicly expressed their concern that the Zebras are not full-time employees. These coaches are convinced that full-time officials will provide a panacea for missed calls, supposedly missed calls and good calls that coaches, players and media people don't know are good calls, because they don't know the rules.

One coach even went so far as to say that he and twenty-seven other coaches were better qualified to officiate than any of the officials now working. This, of course, is ridiculous! That's the same as saying that, because I work full-time building airplanes, I am better qualified to fly them than is a part-time, but highly-trained pilot. If you believe that, then you ride with the guy who spends forty hours a week building the damn plane, but never had a flying lesson, and I'll ride with the guy who learned how to fly during the hours away from his regular job, doesn't know a thing about building the plane, but does have his instrument rating.

What I'm saying is simply this: I don't know the first thing about coaching an NFL team. I leave that highly skilled job to professionals like Tom Landry, Don Shula, Bud Grant and Chuck Noll, just to name a few. I admire them for their expertise as coaches and for what they keep contributing to building the National Football League. But I would like to think that they would respect my contribution, which has come from a quarter of a century of officiating. Our 1978 crew had the combined experience of eighty-six years of officiating in the NFL — and that includes Sid Semon, our head linesman, who was in his rookie year. That comes to a 12.28 year average per man on our crew, in pro football alone.

During a game recently, I threw a flag for a clipping foul. The coach disagreed and said so, punctuating his remarks with, "They pay you $800 a game, just for throwing that damn yellow flag?"

"No, Coach," I replied, "They only pay me $20 a game for throwing the flag, the same as I got in high school football. They pay me $780 a game for knowing when to throw it!"

New officials start at $325 a game, plus expenses. They get a raise every other year, until they reach the maximum pay level of $800 a game, which commences in their eleventh year. This means that an official working a full schedule of four pre-season games and a full sixteen-game regular season schedule would earn from $6,400 a year for a new man to a maximum of $14,000 a year for those with a minimum of eleven years experience.

Post season games are extra and are assigned on a basis of an official's ratings for the year. The Super Bowl pays the most — $3,000 plus expenses. At this wage scale, $17,000 a season is tops, or perhaps $19,000 if he works two post-season games. The real question is not, "How much can the National Football League afford to pay officials?" The question is, "Under what conditions can professional football obtain the services of the very best officials?"

Comparing football officials and baseball umpires is irrelevant, and here's why. Even in the minor leagues, baseball teams play approximately one hundred and forty games a year, plus some games in the "Grapefruit League," before the season opens. The major leagues play one hundred and sixty-two games. In football, sixteen regular season games are played plus four pre-season games or a total of twenty. Now, this means that a baseball umpire can start in his early twenties at a salary of around $800 per month for seven months work and aim at a career in the major league. In football, the "minor leagues" are the high schools and colleges. Back in the sixties, the pay for a high school official was from $15 to $25 a game, and the official usually had to pay his own expenses. So, if a man worked on a Friday and another game on Saturday, he made a gross of $50 per week for a ten-week season — or $500 per year! That is a labor of love, pure and simple!

Now, let's say that our man started at age twenty-three and worked nine years of high school and some small college football. When he reaches the age of thirty-two, he is picked by the Big Ten, the PAC Ten, the Southwest Conference or the Big Eight. His pay now climbs to around $300 a game, for a ten-week season. That gives him a total salary of $3,000 plus ten high school games on Fridays at $30 each. That's another $300 and our man is now making $3,300 per year at the pinnacle of college football.

Meanwhile, he has started working in a bank or as an insurance agent or as a teacher and he has progressed in this full-time profession. By age thirty-eight, his salary off the field may range from $25,000 to $50,000 a year, or even more. What's more, he now has job security, vested pension benefits and what have you. Will he want to leave all this for the relative insecurity of being a full-time professional football official? If not, where would the experienced, full-time men come from?

It seems to me that somewhere between the two extremes lies a sensible solution, and I believe we are near it. Officiating an NFL game may not seem like much of a sacrifice of time, but it is only the tip of the iceberg. Zebras spend many football hours off the field. Remember the weekly test on the rules, between Monday and Saturday? It's tough, and makes Zebras think football all the time, even providing excellent discussion on Saturday evenings. Then there are meetings during the year for all of the men from the various positions. As I write this, I am enroute to St. Louis for a Friday night and Saturday morning meeting of umpires and line judges. More time is spent reviewing the rules and mechanics of officiating than most people would think.

I would estimate that my personal time each week totaled between sixteen and twenty hours, plus travel time. This included physical conditioning time, rules study time, crew meetings, phone calls and the games themselves. So only about one-sixth of the total time is spent on the game; the other eighty-five percent or so is spent in preparation.

I should add that there is also a great benefit in being a part-time official. No official should have to worry about how his calls on the field relate to the grocery bills, the kids' education or the mortgage payments. A man whose primary income is in a field other than football, but who loves the game and is dedicated to being as perfect a football official as he possibly can, is more apt to be objective, in my book, when he puts on that Zebra shirt.

Well, that completes my case for the officials. Certainly Zebras are under fire more since the advent of the instant replay than at any other time in the history of the game. Maybe the solution to the problem would be one official for each player on the field. Twenty-two pairs of eyes just might call the perfect game, but I'll tell you one thing: of the 40,000 or more plays a year in the NFL, we're right on just about 40,000 of them! Officials can live with the bum raps they're getting, for they know that the guy who criticizes the most is the guy who sits in the fortieth row, then goes out to the parking lot after the game and can't find his car. Besides, he paid for his ticket and he has the right to bitch if he chooses.

Another subject for lengthy debate these days is violence in pro football. As I travel the country on my speaking tours, I am always asked how I feel about football brutality, as an official. I can only say that there are many factors which contribute to what is called "violence" on the football field.

Football is a violent game, but I personally believe that there is very little unnecessary violence. Indeed, I have seen more acts of sportsmanship and consideration for an opponent's physical safety than I have acts of brutality. In every game we see players do all in their power, sometimes even endangering their own safety, to miss hitting a man who is already down. If possible, I always try to tell a man that I notice him go out of his way to keep from hitting an opponent after the play has been blown dead.

But this is an intense sport and, yes, there have been instances of late hits and unsportsmanlike acts. It's a game of hard contact. These are big men and their adrenalin flows wildly. They are strong and they play hard. There will, of course, be occasional pilings on, hits out of bounds, striking a man in the head or "clotheslining" a pass receiver. (Clotheslining is the act of a defensive player, usually a halfback, who holds his arm straight out from the shoulder, so that the ball carrier runs into it, neck high, as if it were a clothesline.)

It is the official's job to see these illegal acts and throw that yellow flag. But even with seven officials, some of these infractions are missed. Commissioner Pete Rozell has taken a hard line on these "cheap shots" and has fined the individuals involved, even if their actions were not observed by the officials. Furthermore, you can bet your socks that if Zebras do miss a "cheap shot," they're going to hear about it, and they should.

These players are tough, aggressive, hard-hitting, and they play for keeps. There was a coach once who always had the welcome mat out for the meanest types available. One day a little guy came into his office and asked for a tryout. The coach sized him up, but wasn't about to say, "Forget it!" for he had seen little guys play savagely before, so he interviewed him. "You know," he said, "what we want are players who are big, aggressive, bad-tempered, revengeful and terribly hard hitters! The kind of person who, when aroused, is the devil himself!"

The little guy put on his cap and started to leave.

"Wait a minute!" the coach yelled, "Aren't you interested?"

"Hell, no!" the little guy replied, "You don't want me! You want my wife!"

But, seriously, out on the field, the speed of the players coupled with the hard surfaces of the helmets and shoulder pads makes it mandatory to call anything that even borders on unnecessary roughness. However, I honestly feel that the amount of roughness, brutality, violence, or whatever term you care to use, is less now than when I began my career in the NFL in 1964. For one thing, the simple fact that we have seven sets of eyes watching, instead of five, is a big help. A second factor is the constant improvement of our officiating mechanics, so that we always have at least one official "cleaning up" — watching the action away from the ball.

For example, if a runner goes out of bounds between the back judge and the line judge, whichever official is closest marks the out-of-bounds spot and as he does so, he turns and looks at the out-of-bounds action. At the same time, the other official runs out of bounds to the point where the players are, so that he is right on top of the play. We call that cleaning up. Meanwhile, since our backs are turned on the field, the umpire and the field judge come up behind us, looking for any unnecessary roughness that might occur behind us.

Another change which has helped us do our jobs better is the white six-foot border area in which no one is allowed except the chain crew. Behind that we have another six-foot wide area marked in dotted yellow. Only the coaches and one player may be in that area. This has helped immensely in cleaning up sideline action.

When I began my career in the NFL in 1964, the players and coaches were not the only ones who crowded up to the sidelines. The photographers were always right on the "out of bounds" lines and this, combined with the players, coaches and various other people with sideline passes, made it more difficult to see certain plays, particularly those in which a man was tackled out of bounds. What would appear easy to see from a camera's view in the press box, was almost impossible to see on the field. A runner would come barreling out of bounds, go through the mass of substitutes, and then be hit by a trailing opponent. Coming up on this action from the rear, the official's view was restricted by the ridge of football talent and could miss seeing a man who was hit six or eight feet out of bounds. The new restriction concerning the sideline has made this aspect of cleaning up the game much easier for us.

And so, I repeat, there is less unnecessary roughness in the game today than there was when I began my career in 1964 as an official in the NFL. I believe the incidents of brutality have gone down and not up. You turn twelve hundred football players loose in games all over the country and you're going to have some guys who will hit late, spear with their helmets or slam a forearm across another player's neck. You can't avoid that. But you'll find that type of person in any business or other endeavor you'd care to name. You're going to have people who will take advantage of anyone they can, but I'll put professional football players up against any other group of business people and they'll look good in the comparison. Even most unnecessary-roughness fouls are unintentional.

So what does it all boil down to? Football is a game of strength, speed and skill. It is not a game for dummies, as some wags would have us believe. I remember a game between the Cleveland Browns and the St. Louis Cardinals during my tenure with Norm Schachter's crew. The offensive captain for Cleveland was Quarterback Frank Ryan, who holds a doctor's degree in mathematics. Charley Johnson, captain for the Cardinals held a Ph.D. in engineering. Referee Norm Schachter was also a Ph.D.

We had a foul on a kick, one of those that took some time to explain, and we ended up with both offensive captains on the field, talking it over with Norm. There they were, Dr. Schachter, Dr. Ryan and Dr. Johnson, three Ph.D.'s gathered in the center of the field with eighty thousand Cleveland fans howling. After a lengthy discussion someone accepted the penalty and Norm walked it off. The whole thing struck me as an incongruity. Here we were in a hard-hitting professional football game with three Ph.D.'s talking it over in the center of the field. It does take brains!

But football is more than brains, strength and speed. Football builds character, makes a man develop the winning habit. Football asks men to do more than they think they can do. John Mackey made a great catch in the 1964 Cleveland-Baltimore championship game. The pass was for about 45 yards and Mackey made a diving catch on the two-yard line. Being interviewed later by a CBS sportscaster, John was asked, "That long pass, how on earth did you ever catch it?"

"I don't know," replied Mackey, "I didn't think I could catch it myself!"

But he did, and that's the story of football. Football makes men give everything they have and then a little bit more. The kind of competition exemplified in professional football makes men grow tall and straight where character is concerned.

Plant three trees together and they grow tall and straight, competing for the sunlight. Without competition, there would be little achievement. With it, man must reach higher in his quest for excellence.

If all of us, in whatever fields we toil, could give that great second effort that football demands, we would enjoy greater accomplishment and above all, greater self-pride.

CHAPTER FIFTEEN

IT'S A GRAND OLD GAME

Football has changed a lot since the vacant lot, cinder field games of the 1930's. Back in those deep Depression days, teams were made up of the most rugged kids in various big city neighborhoods and the greatest source of entertainment for strolling citizens on brisk fall afternoons were the free Sunday football games between teams with names to stir the imagination, such as the Lakotas and the Spokes, or the Javelin A. C.'s versus the West Side Panthers.

Though the game has been refined through the years, the one thing that hasn't changed is the game's ability to develop character and the competitive spirit. Those old cinder lot games have long since disappeared from the sports scene, but they developed the team spirit in thousands of young men that would carry them through the worst depression in history and the challenge of World War II.

While college and professional football are much more sophisticated today, the team spirit remains as strong or stronger than it was when the game was an infant. The game teaches young men to eliminate the word "quit" from their vocabularies, and in the process gives them the moral fiber to bring them success in later years off the playing field. The Hall of Fame roster is filled with the names of those men who represent the game at its finest: names such as George Halas, Jim Thorpe, "Red" Grange, Sam Baugh, Mel Hein, Bob Waterfield, Otto Graham, Emlen Tunnel, Jim Brown, Gale Sayers, Bart Starr, Frank Gifford and many others.

Frank Gifford is an excellent choice, if we were to pick one man to exemplify the caliber of men who have played in the NFL. Frank was a star halfback with the New York Giants during the late 50's and early 60's. He was a member of that team when one of their obscure assistant coaches was an intense and tough taskmaster named Vince Lombardi.

Frank, as all sports fans know, is the backbone of ABC's Monday Night Football telecasts. He does play by play while Don Meredith and Francis Tarkenton, two other gifted ex-players, do commentary along with another voice whose name escapes me at the moment.

In addition to all of Frank's other qualities, he is a gentleman. In July of 1977, I was the banquet speaker when Frank was inducted into Pro Football's Hall of Fame at Canton, Ohio. The banquet was held on a Friday evening with induction ceremonies scheduled for the following Saturday, just prior to the Hall of Fame game. After the banquet, which included honoring inductees Gale Sayers, Len Willis, Forrest Gregg and Bart Starr, as well as Frank, there were hundreds of autograph seekers. Frank was the last man to leave the dais, for he continued to sign autographs until all requests were met.

The next day, he was presented for induction by Mr. Wellington Mara, president and principal owner of the New York Giants. As Frank rose to speak, he abandoned his prepared remarks, and in a voice rich with honest emotion, he expressed his gratitude for being selected to receive football's highest honor and to declare to all what the game had done for him.

Frank, of course, was a profile in courage as he came back from a very severe brain concussion in 1962 and a one-year absence to finish a brilliant career. When he finally retired in 1964 at the age of 35, he held several club records. He had scored more points (484) than any other Giant player, caught more passes (387), gained the most yards on receptions (5,434) and scored the most touchdowns (78).

The NFL has been around for about sixty years, and for most of that time has chosen wisely in the selection of its commissioners. Under the leadership of Joe Carr, who took charge in 1921 and ran the league for eighteen years, it grew to be a strong organization. He was succeeded after his death in 1939 by Carl Storck, who in 1941 turned the reins over to one of Notre Dame's famed Four Horsemen, Elmer Layden. Layden managed the league until 1946, when Bert Bell assumed command.

Bell was a fine commissioner and ran things firmly and decisively. A former player, coach and owner, he loved the game and gave it the full measure of his attention. Before he died in the fall of 1959 of a heart attack, while watching a Philadelphia Eagle game, Bell told Tex Maule, football editor of *Sports Illustrated,* "Tex, the one thing we can't forget is that the game was built and made popular by the players. We owe them everything. I don't think that any group of athletes in the world can match pro football players for honesty, character and strength."

To that I say, "Amen." In our present commissioner, Pete Rozelle, we have another fine professional sports administrator. Rozelle had been general manager of the Los Angeles Rams for three years prior to being named the chief administrator of the National Football League.

Although I have not had the opportunity to know Pete Rozelle well, I have a deep-seated respect for him as commissioner. His forward thinking with regard to television coverage and his overseeing the orderly merger with the American Football League are only two examples of his foresight and creative ability to build the NFL into what it is today and what it will be in the future. There were twelve teams in the League when he assumed the commissioner's post in 1960. Now there are twenty-eight and the Super Bowl has become the top single sports attraction in history. Attendance at the game, revenue and number of television viewers tuned in continue to grow. One-hundred-two million, ten thousand TV viewers watched Super Bowl XII live on January 15th, 1978, still the largest live TV audience in history. Imagine, one-hundred and two million people second guessing me!!

The commissioner, of course, bears the ultimate

responsibility for the competency of the officiating and has always demanded the utmost in professionalism from us, yet never fails to back us to the hilt when we are right. During my career as an NFL official, I have seen the film review program become standard procedure for officials. Moreover, a grading procedure has been made a part of the evaluation of officials wherein we are graded on everything from appearance to individual calls — even to details like which way an official's head is turned at a particular time on a particular play. Mr. Rozelle is always open to new ideas without hitting the familiar "panic-button" when controversy rears its ugly head, as it usually does when human judgement is concerned.

For instance, in the current hue and cry to use instant replay as an officiating aid, the commissioner and the owners have adopted a cautious attitude. So, in the 1978 pre-season schedule, selected games were used as a test. After a very careful and professional evaluation, the commissioner and league owners agreed that the use of instant replay as an officiating aid is not feasible at this time.

It has been the tradition, indeed the cornerstone of our American free enterprise system, whereby people solve their problems in the free and competitive market by using their own talents and judgement, good or bad, knowing that a more productive nation will be the result. It is my conviction that pro football is a shining example of this concept. Even in this area the commissioner has had an important function along with the team owners.

Now Congress has stretched its long tentacles into professional sports, and the National Football

League has not escaped. Congressional hearings have been held on such things as the television "blackout" issue wherein games not sold out 72 hours in advance are blacked out locally. Mr. Rozelle must bring the position of the League to both the public and the government on the "blackout" issue, the so-called reserve clause and other issues. I applaud him for his strong positions on the issues. He is a firm man and considers the integrity of the game uppermost. His strong stand against legalizing gambling on professional football games is well known and applauded by the Zebras.

I hasten to add that Commissioner Rozelle and Supervisor of Officials Art McNally always give us the kind of support which enables us to stay independent. No coach, owner or general manager can dictate who will officiate his club's games. The league office does this and we like to think that any crew can work any game, anywhere, regardless of what bearing that particular game has on the championship of a division. Believe me, this kind of support is vital to the game and certainly appreciated by the officials. But just so there is no misunderstanding, please note that we are promptly brought to task when we err. Questionable calls put the spotlight on the officials, where it shouldn't be.

Indeed, page one of the NFL Official Manual declares, "It is the popular belief that during National League Football games, there are only twenty-two men on the field. Let's keep it that way, mathematically inaccurate, but so very right from a spectator standpoint. For while the official is an integral and vital part of the NFL, and of its individual games, the degree of anonymity he can achieve in front of sixty thousand people is a mark of his success."

Some wag once said there is a plaque in the New York League office which states, "To err is human — to forgive is not league policy." But the number of questionable calls in league play is infinitesimal compared to the number of good calls.

In 1977, two fumbles, or non-fumbles, brought much pressure on the officials. The first occurred during the late-season game between the New England Patriots and the Baltimore Colts. Bert Jones, the ball carrier for the Colts, appeared to be bobbling the ball near the goal line. The official ruled, "no fumble" and on the next play, Baltimore scored a touchdown. Fumble or no fumble? It was a judgement call. To the TV viewers, it was a fumble, but they had instant replay on which to base their decision. However, there is one important fact to be considered: the angle and proximity of the viewer to the action can tell two different stories.

The second non-fumble that touched off skyrockets occurred during a game between the Denver Broncos and the Oakland Raiders for the AFC championship. Rob Lytle was the ball carrier and during the action, lost the ball. The official ruled "no fumble," declaring that Lytle's progress may have been stopped before the loose ball was seen by the officials. The question asked, as the officials gathered for a crew conference was, "Did any official see a fumble before Lytle's progress was stopped?" The answer was "No!" from all six officials so it was no fumble. You can't call what you can't see!

The 1978 season was a good one for me. I didn't get mixed up in any really controversial calls, but then why should I make any mistakes? That was the winter I discovered I would walk on water. It was on January 7th 1979, during the AFC championship game between Houston and Pittsburgh that the miracle occurred! The temperature was a bone-chilling thirty-two degrees with a driving, freezing rain falling. Three Rivers Stadium was misnamed that day, because the field was the "fourth" river, making the footing sloppy and treacherous and causing the ball to conduct itself like an elusive, greased pig at a county fair.

For years I have wondered why players would turn my way and scream "Jesus Christ!" at me. But as I walked the waters of Three Rivers Stadium that Sunday, I finally found out. It was a day more for amphibians than humans as Pittsburgh blew Houston out of the water by a score of 34-5. Yes, the rain fell on Coach Bum Phillip's parade as his Houston team only managed to score a field goal and a safety.

It was my two hundred ninety first game as a National Football League official and the conditions were the worst of any under which I have worked. But in spite of the conditions, our job was to officiate the game properly, and putting modesty aside, I submit that is exactly what we did.

There were eleven fumbles in the first half alone and there were twelve in the whole ball game, a new NFL record! It topped the old record of ten set in 1934 by the Bears and the Giants. However, the whole weekend wasn't misery as verified by an incident that occurred on the Saturday prior to the big game, underlining our concern for good calls.

A meeting was called for 7:00 p.m. Friday, January 5th in Pittsburgh with the seven men who were to work the game Sunday, along with two alternate officials and the nine-man crew who were to work the Los Angeles Rams — Dallas Cowboys game following our game. During the meeting, (which incidentally, ran until 11:30 p.m. on Friday and for another two hours on Saturday morning at 7:30 a.m.) Art McNally wrote the words, "SLOW WHISTLE" on the blackboard. To emphasize these important words he would interrupt himself from time to time to exclaim, "Oh, yes, SLOW WHISTLE!" I kept account of the number of times he said that on a small note pad and discovered he had repeated this caution no less than thirty-four times between 7:00 p.m. Friday and 9:30 a.m. Saturday.

After the other crew departed for Los Angeles on Saturday morning, our crew for the Pittsburgh-Houston game held our own conference, which lasted until noon. The meeting was held in the Hilton Hotel, in the Golden Triangle of Pittsburgh. Our conference room was on the eighth floor of the hotel, overlooking a serene and snow-covered Fort Pitt Park.

Suddenly an idea popped! Someone said, "Why don't we tramp the words, SLOW WHISTLE in the snow, with a couple of exclamation points?"

Everyone chuckled at the idea, but thinking it was too good to pass up, I provided vigorous encouragement. To make a long story short, at just after noon on Saturday, January 6th, 1979, the crew that was to officiate the Pittsburgh-Houston championship game the next day, was out in Fort Pitt Park tramping and scraping in the snow the words, "SLOW WHISTLE!"

It was beautiful! In letters about fifteen feet high, it filled about two-thirds of a block in that lovely park.

When we came up from lunch later, Art McNally was back in his room. Not wanting him to miss our snow artistry, I banged on his door and when he responded, I invited him to come to room 806, where Jim Poole (the back judge) and I were rooming together. He said he'd be happy to, and came out and followed us to our room. When I opened the drapes and gave him a full view of our creation, he cracked up laughing; but I'm sure, down deep, he knew he had gotten the message across. We spent an hour and a half that afternoon, with a rented camera, taking photos from a borrowed room on the twentieth floor of the Pittsburgh Hilton.

I'm sure that this exceptional emphasis on the "SLOW WHISTLE," combined with our pregame preparation, paid off the following day. The millions of fans who watched the game on television and the thousands of brave, loyal Pittsburgh fans who attended the game, will remember the brilliant catches by Swann and Stallworth, the passing of Terry Bradshaw and the ice hanging from the goal posts. I know I will. But more than that, I will remember all the loose balls and that picture in my mind of the prophetic snow-stamped warning, "SLOW WHISTLE!"

It seems as if the meaning of an entire officiating career was embodied in that one game. The anticipation, the preparation, the execution, the discipline and yes, even the humor, were all part of a job well done under the most trying circumstances.

As I look back over my fifteen years as an official for the National Football League, as a Sunday Zebra, and as I look back over the fifteen years of speaking to thousands of audiences across this great nation, I am struck by the significance of the game as it relates to life. Football as played in the NFL illustrates the values that we hold dear as Americans, as businessmen, salesmen, professionals, as housewives, men or women, black or white, Catholic, Protestant or Jew. It's a lay-it-on-the-line game. As a player, coach or official, when game time comes all that we know, or profess to know — all of our skills — are laid on the line when the referee blows the whistle for the kickoff. There are no guarantees as to who will win and there never have been in our nation. When our forefathers carved the greatest nation in the world (in spite of all its faults) from a demanding and competitive wilderness and wrested freedom from the bonds of tyranny, they agreed that the opportunity for great reward in a new land carried with it great risk. We are a nation which believes, or at least should believe, that hard competition within the framework of understandable and enforceable rules or laws results in a better life for all of our people. If you and I don't believe this, then we have failed to grasp the real reasons why Americans hold over fifty percent of the world's wealth with only six percent of its population and why hundreds of thousands have given their lives in our country's defense.

This competition is best when as many people as possible participate to the highest level of their competence. The value and dignity of teamwork and the striving for excellence, as Vince Lombardi put it, is as important in business or family life as it is in a football game. The dignity and value of every human being is personified on the football field. It's not a matter of race, creed, color or religion but is a matter of talent. Jim Thorpe was an Indian, Lynn Swann and Gale Sayers are Black; Alex Wojciechowicz and Chuck Bednarik are Polish; Gino Marchetti is Italian; Sid Luckman is a Jew; Bart Starr is from Alabama; Namath and Unitas are from Pennsylvania, and Jerry Kramer came from a farm in Idaho. Talent does not know or care about family background. When Tom Dempsey kicked his 63-yard field goal for New Orleans and beat Detroit, he did it with half of his kicking foot gone. Rocky Bleier of the Pittsburgh Steelers came back from his terrible wounds in Viet Nam to become an outstanding runner for the Steelers.

Lombardi said that every man has the obligation to live up to his maximum potential with the talents God gave him. I would expand that to include every man *and* woman in every kind of work.

When we officiate an NFL game we are so busy with the intricate details of our responsibilities that we don't think about the broader meaning of the game. It is in the preparation and in the afterglow of a job well done that we begin to appreciate the full meaning and dimension of our activities as they relate to others and to life itself. This is the way it should be.

The authors of our Declaration of Independence prepared it well, but as they fought for it they were so busy dodging British musket balls that I'm certain they were unable to appreciate how each skirmish was slowly having a profound change upon the whole world. So it is with all of us. The ability to dream and plan is unique to mankind. It finds its richest productivity in the fertility of a free nation.

It has been a great fifteen years, full of memories of brushes with the immortals of professional football.

The Sunday Zebra. His is not the lush, green, tree-scattered veldt of sunny Africa. Sometimes, for him, it is sunshine, sometimes snow and sometimes rain. His work is always a challenge, often humorous and never dull. You may disagree with him; you will probably "boo" or curse him. That's okay: that's your privilege. But please, don't question his integrity. Despite what you think, he's probably a nice guy. He may be your child's teacher, your insurance man, your lawyer, the president of a bank or even the speaker at your next convention.

What's more, he can walk on water! No other Zebra can do that!

THE NATIONAL FOOTBALL LEAGUE

DIGEST OF RULES

Pete Rozelle
Commissioner

This National Football League Digest of Rules has been prepared to aid players, fans and members of the press, radio and television media in their understanding of the game.

It is not meant to be a substitute for the official rule book. In any case of conflict between these explanations and illustrations and the official rules, the rules always have precedence.

In order to make it easier to coordinate the information in this digest and topics discussed, generally follow the order of the rule book.

OFFICIALS' JURISDICTIONS, POSITIONS AND DUTIES

REFEREE — General oversight and control of game. Gives signals for all fouls and is final authority for rule interpretations. Takes a position in backfield 10 to 12 yards behind line of scrimmage, favors right side (if quarterback is right-handed passer). Determines legality of snap, observes deep back(s) for legal motion. On running play, observes quarterback during and after handoff, remains with him until action has cleared away, then proceeds downfield, checking on runner and contact behind him. When runner is downed, Referee determines forward progress from wing official and if necessary, adjusts final position of ball.

On pass plays, drops back as quarterback begins to fade back, picks up legality of blocks by near linemen. Changes to complete concentration on quarterback as defenders approach. Primarily responsible to rule on possible roughing action on passer and if ball becomes loose, rules whether ball is free on a fumble or dead on an incomplete pass.

During kicking situations, Referee has primary responsibility to rule on kicker's actions and whether or not any subsequent contact by a defender is legal.

UMPIRE — Primary responsibility to rule on players' equipment, as well as their conduct and actions on scrimmage line. Lines up approximately 4 to 5 yards downfield, varying position from in front of weakside tackle to strongside guard. Looks for possible false start by offensive linemen. Observes legality of contact by both offensive linemen while blocking and by defensive players while they attempt to ward off blockers. Is prepared to call rule infractions if they occur on offense or defense. Moves forward to line of scrimmage when pass play develops in order to insure that interior linemen do not move illegally downfield. If offensive linemen indicate screen pass is to be attempted, Umpire shifts his attention toward screen side, picks up potential receiver in order to insure that he will legally be permitted to run his pattern and continues to rule on action of blockers. Umpire is to assist in ruling on incomplete or trapped passes when ball is thrown overhead or short.

HEAD LINESMAN — Primarily responsible for ruling on offside, encroachment and actions pertaining to scrimmage line prior to or at snap. Keys on closest set back on his side of field. On pass plays, Linesman is responsible to clear this receiver approximately 7 yards downfield as he moves to a point 5 yards beyond the line. Linesman's secondary responsibility is to rule on any illegal action taken by defenders on any delay receiver moving downfield. Has full responsibility for ruling on sideline plays on his side, e.g. — pass receiver or runner in or out of bounds. Together with Referee, Linesman is responsible for keeping track of number of downs and is in charge of mechanics of his chain crew in connection with its duties.

Linesman must be prepared to assist in determining forward progress by a runner on plays directed toward middle or into his side zone. He, in turn, is to signal Referee or Umpire what forward point ball has reached. Linesman is also responsible to rule on legality of action involving any receiver who approaches his side zone. He is to call pass interference when the infraction occurs and is to rule on legality of blockers and defenders on plays involving ball carriers, whether it is entirely a running play, a combination pass and run or a play involving a kick.

LINE JUDGE — Straddles line of scrimmage on side of field opposite Linesman. Keeps time of game as a backup for clock operator. Along with Linesman is responsible for offside, encroachment and actions pertaining to scrimmage line prior to or at snap. Line Judge keys on closest set back on his side of field. Line Judge is to observe his receiver until he moves at least 7 yards downfield, Judge then moves toward backfield side being especially alert to rule on any back in motion and on flight of ball when pass is made (he must rule whether forward or backward). Line Judge has primary responsibility to rule whether or not passer is behind or beyond line of scrimmage when pass is made. He also assists in observing actions by blockers and defenders who are on his side of field. After pass is thrown, Line Judge directs attention toward activities which occur in back of Umpire. During punting situations, Line Judge remains at line of scrimmage to be sure that only the end men move downfield until kick has been made, he also rules whether or not the kick crossed line and then observes action on members of the kicking team who are moving downfield to cover the kick.

BACK JUDGE — Operates on same side of field as Line Judge 17 yards deep. Keys on wide receiver on his side. Concentrates on path of end or back, observing legality of his potential block(s) or of actions taken against him. Is prepared to rule from **deep** position on holding or illegal use of hands by end or back or on defensive infractions committed by player guarding him. Has primary responsibility to make decisions involving sideline of his side of field, e.g. — pass receiver or runner in or out of bounds.

Back Judge makes decisions involving catching, recovery or illegal touching of a loose ball beyond line of scrimmage; rules on plays involving pass receiver, including legality of catch or pass interference; assists in covering actions of runner, including blocks by teammates and that of defenders; calls clipping on punt returns and, together with Field Judge, rules whether or not field goal attempts are successful.

SIDE JUDGE — operates on same side of field as Linesman 17 yards deep. Keys on wide receiver on his side. Concentrates on path of end or back, observing legality of his potential block(s) or of actions taken against him. Is prepared to rule from **deep** position on holding or illegal use of hands by end or back or on defensive infractions committed by player guarding him. Has primary responsibility to make decisions involving sideline of his side of field, e.g. — pass receiver or runner in or out of bounds.

Side Judge makes decisions involving catching, recovering or illegal touching of a loose ball beyond line of scrimmage; rules on plays involving pass receiver, including legality of catch or pass interference; assists in covering actions of runner, including blocks by teammates and that of defenders and calls clipping on punt returns.

FIELD JUDGE — Takes a position 25 yards downfield. In general, favors the tight end's side of field. Keys on tight end, concentrates on his path and observes legality of tight end's potential block(s) or of actions taken against him. Is prepared to rule from **deep** position on holding or illegal use of hands by end or back or on defensive infractions committed by player guarding him.

Field Judge times intervals between plays on 30-second clock plus intermission between two periods of each half; makes decisions involving catching, recovery or illegal touching of a loose ball beyond line of scrimmage; is responsible to rule on plays involving end line, calls pass interference, fair catch infractions and clipping on kick returns and together with Back Judge, rules whether or not field goal attempts are successful.

The diagrams on the following five pages illustrate the positions on the field of play of the seven game officials in five different situations that occur in the course of NFL games.

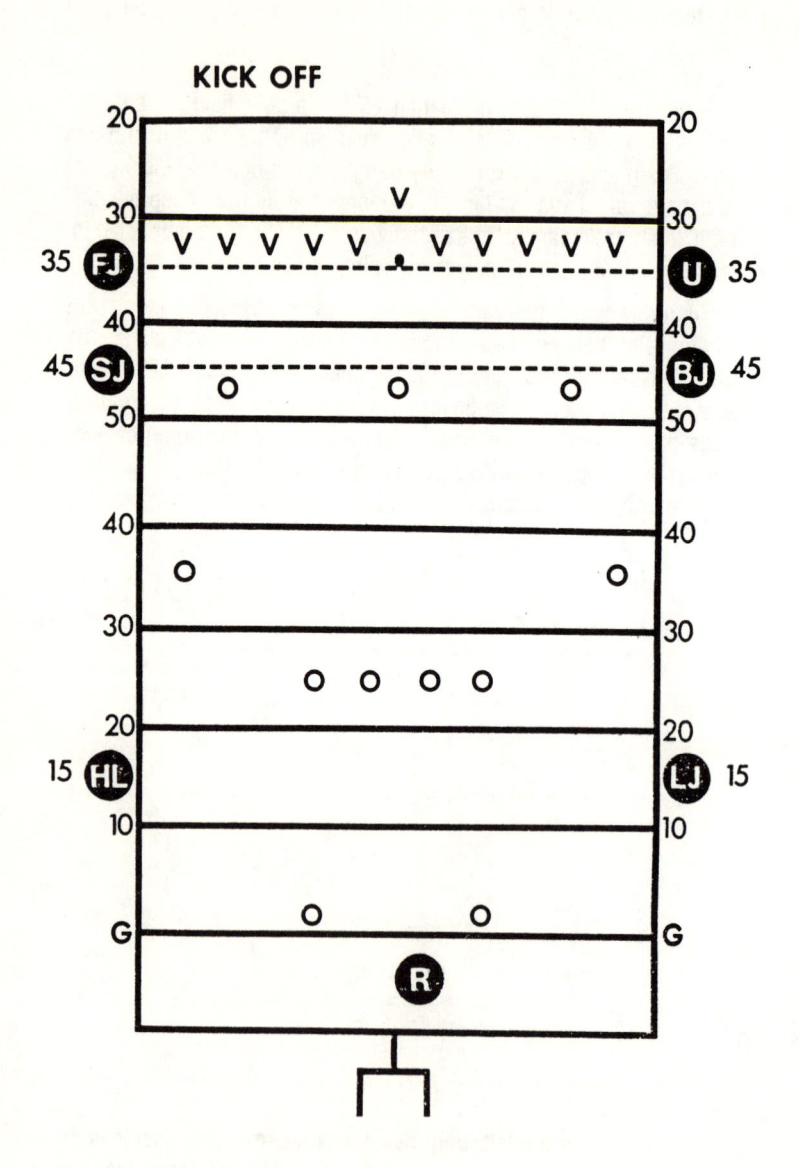

KICK OFF

BEFORE THE PASS

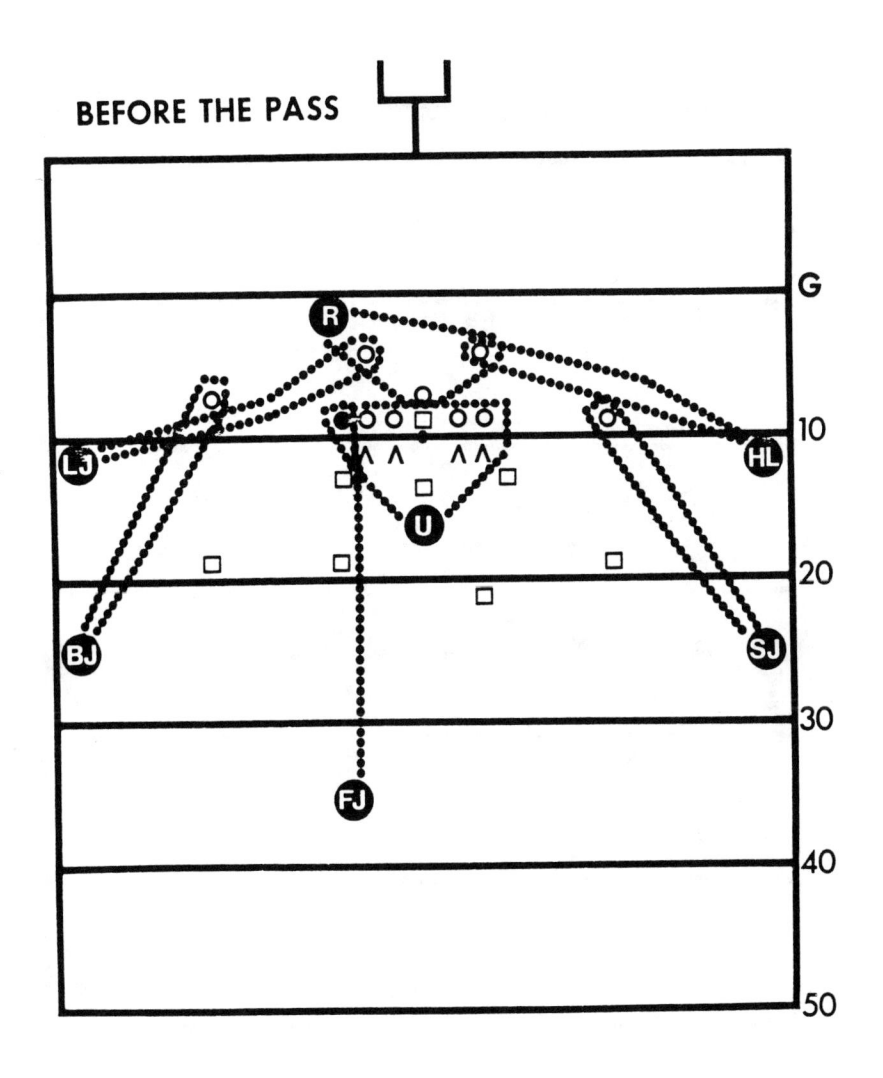

AFTER THE PASS

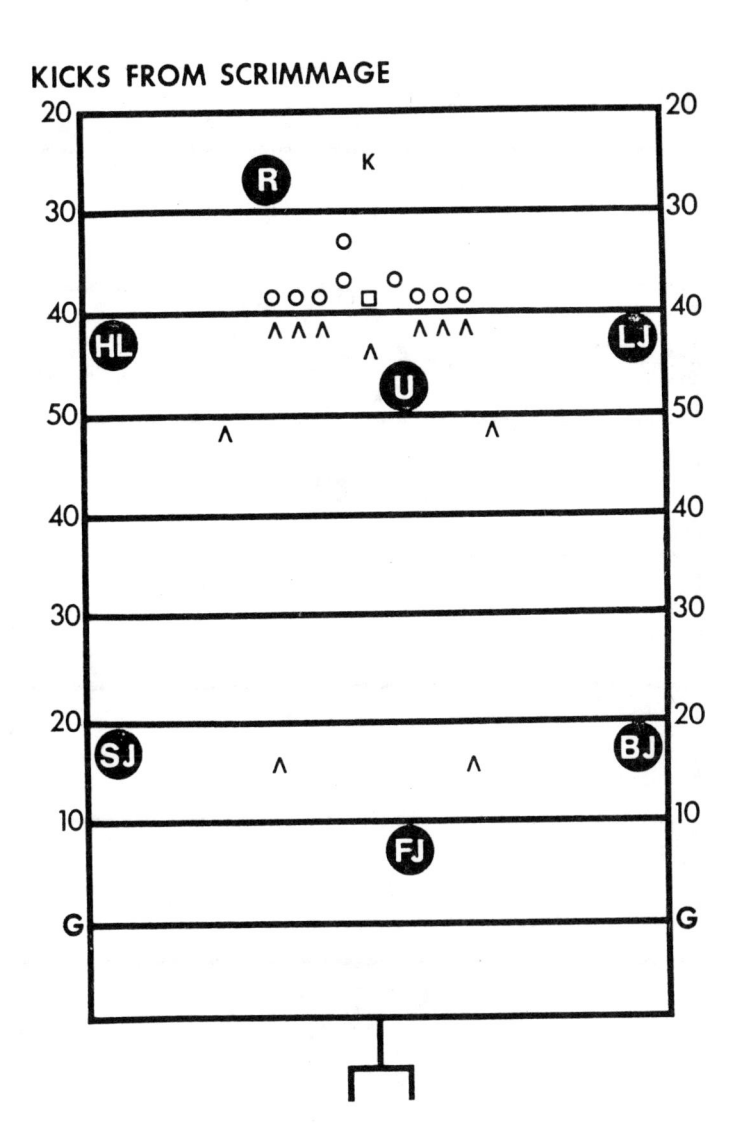

KICKS FROM SCRIMMAGE

FIELD GOAL ATTEMPT

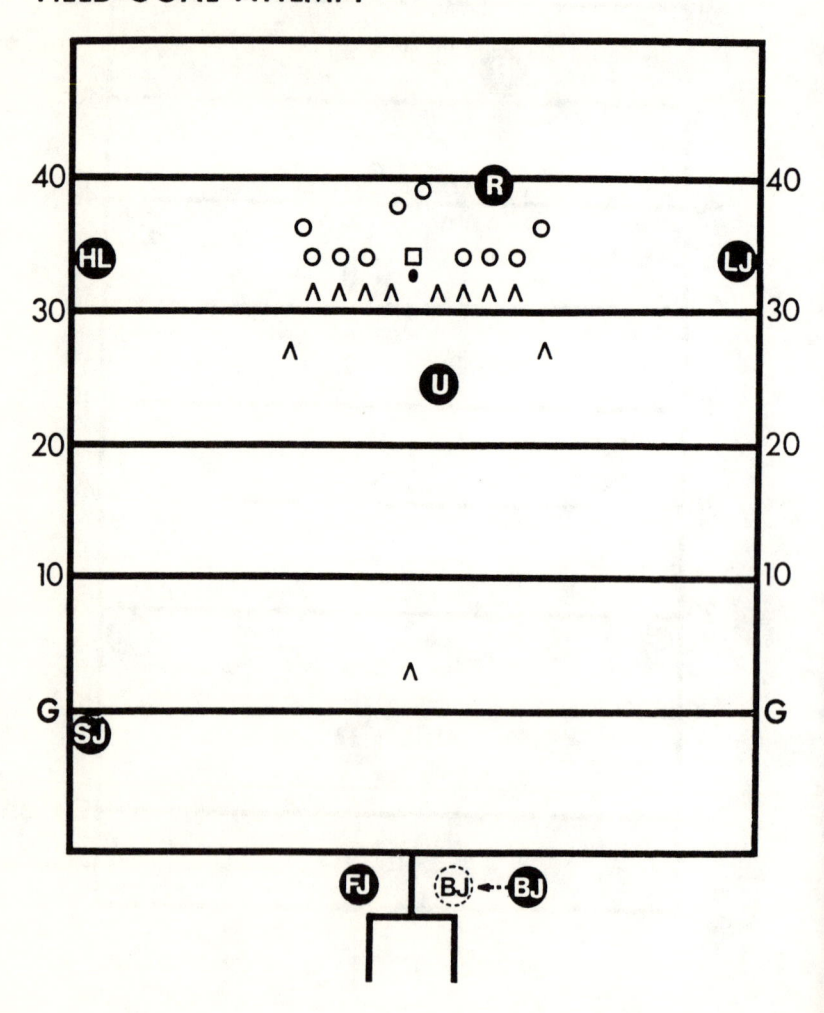

DEFINITIONS

1. **CHUCKING:** Warding off an opponent who is in front of a defender by contacting him with a quick extension of arm or arms, followed by the return of arm(s) to a flexed position, thereby breaking the original contact.
2. **CLIPPING:** Throwing the body across the back of an opponent's leg or hitting him from the back while moving up from behind unless the opponent is a runner or the action is in close line play.
3. **CLOSE LINE PLAY:** The area between the positions normally occupied by the offensive tackles, extending three yards on each side of the line of scrimmage.
4. **CRACKBACK:** Eligible receivers who take or move to a position more than two yards outside the tackle may not block an opponent below the waist if they then move back inside to block.
5. **DEAD BALL:** Ball not in play.
6. **DOUBLE FOUL:** A foul by each team during the same down.
7. **DOWN:** The period of action that starts when the ball is put in play and ends when it is dead.
8. **ENCROACHMENT:** When a player is in the neutral zone at the time of the snap or makes contact with an opponent **before** the ball is snapped.
9. **FAIR CATCH:** An unhindered catch of a kick by a member of the receiving team who must raise one arm full length above his head while the kick is in flight.
10. **FOUL:** Any violation of a playing rule.
11. **FREE KICK:** A kickoff, kick after a safety or kick after a fair catch. It may be a placekick, dropkick or punt except a punt may **not** be used on a kickoff.
12. **FUMBLE:** The loss of possession of the ball.
13. **IMPETUS:** The action of a player which gives momentum to the ball.
14. **LIVE BALL:** A ball legally free-kicked or snapped. It continues in play until the down ends.

15. **LOOSE BALL:** A live ball not in possession of any player.
16. **MUFF:** The touching of a loose ball by a player in an **unsuccessful** attempt to obtain possession.
17. **NEUTRAL ZONE:** The space the length of a ball between the two scrimmage lines. The offensive team and defensive team must remain behind their end of the ball. **Exception: The offensive player who snaps the ball.**
18. **OFFSIDE:** A player is offside when any part of his body is beyond his scrimmage or free kick line **when the ball is snapped.**
19. **OWN GOAL:** The goal a team is guarding.
20. **POSSESSION:** When a player holds the ball long enough to give him control to perform any act common to the game.
21. **PUNT:** A kick made when a player drops the ball and kicks it while it is in flight.
22. **SAFETY:** The situation in which the ball is dead on or behind a team's own goal if the **impetus** comes from a player on that team. Two points are scored for the opposing team.
23. **SHIFT:** The movement of two or more offensive players at the same time before the snap.
24. **STRIKING:** The act of swinging, clubbing or propelling the arm or forearm in contacting an opponent.
25. **SUDDEN DEATH:** The continuation of a tied game into sudden death overtime in which the team scoring first (by safety, field goal or touchdown) wins.
26. **TOUCHBACK:** When a ball is dead on or behind a team's own goal line, provided the impetus came from an opponent and provided it is not a touchdown or a missed field goal.
27. **TOUCHDOWN:** When any part of the ball, legally in possession of a player inbounds, is on, above or over the opponent's goal line, provided it is not a touchback.
28. **UNSPORTSMANLIKE CONDUCT:** Any act contrary to the generally understood principles of sportsmanship.

SUMMARY OF PENALTIES

AUTOMATIC FIRST DOWN

1. Awarded to offensive team on **all defensive fouls** with these exceptions:
   (a) Offside
   (b) Encroachment
   (c) Delay of game
   (d) Illegal substitution
   (e) Excessive time out(s)

LOSS OF DOWN (No yardage)

1. Second forward pass **behind** the line.
2. Forward pass strikes ground, goal post or crossbar.
3. Forward pass goes out of bounds.
4. Forward pass is first touched by eligible receiver who has gone out of bounds and returned.
5. Forward pass accidentally touches ineligible receiver on or behind line.
6. Forward pass thrown from behind line of scrimmage after ball once crossed the line.

FIVE YARDS

1. Crawling.
2. Defensive holding or illegal use of hands (automatic first down).
3. Delay of game.
4. Encroachment.
5. Too many time outs.
6. False start.
7. Illegal formation.
8. Illegal shift.
9. Illegal motion.
10. Illegal substitution.
11. Kickoff out of bounds between goal lines and not touched.
12. Invalid fair catch signal.
13. More than 11 players on the field at snap for either team.
14. Less than seven men on offensive line at snap.
15. Offside.

16. Failure to pause one second after shift or huddle.
17. Running into kicker (automatic first down).
18. More than one man in motion at snap.
19. Grasping face mask of opponent (if by defense, automatic first down).
20. Player out of bounds at snap.
21. Ineligible member(s) of kicking team going beyond line of scrimmage before ball is kicked.
22. Illegal return.
23. Failure to report change of eligibility.
24. Helping the runner.

TEN YARDS

1. Offensive pass interference.
2. Ineligible player downfield during passing down.
3. Holding, illegal use of hands by offense.
4. Tripping by a member of either team.

FIFTEEN YARDS

1. Clipping.
2. Fair catch interference.
3. Illegal batting or punching loose ball.
4. Deliberately kicking a loose ball.
5. Illegal crackback block by offense.
6. Piling on (automatic first down).
7. Roughing the kicker (automatic first down).
8. Roughing the passer (automatic first down).
9. Twisting, turning or pulling an opponent by the face mask.
10. Unnecessary roughness.
11. Unsportsmanlike conduct.
12. Delay of game at start of either half.
13. Illegal blocking below the waist.
14. A tackler using his helmet to butt, spear or ram an opponent.
15. Any player who uses the top of his helmet unnecessarily.

FIVE YARDS AND LOSS OF DOWN

1. Forward pass thrown from **beyond** line of scrimmage.

TEN YARDS AND LOSS OF DOWN

1. Forward pass intentionally touched by ineligible receiver on or behind line.
2. Forward pass intentionally or accidentally touched by ineligible receiver beyond the line of scrimmage.
3. Intentional grounding of forward pass (safety if passer is in own end zone).

FIFTEEN YARDS AND LOSS OF COIN TOSS OPTION

1. Team's late arrival on the field prior to scheduled kickoff.

FIFTEEN YARDS (AND DISQUALIFICATION IF FLAGRANT)

1. Striking an opponent with fist.
2. Kicking or kneeing opponent.
3. Striking opponent on head or neck with forearm, elbow or hands.
4. Roughing kicker.
5. Roughing passer.
6. Malicious unnecessary roughness.
7. Unsportsmanlike conduct.
8. Palpably unfair act (distance penalty determined by the Referee after consultation with other officials).

SUSPENSION FROM GAME

1. Illegal equipment. (Player may return after one down when legally equipped.)

TOUCHDOWN

1. When Referee determines a palpably unfair act deprived a team of a touchdown. (Example: Player comes off bench and tackles runner apparently enroute to touchdown.)

DIGEST OF RULES

FIELD

1. Side lines and end lines are out of bounds. The **goal line** is **actually in the end zone**. A player with the ball in his possession scores when the ball is **on, above** or **over** the goal line.

2. The field is rimmed by a white border, six feet wide, along the side lines. All of this is **out of bounds.**
3. The hash marks (inbound lines) are 70 feet, 9 inches from each side line.
4. Goal posts must be single-standard type, offset from the **end** line and painted bright gold. The goal posts must be 18 feet, 6 inches wide and the top face of the crossbar must be 10 feet above the ground. Vertical posts extend at least 30 feet above the crossbar. A ribbon 4'' by 42'' long is to be attached to the top of each post. The actual goal is the plane extending indefinitely **above** the crossbar and between the **outer** edges of the posts.
5. The field is 350 feet long and 160 feet wide. The end zones are 30 feet deep. The line used in try-for-point plays is 2 yards out from the goal line.
6. Chain crew members and ball boys must be uniformly identifiable.
7. All clubs must use standardized sideline markers. Pylons must be used for goal line and end line markings.
8. End zone markers and club identification at 50-yard line must be approved by the Commissioner to avoid any confusion as to delineation of goal lines, side lines and end lines.

BALL
1. The home club must have 24 balls available for testing by the Referee one hour before game time. In case of bad weather, a playable ball is to be substituted on request of the offensive team captain.

COIN TOSS
1. The toss of coin will take place within 3 minutes of the kickoff in the center of the field. The toss will be called by the visiting captain. The winner may choose one of two privileges and the loser gets the other:
   (a) Receive or kick
   (b) Goal his team will defend

2. Immediately prior to start of second half, the captains of both teams must inform the officials of their respective choices. The loser of the original coin toss gets first choice.

TIMING

1. The stadium clock is official. In case it stops or is operating incorrectly, the **Line Judge** takes over the official timing on the field.
2. Each period is 15 minutes. The intermission between the periods is two minutes. Halftime is 15 minutes, unless otherwise specified.
3. On charged team time outs, the Field Judge starts watch and blows whistle after 1 minute 30 seconds. However, Referee may allow two minutes for injured player and three minutes for equipment repair.
4. Each team is allowed three time outs each half.
5. Offensive team has 30 seconds to put the ball in play. The time is displayed on two 30-second clocks which are visible to the players, officials and fans. Field Judge is to call a delay of game penalty (5 yards) when the time limit is exceeded. In case 30-second clocks are not operating, Field Judge takes over the official timing on the field.
6. Clock will start running when ball is snapped following all changes of team possession.

SUDDEN DEATH

1. The sudden death system of determining the winner shall prevail when score is tied at the end of the regulation playing time of **all NFL games.** The team scoring first during overtime play shall be the winner and the game automatically ends upon any score (by safety, field goal or touchdown) or when a score is awarded by Referee for palpably unfair act.
2. At the end of regulation time the Referee will immediately toss coin at center of field in accordance with rules pertaining to the usual pre-game toss. The captain of the visiting team will call the toss.

3. Following a 3-minute intermission after the end of the regulation game, play will be continued in 15-minute periods or until there is a score. There is a 2-minute intermission between subsequent periods. The teams change goals at the start of each period. Each team has 3 time outs and general provisions for play in the last 2 minutes of a half shall prevail. Disqualified players are not allowed to return.

Exception: In preseason and regular season games there shall be a maximum of 15 minutes of sudden death with 2 time outs instead of 3. General provisions for play in the last 2 minutes of a half will be in force.

TIMING IN FINAL TWO MINUTES OF EACH HALF

1. On kickoff, clock does not start until the ball has been legally touched by player of either team **in the field of play.** (In all other cases, clock starts with kickoff.)
2. A team cannot ''buy'' an excess time out for a penalty.

However, a **fourth time out** is allowed without penalty for an injured player, who must be removed immediately. A **fifth time out** or more is allowed for an injury and a five-yard penalty is assessed if the clock was running. Additionally, if the clock was running and the score is tied or the team in possession is losing, the ball cannot be put in play for at least 10 seconds on the fourth or more time out. The half or game can end while those 10 seconds are run off on the clock.

TRY-FOR-POINT

1. After a touchdown, the scoring team is allowed a try-for-point during one scrimmage down. The ball may be spotted anywhere between the inbounds lines, two or more yards from the goal line. The successful conversion counts one point, whether by run, kick or pass.
2. The **defensive team never can score** on a try-for-point. As soon as defense get possession, or kick is blocked, ball is dead.
3. Any distance penalty for fouls committed by the defense which prevent the try from being attempted can be enforced

on the succeeding kick-off. Any foul committed on a successful try will result in a distance penalty being assessed on the ensuing kickoff.

PLAYERS-SUBSTITUTIONS

1. Each team is permitted 11 men on the field at the snap.
2. Unlimited substitution is permitted. However, players may enter the field only when the ball is dead. Players who have been substituted for are not permitted to linger on the field. Such lingering will be interpreted as unsportsmanlike conduct.
3. Players leaving the game must be out of bounds **on their own side,** clearing the field **between the end lines,** before a snap or free kick. If player crosses end line leaving field it is delay of game (5-yard penalty).

KICKOFF

1. The kickoff shall be from the kicking team's 35-yard line at the start of each half and after a field goal and try-for-point. A kickoff is one type of free kick.
2. Either a 1, 2 or 3 inch tee may be used (no tee permitted for field goal or try-for-point plays). The ball is put in play by a placekick or dropkick.
3. If kickoff clears the opponent's goal posts it is **not a field goal.**
4. A kickoff is illegal unless it travels 10 yards OR is touched by the **receiving** team. Once the ball is touched by the receiving team it is a free ball. Receivers may recover and advance. Kicking team may recover but **NOT** advance **UNLESS** receiver had possession and lost the ball.
5. When a kickoff goes out of bounds between the goal lines without being touched by the receiving team, it must be kicked again. There is a 5-yard penalty for a short kick or an out-of-bounds kick.
6. When a kickoff goes out of bounds between the goal lines and is **touched last** by receiving team, it is receiver's ball at out-of-bounds spot.

FREE KICK

1. In addition to a kickoff, the other free kicks are a kick after a safety and a kick after a fair catch. In both cases, a dropkick, placekick or punt may be used. (A punt may **not** be used on a kickoff.)
2. On free kick **after a fair catch,** captain of receiving team has the option to put ball in play by punt, dropkick or placekick **without** a tee, or by snap. If the placekick or dropkick goes between the uprights a field goal is scored.
3. On a free kick after a safety, the team scored upon puts ball in play by a punt, dropkick or placekick without a tee.

    No score can be made on a free kick following a safety, even if a series of penalties place team in position. (A field goal can be scored only on a play from scrimmage or a free kick after a fair catch.)

FIELD GOAL

1. All field goals attempted and missed from scrimmage line beyond the 20-yard line will result in the defensive team taking possession of the ball at the scrimmage line. On any field goal attempted and missed from scrimmage line inside the 20-yard line, ball will revert to defensive team at the 20-yard line.

SAFETY

1. The important factor in a safety is impetus. Two points are scored for the opposing team when the ball is dead on or behind a team's own goal line **if the impetus came from a player on that team.**

    Examples of safety:
    (a) Blocked punt goes out of kicking team's end zone. Impetus was provided by punting team. The block only changes direction of ball, not impetus.
    (b) Ball carrier retreats from field of play **into his own end zone** and is downed. Ball carrier provides impetus.
    (c) Offensive team commits a foul and spot of enforcement is **behind its own goal line.**

(d) Player on receiving team muffs punt and, trying to get ball forces or illegally kicks it into end zone where he or a teammate recovers. He has given new impetus to the ball.

Examples of non-safety:
(a) Player intercepts a pass inside his own 5-yard line and his momentum carries him into his own end zone. Ball is put in play at spot of interception.
(b) Player intercepts a pass **in his own end zone** and is downed. Impetus came from passing team, not from defense (Touchback).
(c) Player passes from **behind his own goal line.** Opponent bats down ball in end zone (Incomplete pass).

MEASURING
1. The forward point of the ball is used when measuring.

POSITION OF PLAYERS AT SNAP
1. Offensive team must have **at least seven** players on line.
2. Offensive players, not on line, must be at least one yard back at snap. (Exception, player who takes snap.)
3. No interior lineman may move after taking or simulating a three-point stance.
4. No player of either team may invade neutral zone before snap.
5. No player of offensive team may charge or move, after assuming set position, in such manner as to lead defense to believe snap has started.
6. If a player changes his eligibility, the Referee must alert the defensive captain after player has reported to him.
7. All players of offensive team must be stationary at snap, except one back who may be in motion paralled to scrimmage line or backward (not forward).
8. After a shift or huddle all players on offensive team must come to an absolute stop for **at least one second** with no movement of hands, feet, head or swaying of body.
9. A double shift is legal after it has been shown three times in the game outside an opponent's 20-yard line.

10. Linemen may lock legs **only** with the snapper.
11. Quarterbacks can be called for a false start penalty (5 yards) if their actions are judged to be an obvious attempt to draw an opponent offside.

USE OF HANDS, ARMS AND BODY

1. No player on offense may assist a runner except by blocking for him. There shall be no interlocking interference.
2. A runner may ward off opponents with his hands and arms but no other player on offense may use hands or arms to obstruct an opponent by grasping with hands, pushing or encircling any part of his body during a block.
3. Pass blocking is the obstruction of an opponent by the use of that part of the body above the knees. During a legal block, hands (open or closed) must be inside the blocker's elbows and can be thrust forward to contact an opponent as long as the contact is inside the frame. Hands cannot be thrust forward above the frame to contact an opponent on the neck, face or head. (**Note:** The frame is defined as that part of the opponent's body below the neck that is presented to the blocker.) Blocker cannot use his hands or arms to push from behind, hang onto, or encircle an opponent in a manner that restricts his movements as the play develops. By use of up and down action of arm(s), the blocker is permitted to ward off the opponent's attempt to grasp his jersey or arm(s) and prevent legal contact to the head.
4. A **defensive** player may not tackle or hold any opponent other than a runner. Otherwise, he may use his hands, arms or body only:
   (a) To defend or protect himself against an obstructing opponent.

   Exception — An eligible receiver is considered to be an obstructing opponent ONLY to a point 5 yards beyond the line of scrimmage unless the player who receives the snap clearly demonstrates no further intention to pass the ball. Within this 5-yard zone, a defensive player may make contact with an eligible receiver which may be maintained as long as it is continuous and unbroken. The defensive player cannot use his hands or arms to push from behind, hang onto, or encircle an eligible receiver in a manner that restricts movement as the play develops. Beyond this 5-yard limitation, a defender may use his hands or arms ONLY to defend or protect himself against impending contact caused by a receiver. In such reaction, the defender may not contact a receiver who attempts to take a path to evade him.

(b) To push or pull opponent out of the way on line of scrimmage.

(c) In actual attempt to get at or tackle runner.

(d) To push or pull opponent out of the way in a legal attempt to recover a loose ball.

(e) During a legal block on an opponent who is not an eligible pass receiver.

(f) When legally blocking an eligible pass receiver above the waist.

Exception — Eligible receivers lined up within 2 yards of the tackle, whether on or immediately behind the line, may be blocked below the waist AT or behind the line of scrimmage. NO eligible receiver may be blocked below the waist after he goes beyond the line.

5. A defensive player must not contact an opponent above the shoulders with the palm of his hand **except** to ward him off on the line. This exception is permitted only if it is not a repeated act against the same opponent during any one contact. In all other cases the palms may be used on head, neck or face **only** to ward off or push an opponent in legal attempt to get at the ball.

6. Any offensive player who pretends to possess the ball or to whom a teammate pretends to give the ball may be tackled provided he is **crossing** his scrimmage line between the ends of a normal tight offensive line.

7. An offensive player who lines up more than 2 yards outside his own tackle or a player who, at the snap, is in a backfield position and subsequently takes a position more than 2 yards outside a tackle may not clip an opponent anywhere nor may

he contact an opponent below the waist if the blocker is moving toward the ball and if contact is made within an area 5 yards on either side of the line.

8. A player of either team may block at any time provided it is not pass interference, fair catch interference or unnecessary roughness.

9. A player may not bat or punch:
   (a) A loose ball (in field of play) **toward** his opponent's goal line or in any direction in either end zone.
   (b) A ball in player possession or attempt to get possession.
   (c) A pass in flight forward toward opponent's goal line.
   Exception — A forward or backward pass may be batted in any direction at any time by the defense.

10. No player may deliberately kick any ball except as a punt, dropkick or placekick.

FORWARD PASS

1. A forward pass may be touched or caught by any eligible receiver. All members of the defensive team are eligible. Eligible receivers on the offensive team are players on either end of line (other than center, guard or tackle) or players at least one yard behind the line at the snap. A T-Formation quarterback is **not** eligible to receive a forward pass during a play from scrimmage.

   Exception — T-Formation quarterback becomes eligible if pass is previously touched by an eligible receiver.

2. An offensive team may make only **one** forward pass during each play from scrimmage (Loss of down).

3. The passer must be behind his line of scrimmage (Loss of down and 5 yards, enforced from the spot of pass).

4. Any eligible offensive player may catch a forward pass. If a pass is touched by one offensive player and touched or caught by a second eligible offensive player, pass completion is legal. Further, all offensive players become eligible once a pass is touched by an eligible receiver or any defensive player.

5. The rules concerning a forward pass and ineligible receivers:
   (a) If ball is touched **accidentally** by an ineligible receiver **on or behind his line** (Loss of down).
   (b) If touched or caught **intentionally** by an ineligible receiver **on or behind his line** (Loss of down and 10 yards).
   (c) If touched or caught (intentionally or accidentally) by ineligible receiver **beyond** the line (Loss of down and 10 yards).
   (d) If ineligible receiver is illegally downfield (10 yards).

6. If a forward pass is caught simultaneously by eligible players on **opposing teams**, possession goes to passing team.

7. Any forward pass becomes incomplete and ball is dead if:
   (a) Pass hits the ground or goes out of bounds.
   (b) Hits the goal post or the crossbar of either team.
   (c) Is caught by offensive player after touching ineligible receiver.
   (d) An illegal pass is caught by the passer.

8. A forward pass is complete when a receiver touches the ground with **both feet** inbounds while in possession of the ball. If a receiver is carried out of bounds by an opponent while in possession in the air, pass is complete at the out-of-bounds spot.

9. If an eligible receiver goes out of bounds accidentally or is forced out by a defender and returns to catch a pass, the play is regarded as a pass caught out of bounds. (Loss of down, no yardage).

10. On a **fourth down** pass — when the offensive team is **inside** the **opposition's 20-yard line** — an incomplete pass in the field of play or in the end zone results in a loss of down at the line of scrimmage.

11. If a personal foul is committed by the **defense prior to** the completion of a pass, the penalty is 15 yards from the post where ball becomes dead.

12. If a personal foul is committed by the **offense prior to** the completion of a pass, the penalty is 15 yards from the previous line of scrimmage.

INTENTIONAL GROUNDING OF FORWARD PASS

1. Intentional grounding of a forward pass is a foul (Loss of down and 10 yards from previous spot if passer is in the field of play or safety if passer is in his own end zone when ball is released).
2. It is considered intentional grounding of a forward pass when the ball strikes the ground after the passer throws, tosses or lobs the ball to prevent a loss of yards by his team.

PROTECTION OF PASSER

1. By interpretation, a pass begins when the passer — with possession of ball — starts to bring his hand forward. If ball strikes ground after this action has begun, play is ruled as an incomplete pass. If passer loses control of ball prior to his bringing his hand forward, play is ruled a fumble.
2. No defensive player may run into a passer of a legal forward pass after the ball has left his hand (15 yards). The Referee must determine whether opponent had a **reasonable chance to stop his momentum** during an attempt to block the pass or tackle the passer while he still had the ball.
3. Officials are to blow the play dead as soon as the quarterback is clearly in the grasp of any tackler.

PASS INTERFERENCE

1. There shall be no interference with a forward pass thrown from behind the line. The restriction for the **passing team** starts **with the snap**. The restriction on the **defensive team** starts **when the ball leaves the passer's hand**. Both restrictions **end when the ball is touched by anyone.**
2. The penalty for **defensive** pass interference is an automatic first down at the spot of the foul. If interference is in the end zone, it is first down for the offense on the defense's 1-yard line. If previous spot was inside the defense's 1-yard line, penalty is half the distance to the goal line.
3. The penalty for **offensive** pass interference is 10 yards from the previous spot.

4. It is interference when **any player's** movement **beyond** the passing team's line hinders the progress of an eligible opponent in his attempt to reach a pass.

   Exception — Such incidental movement or contact when two or more eligible players make a **simultaneous and bona fide** attempt to catch or bat the ball is permitted. **"Simultaneous and bona fide"** means the contact of an eligible receiver and a defensive player when each is playing the ball and contact is unavoidable and incidental to the act of trying to catch or bat the ball.

5. It must be remembered that defensive players have as much right to the **path of the ball** as eligible receivers. Any bodily contact, however severe, is not interference by a player in making a bona fide and simultaneous attempt to catch or bat the ball.

BACKWARD PASS

1. Any pass not a forward pass is regarded as a backward pass or lateral. A pass parallel to the line is a backward pass. A runner may pass backward at any time. **Any player on either team** may catch the pass or recover the ball after it touches the ground.

2. A backward pass that strikes the ground can be recovered and advanced by the offensive team.

3. A backward pass that strikes the ground can be **recovered** but **cannot be advanced** by the **defensive** team.

4. A backward pass **caught in the air** can be advanced by the **defensive team.**

FUMBLE

1. The distinction between a **fumble** and a **muff** should be kept in mind in considering rules about fumbles. A **fumble** is the **loss of possession** of the ball. A **muff** is the touching of a loose ball by a player in an **unsuccessful attempt to obtain possession.**

2. A fumble may be advanced by any player on either team regardless of whether recovered before or after ball hits the ground.

3. If an offensive player fumbles anywhere on the field during a fourth down play, or if a player fumbles on any down after the two minute warning in a half, only the fumbling player is permitted to recover and/or advance the ball. If recovered by any other offensive player, the ball is dead at the spot of fumble unless it is recovered behind the spot of fumble. In that case, the ball is dead at the spot of recovery. Any defensive player may recover and/or advance any fumble.

KICKS FROM SCRIMMAGE

1. Any punt or missed field goal that touches a goal post is dead.
2. During a kick from scrimmage, only the end men, as eligible receivers on the line of scrimmage at the time of the snap, are permitted to go beyond the line before the ball is kicked.

   Exception — An eligible receiver who, at the snap is aligned or in motion behind the line and more than one yard outside the end man on his side of the line, clearly making him the outside receiver, REPLACES that end man as the player eligible to go downfield after the snap. All other members of the kicking team must remain at the line of scrimmage until the ball has been kicked.
3. Any punt that is blocked and does **not** cross the line of scrimmage can be recovered and advanced by either team. However, if the offensive team recovers it must make the yardage necessary for its first down to retain possession if punt was on fourth down.
4. The kicking team may never advance its own kick even though legal recovery is made beyond the line of scrimmage. Possession only.
5. A member of the receiving team may not run into or rough a kicker who kicks from behind his line unless contact is:
   (a) Incidental to and **after** he had touched ball in flight.
   (b) Caused by kicker's own motions.
   (c) Occurs during a quick kick or a kick made after a run or after kicker recovers a loose ball. Ball is loose when kicker muffs snap or snap hits ground.

(The penalty for **running into** the kicker is 5 yards. For **roughing** the kicker 15 yards and disqualification if flagrant.)

6. If a member of the kicking team attempting to down the ball on or inside opponent's 5-yard line carries the ball into the end zone, it is a touchback.

7. Fouls during a punt are enforced from the previous spot (line of scrimmage).

   Exception — Illegal touching, illegal fair catch, invalid fair catch signal and fouls by the receiving team during loose ball after ball is kicked.

8. While the ball is in the air or rolling on the ground following a punt or field goal attempt and receiving team commits a foul before gaining possession, receiving team will retain possession and will be penalized for its foul.

9. It will be illegal for a defensive player to jump on or stand on any player or be picked up by a teammate or to use a hand or hands on a teammate to gain additional height in an attempt to block a kick (Penalty 15 yards, unsportsmanlike conduct).

10. A punted ball remains a kicked ball until it is declared dead or in possession of either team.

11. Any member of the punting team may **down** the ball anywhere in the field of play. However, it is **illegal touching** (Official's time out and receiver's ball at spot of illegal touching). This foul does **not** offset any foul by receivers during the down.

12. Defensive team may advance all kicks from scrimmage (including unsuccessful field goal) whether or not ball crosses defensive team's goal line. Rules pertaining to kicks from scrimmage apply until defensive team gains possession.

FAIR CATCH

1. The member of the receiving team must raise one arm full length above his head while kick is in flight. (Failure to give proper sign, receiver's ball five yards behind spot of signal.)

2. No opponent may interfere with the fair catcher, the ball or his path to the ball (15 yards from spot of foul and fair catch is awarded).

3. A player who signals for a fair catch is **not** required to catch the ball. However, if a player signals for a fair catch, he may not block or initiate contact with any player on the kicking team **until the ball touches a player** (Penalty, snap 15 yards behind spot of foul).
4. If ball hits ground or is touched by member of kicking team in flight, fair catch signal is off and all rules for a kicked ball apply.
5. Any **undue advance** by a fair catch receiver is delay of game. No specific distance is specified for ''undue advance'' as ball is dead at spot of catch. If player comes to a reasonable stop no penalty (For violation, 5 yards).
6. If time expires while ball is in play and a fair catch is awarded, receiving team may choose to extend the period with one free-kick down. However, placekicker may **not** use tee.

FOUL ON LAST PLAY OF HALF OR GAME

1. On a foul by **defense** on last play of half or game, the **down is replayed** if penalty is accepted.
2. On a foul by the **offense** on last play of half or game, the **down is not replayed** and the play in which the foul is committed is nullified.

    Exception — Fair catch interference, foul following change of possession, illegal touching. **No score by offense counts.**
3. On **double foul** on last play of half or game, **down is replayed.**

SPOT OF ENFORCEMENT OF FOUL

There are four basic spots at which a penalty for a foul is enforced:
1. Spot of foul: The spot where the foul is committed.
2. Previous spot: The spot where the ball was put in play.
3. Spot of snap, pass, fumble, return kick or free kick: The spot where the act connected with the foul occurred.
4. Succeeding spot: The spot where the ball next would be put in play if no distance penalty were to be enforced.
    Exception — If foul occurs after a touchndown and before the whistle for a try-for-point, succeeding spot is spot of next kickoff.

5. All fouls committed by **offensive** team **behind** the line of scrimmage in the field of play shall be penalized from the **previous spot**.

6. When the spot of enforcement for fouls involving defensive holding or illegal use of hands by the defense is behind the line of scrimmage, any penalty yardage to be assessed on that play shall be measured from the line.

DOUBLE FOUL

1. If there is a double foul **during** a down in which there is a change of possession, the team last gaining possession may keep the ball unless its foul was committed prior to the change of possession.

2. If double foul occurs **after** a change of possession, the defensive team retains the ball at the spot possession was gained.

3. If one of the fouls of a double foul involves disqualification, that player must be removed, but no penalty yardage is to be assessed.

4. If the kickers foul during a punt before possession changes and the receivers foul after possession changes, penalties will be offset and the down replayed.

PENALTY ENFORCED ON FOLLOWING KICKOFF

1. When a team scores by touchdown, field goal, extra point or safety and either team commits a personal foul, unsportsmanlike conduct or obvious unfair act during the down, the penalty will be assessed on the following kickoff.

1979 NFL RULES CHANGES

1. Provided for the captain who lost the pre-game coin toss to delay his second half choice until immediately prior to start of second half kickoff.

2. A team whose player is injured as the result of a personal foul committed during the last two minutes of a half will no longer be charged with a time out if he is disabled after the penalty has been assessed.

3. Clarified the automatic referee's time out whenever a quarterback is sacked behind the line in order to provide for a consistent length of time for the clock to be stopped before it is restarted again.
4. A period can be extended to permit a team whose opportunity to catch a scrimmage kick has been interfered with on the last play of a half (but no fair catch signal was given). That team will be allowed to run one play for scrimmage or attempt a field goal from free kick instead of only being permitted to attempt a free kick as in the past.
5. Adjusted numbering of players to allow defensive linemen to wear numbers in the nineties.
6. Any time a player, who has been substituted for, leaves the field on the wrong side of the field or over the end line in the end zone, his team will be penalized five yards from the **previous** spot whether or not the violation is discovered during the down or at the end of the down. In previous years if the violation was discovered after the down was over, the play had to count and the team was then penalized.
7. Stipulated mandatory equipment for all players to wear when they participate in any game.
8. If an offensive player fumbles anywhere on the field during a fourth down play or if a player fumbles on any down after the two minute warning in a half, only the fumbling player is permitted to recover and/or advance the ball.
9. Stipulated that if a member of the receiving team touches a scrimmage kick in the field of play or in the end zone and a member of the kicking team legally recovers the ball in the end zone, the kicking team will retain possession either at the spot of first touch by receivers, or at one yard line.
10. Prohibited all players on the receiving team from blocking opponents below the waist during kickoffs, punts and field goals attempts.
11. Extended the prohibited crackback zone from 3 yards on either side of the line of scrimmage to 5 yards on either side of the line in order to provide a greater measure of protection for the players.

12. Officials are to blow the play dead as soon as the quarterback is clearly in the grasp of any tackler.
13. A player may be penalized for unsportsmanlike conduct when he commits a non-contact act such as throwing a punch, or a forearm or kicking at an opponent.
14. Clarified unnecessary roughness rule to make it illegal for a player to use his helmet to butt or ram an opponent or to use the crown of the helmet unnecessarily.
15. For better understanding by fans, current NFL Officials' signals will be brought into closer synchronization with those that are used on a collegiate level for:
    (a) Intentional grounding.
    (b) Ineligible player downfield on pass or kick.
    (c) Ball illegally touched, kicked or batted.
    (d) Player disqualified.
    (e) Illegally blocking below the waist.
    (f) Touching a forward pass or scrimmage kick.
    (g) Loss of down.

HISTORY OF NFL RULE CHANGES

1925 — Player limit set at 16 men.

1926 — Player limit increased to 18 men.

1929 — Adoption of rule to employ fourth official, a field judge.

1930 — Player limit increased to 20 men.

1933 — Ball moved in 10 yards whenever it is in play within five yards of the sidelines.
— Clipping penalty increased to 25 yards.
— Goal posts returned to goal line.

1934 — Player entering game may communicate with teammates immediately instead of waiting until one play is completed.
— Officials must notify coach when team has exhausted three legal time outs in each half.
— A forward pass made hand-to-hand behind the line of scrimmage which becomes incomplete is a fumble and may be advanced by either team.

- Within 10 yards of goal, defensive team can be penalized only half distance for offside violations.
- The second incomplete pass over the goal line in the same series or a fourth down incompletion in the end zone results in a touchback (Previously, any incomplete pass over the goal line was a touchback).
- Forward passing legalized from any spot behind line of scrimmage.
- A runner who falls to the ground, or who is tackled, may advance unless a defender continues to hold him on the ground.
- Flying blocks and flying tackles are permitted during the game.
- Players of the receiving team may be stationed at any place on the field, so long as they do not advance within 10 yards of the ball before it is kicked.
- At the kickoff, the ball may be kicked from a dirt tee.
- A fumbled ball, except fumbles resulting from lateral passes, may be advanced by either team, no matter whether the ball strikes the ground or not. If the defense recovers a fumbled lateral, the ball is dead; if the offense recovers a fumbled lateral, it may advance.
- When a team completes on legal forward pass, which is in turn followed by second forward pass, penalty will be loss of 5 yards from the point of the second and illegal forward pass.

1935 — Player limit increased to 24 men.
- All penalties will be inflicted from the point where the ball was put in play and not from the point where the foul occurred.
- A pass thrown beyond the line of scrimmage intended as a lateral but going forward shall be declared downed at the point of throwing.
- The ball, when fumbled, is free except when kicked or thrown.
- The fourth down incomplete pass, or a second incomplete pass in the same series, that goes into the end zone is returned to the point where the ball was put in play, except when the previous play originated inside the 20-yard line.

— A ball out of bounds shall be brought in 15 yards.

1936 — Player limit increased to 25 men.
— When the goal posts interfere with the play of the team who is in possession of the ball, said team shall have the privilege of moving the ball 5 yards to either side of the goal posts without penalty.

1938 — Player limit increased to 30 men.
— A kickoff that goes out of bounds shall cause the ball to be put into play on the receiving team's 45-yard line (previously 35).
— Any two players withdrawn from game during fourth quarter may re-enter once.
— All penalties against defense within the 10-yard line shall be half the distance to the goal.
— Referee empowered to penalize 15 yards for deliberate roughing of a forward passer after the ball has left his hand.
— Penalty for a second forward pass behind the line of scrimmage is loss of down instead of loss of down and 5 yards as heretofore.
— If a kickoff goes out of bounds between the goal lines, the opponents shall have option of putting it in play by a scrimmage anywhere on their 45-yard line or at a point 15 yards in from where the ball crossed the sidelines. If ball is last touched by receivers, they shall put the ball in play at the inbounds spot.

1939 — During the last two minutes of the second half, additional time outs by Team A after their third legal one are not allowed unless it is for a designated injured player who is to be removed. A fourth time out under these conditions is not penalized, but thereafter they are treated as excess time outs.
— During a kickoff, the kicking team may use only a natural tee made of the soil in the immediate vicinity of the point of such a kick and it shall not be more than 3 inches in height.
— The penalty for a forward pass touching an ineligible player **on or behind** his line of scrimmage is loss of down

and 15 yards from previous spot, and this penalty may not be declined.
— Penalty for forward pass striking an ineligible player beyond the line of scrimmage shall be **loss** of ball at previous spot.
— Before a forward pass is thrown from behind the line of scrimmage, ineligible players may not legally cross that line except in an initial line charge while blocking an opponent. Penalty: Loss of down and 15 yards.

1940 — Player limit increased to 33 maximum and 22 minimum.
— Clipping penalty reduced to 15 yards.
— Team B has choice of loss of down and 15 yards from previous spot or a touchback for pass interference by Team A behind B's goal line.
— Adoption of rule prohibiting sale or trading of Team's first two selections in a player draft without unanimous consent of league until one playing season after player's selection.
— Three and one method of enforcing penalties is in effect.
— Penalty for a forward pass not from scrimmage is 5 yards.
— A penalty enforced in the field of play cannot carry the ball more than one half the distance to the offenders' goal line.
— Penalty for a foul prior to a kick or pass from behind line is enforced from previous spot or behind that spot if offensive team commits a foul behind previous spot.

1941 — Penalty for illegal shift is 5 yards.
— A kick from scrimmage or return kick crossing receivers' goal line from impetus of kick is a touchback.
— Penalty for personal foul by opponents of scoring team is enforced on kickoff.
— Illegal touching of kicked ball is not an offset foul and ball is dead when illegally recovered.
— Distance penalty for disqualifying foul is 15 yards.
— Penalty for an illegal bat or kick is 15 yards.
— Umpire is to time game. Linesman and Field Judge are to supervise substitutions.

1942 — Snapper is not offside unless some portion of his body is ahead of B's line.
— Free kick cannot be made in a side zone.
— A detachable kicking toe is illegal.
— Pass interference by A in B's end zone is a touchback during any down.
— A forward pass which has touched a second eligible or an ineligible player may be intercepted.
— The coach's area is to extend 10 yards in both directions from the center of his team's bench.

1943 — Adoption of the free substitution rule.
— Time out rule to apply at end of both halves.
— Players must wear head protectors.
— Team A may intercept and advance B's illegal pass from end zone.
— Adoption of ten-game schedule.
— Player limit reduced to 28 men for one year.

1944 — The free substitution rule is continued for 1944 only. A substitute is not required to report to an official and he becomes a player when he informs a teammate that he is replacing him or when he communicates with any teammate.
— Loss of 5 by A for kicking a free kick out of bounds between goal lines (unless last touched by B before going out of bounds) and a re-kick must be made (no declination). If last touched by B, B must snap at inbounds spot. While B may not decline A's obligation to re-kick, it has a choice of distance penalties in case of a multiple foul.
— All enforcements for fouls during a free kick except fair catch interference, are from previous spot.
— Communication between players and coach is legal provided coach is in his prescribed area and provided it does not cause delay.
— Pass interference by A in B's end zone is not a touchback.
— Player limit of 28 reaffirmed for one year.
— A designated center, guard or tackle or one shifted to an end or back position may return to any position if withdrawn for one play.

- Fouls during free kick, except fair catch interference, are enforced from previous spot.

1945
- Inbounds lines to be 20 yards from sideline.
- All players must wear stockings.
- Mandatory to enforce penalty for encroachment if defensive signal caller is beyond his line after neutral zone is established.
- A player under center who extends hands must receive snap, otherwise it is a false start. If he receives a hand to hand pass, he becomes an ineligible player.
- When snap in flight is muffed by receiver and then touches ground, B may recover and advance.
- Pre-war player limit of 33 men restored.
- Ball is dead when any receiver catches after a fair catch signal unless kick is touched in flight by kickers. Penalty for two steps abolished and undue advance is delay but does not preclude fair catch.
- It is 1st and 10 for A when they recover a kick from scrimmage any where in field of play after it has first been touched by B beyond line.
- A player in blocking, may not strike an opponent below shoulders with elbows by pivoting or turning trunk at waist.
- During try, snap may be made 2 or more yards from B's goal line.
- Free substitution rule renewed for one year.
- Referee to designate offending player when known.
- Rule regarding attempts to consume or conserve time at the end of the second and fourth periods extended to include first and third periods also.
- On a personal foul prior to a completion or interception of a legal pass by offended team, they shall have choice of (a) usual penalty or (b) 15 yards from spot of dead ball. If offended team loses possession, enforcement of penalty (b) is from spot where possession was lost.

1946
- When A fumbles (unintentional) inside B's 10, during a 4th down play from scrimmage, only the runner may advance if recovery is by A. Otherwise, if they recover, ball

— is next put in play at spot of fumble unless spot of recovery is behind that spot (spot of recovery). No change in rule in regard to advance by B or to an intentional fumble forward (forward pass).
— A is on his line provided one hand is touching ground and it is on or within one foot of his line. No change in rule if neither hand is touching ground.
— When a forward pass from behind line touches either team's goal post or crossbar it is incomplete. Penalty: Loss of down at previous spot. Penalty for pass touching ineligible A: Loss of down and 15 from previous spot, unless accidentally touched behind line in which case it is loss of down only.
— Toss of coin for choice ordered before teams leave field at conclusion of pre-game warmups.
— Captains are to meet at center of field at the usual three minutes before game time, but only the receivers and their goal are to be indicated at this time.
— Penalty for invalid fair catch signal: 5 yards from spot of signal.
— Penalty for illegal equipment: Loss of 5 for delay and suspension for at least one down.
— Substitutions limited to no more than three men at one time.
— Receiving team permitted to run punts and unsuccessful field goal attempts out from behind goal line.

1947 — Officials are to automatically re-spot ball on nearest inbounds line, when spot of snap by A is between inbounds lines and inside their 10 (not a time out).
— Illegal use of hands by defense, when used to block vision of an A receiver during any pass behind A's line.
— When a team has less than eleven players on field prior to snap or free kick, officals are not to inform them.
— When spot of incompletion (includes intentional) pass violation or interference, by A, is behind B's goal line during fourth down, it is a touchback if usual enforcement leaves ball inside B's 20.
— During a try, if try-kick is not successful, ball becomes dead as soon as failure is evident.

- When a scrimmage or return kick crosses receiver's goal line from impetus of kick it is a touchback.
- Kicker loses his usual protection if he kicks after recovering a loose ball on ground.
- A fifth official known as back judge, with prescribed duties, is to be used on field of play.
- During a forward pass if spot of a pass violation is behind A's goal line the usual penalty is enforced from previous spot.
- During a forward pass if spot of a pass violation by A is behind B's goal line, during fourth down, it is a touchback if the usual enforcement leaves the ball inside B's 20. If pass interference by A, behind B's goal line, during fourth down and previous spot was inside B's 5, it is a touchback.
- Field judge may use whistle to assist referee or other officials in declaring ball dead.
- Sudden death method of deciding tie game in divisional playoff or championship game adopted.
- Player limit set at 35 for first three games and 34 for remainder of season.

1948 — Officials notifying each team of 5 minutes before start of second half must notify head coach personally.
- If an intended pass is downed behind line, it is a referee's time out until any players who have gone down field for a pass have had a reasonable time to return.
- Use of plastic head protectors is prohibited and coaches are to assume primary responsibility for the use of equipment which endangers their own or opponents' players.
- Use of a flexible artificial tee is permitted at the kickoff.
- If a foul occurs beyond line, during backward pass or fumble from scrimmage, basic spot of enforcement is spot of pass or fumble.
- Batting or punching of a ball in any direction while in player's possession is illegal (loss of 15).
- When a player is disqualified, referee must verbally notify such player's coach of this fact.
- Player limit increased to 35 for the entire season.

1949 — Any number of substitutes may enter while ball is dead during time in (for 1949 only).
 — It is optional that all eligible pass receivers of a given team may wear different color head protectors than their teammates. If a different color is used by any such receiver, then all such receivers must wear the same color.
 — At the option of the home team, both the player's benches may be located on the same side of the field. In such a case the end of each bench shall start at the 45 and continue to goal line.
 — Plastic head protectors are to be permitted.
 — Player limit of 32 adopted.

1950 — The free substitution rule was readopted for an indefinite term.
 — Player limit of 32 retained. A minimum of 25 players must be dressed for a championship game.
 — A backward pass going out of bounds between the goal lines shall belong to the team last in possession.
 — Any team may option any number of players above the 25 minimum and within the player limit.

1951 — Aluminum shoe cleats are illegal.
 — A center, guard or tackle is not eligible to touch a forward pass from scrimmage even when on end of line.
 — Player limit of 33 voted. A minimum of 25 players must be dressed for a championship game.
 — Illegal touching violation by a member of kicking team does not offset a foul by receivers.

1952 — All players must be numbered according to their position except as provided for nationally known players.
 — A player is not considered to be illegally in motion provided he is not going forward at snap.
 — The tackle eligible rule was made permanent.
 — On pass interference on the part of the offense, the penalty shall be 15 yards from the previous spot and not loss of down. Penalty for palpably unfair act: Player is also disqualified.

1953 — Withdrawn players and substitutes do not have to participate for at least one play or down.
— A foul between downs must occur after play has definitely ended.
— Elimination of the "dead ball" plays rule except (1) 30 second delay; (2) official not in position at snap.
— A player limit of 33 retained.
— Hurdling clarified to cover only act of a runner.
— Player(s) must be moving forward to be considered illegally in motion.

1954 — Referee is sole judge of and must pressure gauge all game balls on the field prior to start of game.
— In case of rain, wet or slippery field, playable balls can be requested at any time by the offensive team, and are to be furnished by home team attendant from sideline(s).
— Fourth down fumble inside B's 10-yard line rewritten and now covers T-formation Quarterback.
— Referee time out for at least 10 seconds during change of possession; longer if and when required.
— Use of tee for free kick after fair catch prohibited.
— Possibility of field goal after safety eliminated.
— The player limit of 33 was retained.
— Illegal "kicking" of ball must be with foot to be considered a foul.

1955 — Intercepting momentum causing ball to be declared dead in end zone in interceptor's possession is put in play at spot of interception.
— New rule regarding running of 10 seconds off clock for team in possession during last 2 minutes of a half — if behind in score or game tied.
— If a player touches ground with any part of his body, except his hands or feet, while in the grasp of opponent and irrespective of grasp being broken, ball is declared dead immediately.
— Player of kicking team, who has been out of bounds may not touch, recover or advance a scrimmage kick beyond line.

— Interpretation of false starts calls for penalty for any movement by an interior lineman after he has taken three-point stance on the scrimmage line.

1956 — A runner who is contacted by a defensive player and he touches the ground with any part of his body except his hands or feet, ball shall be declared dead immediately.
— Brown ball with white stripes to be used for night games.
— No artificial material shall be permitted to assist in the execution of a field goal and/or try-for-point.
— Intermission between halves 20 minutes.
— Grabbing or grasping of face guards illegal except ball carrier.
— Loudspeaker coaching from sidelines not permitted.
— When an interior lineman takes a three-point stance and moves after taking that stance, he must be ruled offside or illegally in motion.

1957 — On all requested time outs the referee shall not sound his whistle for play to start prior to sixty seconds of elapsed time.
— Player limit increased to 35 men.
— All Head Linesmen shall use a clamp on the chains when measuring for first down.

1958 — The back judge was designated as the official timer of the game.
— On all requested time outs, the referee shall not signify that the ball will be put in play prior to one minute and thirty (30) seconds of elapsed time.

1959 — Player limit increased to 36 men.
— No changes in rules.

1960 — Player limit increased to 38 men.
— No changes in rules.

1961 — No changes in rules. Player limit reduced to 36 men.

1962 — No player shall grasp the face mask of an opponent. Penalty: 15 yards. Flagrant offender shall be disqualified.
— Sudden death rule applies to all postseason games including Pro Bowl.

1963 — Player limit increased to 37 for 1963 season.
— When spot of snap by A is inside A's 15, and between inbounds line, ball is spotted at nearer inbound line.

1964 — Player limit raised by three to 40.
— No change in rules.

1965 — The player limit was again set at 40 for 1965.
— Color of officials' flags now bright gold.
— Addition of sixth official — the Line Judge.
— Wording of the Shift Rule changed. Shift will begin after players assume set position rather then coming out of huddle.

1966 — No rule changes. However, by resolution, all goal posts will be offset from the goal line, the uprights will extend a minimum of 20 feet above crossbar and will be painted bright gold in color.

1967 — A player who signals for a fair catch may not block or initiate contact with one of the kickers until the ball touches a player.
— By resolution, NFL goal posts will be of the single, standard type and playing fields will be rimmed by a white border, six feet wide, along the sidelines.

1968 — AFL differences in the rules were listed:
a.) Two-point conversion.
b.) Official time in AFL is kept on scoreboard clock.
c.) Official AFL ball is a Spalding J5V.

1969 — All kicking shoes will be those of a standard production and cannot subsequently be modified in any manner.
— Referee can charge a team time out when it is apparent an injured player cannot leave the field under his own power. Official no longer has to wait until the team captain requests the team time out.
— **Kicker** as well as holder may be beyond line when placekick is made.

1970 — The stadium electric clock shall be the official time.

1971 — A team will not be charged a time out for an injured player unless the injury occurs in the last two minutes of either half.

- Defensive team may advance unsuccessful field goal attempt after ball crosses B's goal line.
- Holding, illegal use of hands and clipping fouls committed by the offensive team behind the line of scrimmage **DURING FORWARD PASS PLAYS** shall be penalized from the previous spot.
- Clean hands rule went into effect. If there is a double foul during a down in which there is a change of possession, the team last gaining possession may keep the ball after enforcement for its foul, provided its foul was not prior to the final change of possession.
- New pass blocking definition added to rule book.
- Intentional grounding rule clarified so that a passer can be penalized when he throws, tosses or lobs the ball away with a deliberate attempt to prevent a loss of yardage by his team.

1972 — Inbounds markers moved to 70 feet, 9 inches from sideline. Exception: On fourth down (with team A at or inside its 15-yard line), ball will be spotted 20 yards inbounds from the nearest sideline.
- Penalty for illegal receiver accidentally going out of bounds and returning to touch pass is reduced to loss of down (rather than loss of down and 15 yards).
- Penalty reduced to 5 yards for grasping face mask, unless flagrant.
- Commissioner's Office will notify competing teams when a brown ball with white stripe will be used for late starting games.
- Any kick from scrimmage which crosses goal line may be advanced by defensive team into field of play.
- All fouls committed by the offensive team behind the line of scrimmage in the **field of play** shall be penalized from the previous spot.
- Clarification: Disqualified player(s) may not re-enter during overtime period(s).

1973 — Clock to start on snap following all changes of team possession.
- Period can be extended if, after a foul by the offense, there is a change of team possession.

- All players numbered according to their positions.
- Close line play defined as the area ordinarily occupied by **offensive tackles** and longitudinally three years on either side of scrimmage line.
- A defensive player who jumps or stands on a teammate or who is picked up by a teammate cannot attempt to block an opponent's kick. Penalty: 15 yards.
- A receiving team that commits a foul during a kick from scrimmage after the ball is kicked will not lose the ball as part of its penalty.

1974 — Player limit increased to 47 for one year.
- Goal post moved from goal line back to end line.
- Team A's kickoff line moved from 40 to 35-yard line.
- During a kick from scrimmage, only the end men are permitted to go beyond the line of scrimmage before the ball is kicked.
- Field goals attempted and missed from scrimmage line beyond the 20-yard line will result in the defensive team taking possession of the ball at the scrimmage line. Field goals attempted and missed from scrimmage line inside 20-yard line will result in defensive team taking possession at the 20-yard line.
- When spot of enforcement for holding, illegal use of hands, arms or body of offense as well as tripping fouls is not in the field of play at or behind the line of scrimmage or no deeper than 3 yards beyond line of scrimmage, penalty will be reduced from 15 yards to 10 yards.
- Eligible pass receivers can only be chucked once by any defender after the receiver has proceeded to a point 3 yards beyond line of scrimmage.
- Eligible receiver who lines up in a position within 2 yards of a tackle may be legally blocked below the waist "at the line of scrimmage."
- Eligible receivers who take a position more than 2 yards from the tackle may not be blocked below the waist at or behind line of scrimmage.
- No receiver can be blocked below the waist once he clearly moves beyond line of scrimmage.

- It is illegal for an offensive player to block an opponent below the waist within an area 3 yards on either side of line of scrimmage if the blocker is aligned in a position more than 2 yards outside his tackle and is moving in toward position of ball, either at snap or after it is made. Penalty: 15 yards for illegal crackback.
- The sudden death system of determining the winner when score is tied at end of regulation of playing time is in effect for preseason and regular season games with the exception that playing time will be limited to a maximum of one 15-minute period. Two time outs are permitted each team during this extra period.
- Except in coaching areas, a broken limit line 2 feet outside white border is to encompass entire field.

1975 — Player limit reduced to 43 men.
- Further standardized markings of playing field by requiring that end zone marking and club identification at the 50-yard line must be approved by the Commissioner so as not to cause any confusion as to delineation of goal lines, side lines and end lines. In addition, pylons will replace flags for goal line and end line markings, chain crews will be uniformly attired, ball boys will be clearly identifiable and all clubs must use standard sideline markers.
- Directed officials to interpret current unsportsmanlike language in Rule 12, Section 2, Article 15 (3) as covering any lingering by players leaving the field when being substituted for. Current language reads: "Using entering substitutes, legally returning players, substitutes on sidelines or withdrawn players to confuse opponents." (NOTE: This does not represent a change as such, but broadens the interpretation of existing language in the rule book to prohibit the coaching of multiple substitution in a manner designed to deceive.)
- Provides that a team may use a double shift on or inside the opponent's 20-yard line after it has been shown at least three times previously **in the game**. In the past, team could not use double shift at or inside 20 unless it was shown at least three times **in a quarter**.

- Any fourth down pass that is incomplete in or through the end zone when the line of scrimmage is inside the 20 will result in the opponent taking possession at the previous line of scrimmage. In the past, such incomplete pass resulted in a touchback with the opponent taking possession at the 20.
- When there are penalties on each team on the same play and one results in disqualification, the penalties will be offsetting, but the disqualification will stand. In the past, the penalty involving disqualification took precedence and both 15 yards and disqualification were required while the other team was not penalized.
- Penalty for an ineligible player downfield on a forward pass play reduced from 15 to 10 yards.
- Penalty for offensive pass interference reduced from 15 to 10 yards.
- In the case of defensive holding or illegal use of hands, the penalty will be assessed from the previous line of scrimmage rather than from the spot where the ball is blown dead if that spot is behind the line of scrimmage.

1976 — Increased number of footballs available for use in each game from 12 to 24.
- A football with stripes will no longer be used during any game.
- Coin toss ceremony changed from 30 minutes to 3 minutes before kickoff.
- A delay of game penalty will no longer be enforced when a runner carries the ball in a manner clearly designed to consume playing time.
- Any foul committed by the defense which prevents the point-after-touchdown from being attempted will result in the down being replayed and the kicking team having the option as to when the yardage penalty will be assessed — on the next try or on the ensuing kickoff. Any foul committed by the defense on a successful try will result in a distance penalty being assessed on the following kickoff.
- Clarified penalty for striking with fists or kicking or kneeing opponent.
- Clarified degrees of the face mask violations.

- Made it illegal for a defender to use a hand or hands on a teammate to gain additional height in an attempt to block a kick.
- Specified that each team is not permitted to have more than 15 persons in addition to its uniformed players on each sideline.
- Stipulated that whenever spectators enter the playing field before the game is over, the field must be cleared in order that the game can be completed.
- Two 30-second clocks visible to players, officials and fans will be displayed, noting the official time between the ready-for-play signal and the snap of the ball. Field Judge continues to be responsible to rule on any violation.
- A ribbon 2'' by 36'' long is to be attached to the top of each goal post as an assist in determining wind direction.
- A player who reports a change in his eligibility, prior to a touchdown, can legally return to his original position for a point-after-touchdown attempt without having to leave the field for one play.
- A defender is not permitted to rough a ball carrier who falls to the ground untouched by running or diving into him.
- Whenever a disqualified player is banished from a game, he must leave the entire playing field area within a reasonable period of time.

1977
- Clarified restrictions on offensive blocking to include the thrust of a blocker's hands and arms forward to contact an opponent above the shoulders.
- Made it illegal to strike an opponent above the shoulders (head slap) during the initial charge of a defensive lineman.
- Coin toss may be held at any time within 3 minutes of kickoff.
- Made it illegal for a back who lines up inside a tight end to move to the outside and then back inside again to crackback below the waist.
- An offensive lineman who takes a two point stance must have some part of his body (which could include his head) within 1 foot of his end of the ball to be legally on

the line of scrimmage.
— Any shoe that is worn by a player with an artificial limb must have its kicking surface conform to that of a normal kicking shoe.
— If the kickers foul during a punt before possession changes and the receivers foul after possession changes, penalties will be offset and the down replayed.
— Provided that a defender will be permitted to contact an eligible receiver **either** in the three yard zone at or beyond the line of scrimmage or **once** beyond that zone, but not both.
— Provided that a team will lose its coin toss option in addition to sustaining a 15-yard penalty if it does not arrive on the field for warmup at least 15 minutes prior to the scheduled kickoff.
— Made it illegal for a wide receiver to clip an opponent anywhere (including in the legal clipping zone).
— Made kicking a loose ball with the foot a foul only if the act is ruled to be deliberate.

1978 — Further clarified pass blocking rule interpretation to permit extended arms and open hands.
— During last two minutes of a half, placed responsibility on defensive team to line up properly when referee signals ready for play after offensive team is set in position.
— Clarified officials right not to stop the clock, or if stopped, to run 10 seconds off the clock during the last two minutes of a half when a team deliberately attempts to conserve time.
— Whenever the ball is carried across the line of scrimmage, no legal forward pass can be thrown.
— Legalized double touch of a forward pass and made it illegal to bat a pass in flight forward toward opponent's goal line.
— Reduced penalty for intentional grounding in the field of play from a loss of down and 15, to loss of down and 10, and assessed a penalty of a safety when passer illegally grounds a ball in the end zone.
— Permitted defenders to maintain contact on receivers in a 5-yard zone beyond the line of scrimmage, but restricted

their contact on receivers beyond that point.
— Eliminated hurdling as a foul.
— Clarified the unsportsmanlike conduct rule to include forms of taunting or baiting by players towards opponents as violations at any time during a game.
— Stipulated that a 15-yard penalty be assessed during a down involving a double foul without change of possession when one foul carries a penalty of 15 yards and the other 5 **ONLY**.
— Increased crew of game officials from six to seven.
— Reduced 15 yard penalties to 10 yards for all fouls except those involving unnecessary roughness, unsportsmanlike conduct, personal fouls, disqualification or palpably unfair acts.
— In the event of a defensive foul behind the line of scrimmage on which a runner is downed behind the line, the offensive team will be awarded sufficient penalty yardage to advance the ball to at least the former line of scrimmage and a first down.
— Clarified the spot of enforcement for plays in which double fouls are committed after an exchange of possession to ensure that the receiving or recovering team is not placed at a disadvantage because of a foul committed by its opponent during the same play.
— Developed a definition for run blocking to provide a clear distinction with the technique used on pass blocking.

1979 — (See page xxxi)

To order more copies
of SUNDAY ZEBRAS
please contact

Forest Publishing
222 Wisconsin Avenue
Lake Forest, Illinois 60045
312/295-1122